FOREWORD

The Hidden Places series is a collection of easy to use travel guides taking you, in this instance, on a relaxed but informative tour of Dorset and Hampshire, two counties which are blessed with an impressive coastline and beautiful countryside. Dorset is a county that encompasses rolling chalk downs, dark heathland (so beloved of Thomas Hardy), the long ridge of the Purbeck Hills and an incomparable coastline with its wealth of magnificent rock formations sculptured by the sea. Hampshire and the Isle of Wight offer the visitor a combination of seafaring tradition in the many coastal towns and villages as well as wonderful countryside epitomised by the New Forest and the rolling hills of northeast Hampshire. Both counties are a haven for "hidden places" and we hope this book provides the reader with plenty of interesting historical facts.

Our books contain a wealth of interesting information on the history, the countryside, the towns and villages and the more established places of interest in the counties. But they also promote the more secluded and little known visitor attractions and places to stay, eat and drink many of which are easy to miss unless you know exactly where you are going.

We include hotels, inns, restaurants, public houses, teashops, various types of accommodation, historic houses, museums, gardens, garden centres, craft centres and many other attractions throughout Dorset, Hampshire and the Isle of Wight, all of which are comprehensively indexed. Most places have an attractive line drawing and are cross-referenced to coloured maps found at the rear of the book. We do not award merit marks or rankings but concentrate on describing the more interesting, unusual or unique features of each place with the aim of making the reader's stay in the local area an enjoyable and stimulating experience.

Whether you are visiting the area for business or pleasure or in fact are living in the counties we do hope that you enjoy reading and using this book. We are always interested in what readers think of places covered (or not covered) in our guides so please do not hesitate to use the reader reaction forms provided to give us your considered comments. We also welcome any general comments which will help us improve the guides themselves. Finally if you are planning to visit any other corner of the British Isles we would like to refer you to the list of other *Hidden Places* titles to be found at the rear of the book.

CONTENTS

1 Northeast Hampshire

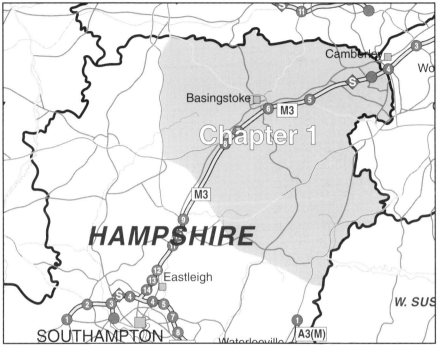

© MAPS IN MINUTES ™ (1998)

You only have to travel a dozen or so miles from the M25 near Staines before you cross the county boundary into Hampshire. So it's not surprising that this corner of the county is quite heavily populated, dotted with prosperous, sprawling towns such as Farnborough, Aldershot and Basingstoke. What *is* surprising is that, once you turn off the busy main roads, you can find yourself driving along narrow country lanes where, if you meet an approaching vehicle, a diploma in Advanced Driving Skills could be very helpful.

This area forms part of the North Downs. Honouring the perverse tradition of English place-names, the Downs are actually uplands, softly-rolling, wooded hills in whose folds lie scores of picturesque villages. As the crow flies, central London is little more than 30 miles away; for many of the northeastern Hampshire villages, even today, the metropolis might just as well be 300 miles distant.

There are few grand houses in the area, although The Vyne near Basingstoke and the Duke of Wellington's home, Stratfield Saye House, are both very imposing. Two smaller dwellings, however, attract hundreds of thousands of visitors to this corner of the county: Jane Austen's House at Chawton, near Alton, and a few miles to the south in the village of Selborne, The Wakes, home of the celebrated naturalist, Gilbert White. Lovers of steam railways can combine a visit to these two houses with a ride on the Watercress Line which runs between Alton and Alresford.

We begin this tour of northeastern Hampshire at Basingstoke, a vibrant, modern town whose name goes back to Saxon times. It was then that a farmer with a name something like Base, along with his extended family, or 'ing', established a 'stok', (stock or farm-house) beside the River Lodden.

BASINGSTOKE

It comes as something of a surprise to discover that this busy, prosperous town with its soaring multi-storey buildings can boast no fewer than 25 parks and open spaces. A useful leaflet available from the Tourist Information Centre gives details of them all, ranging from the 16-hectare **War Memorial Park**, an 18th century park complete with bandstand, aviary and sports facilities, to **Southview Cemetery**, a site with a fascinating history. Some 800 years ago, during the reign of King John, England languished under an Interdict pronounced by the Pope. Throughout the six years from 1208 to 1214, any baby christened, or dead person buried, lacked the official blessing of Mother Church. At Basingstoke during those years, the deceased were interred in a graveyard known as **The Liten** and when the Interdict was finally lifted, the ground was consecrated and a chapel built, the **Chapel of the Holy Ghost**. Today, it's a striking ruin surrounded by a well-managed site which provides a peaceful refuge from the bustling town.

As befits such a thriving place, Basingstoke offers visitors a wide choice of attractions: theatre, cinema, a vast Leisure Park, and an "Old Town" area which is a lively cosmopolitan mix of bars, theme pubs and restaurants. Here too is the excellent **Willis Museum** (free) which charts the town's history with lively displays featuring characters such as "Fred", a Roman skeleton, and "Pickaxe", a 19th century farm worker "forced to scrape a living from the streets of Basingstoke as a scavenger".

Close by and enjoying a unique position as the only town centre hotel in Basingstoke, the **Red Lion Hotel** is also the most historic, dating back to the 17th century. Combining an original coaching inn with a modern bedroom wing, the Red Lion offers visitors a great variation in decorative styles. From the subtle Mediterranean feel of the Reception area to the classic oak beams of the hotel bar the Red Lion is ideal for either business or leisure travellers. The hotel restaurant offers an excellent variety of superb cuisine, complemented by an

Red Lion Hotel, London Street, Basingstoke, Hampshire RG21 7NY
Tel: 01256 328525

extensive list of fine wines from around the world, guaranteed to suit even the most discerning connoisseur. For those seeking a more relaxed meal, the hotel's main bar serves light lunches and coffee in traditional surroundings with wood beams a-plenty. If relaxing in front of a roaring fire is more to your liking, the ground floor lounge is the ideal place to enjoy that after dinner drink, or to simply while away the time. To enhance your enjoyment, a full lounge service is available 24 hours a day.

The hotel has 59 well-appointed bedrooms, all en suite, each equipped with remote control colour television with satellite channels, radio, direct dial telephone, full tea and coffee-making facilities, and 24 hour room service. A number of rooms, including the executive Vyne Suite, feature rich wood panelling, offering traditional warmth and character. Whichever room you stay in, you will be impressed by the hotel's commitment to service and attention to detail. For any special occasion, be it business or pleasure, the Marlborough Suite is suitable for functions of up to 80 people. Featuring a dance floor and a fully adjustable lighting system, complemented by a range of table linen colours, the suite can be set to any number of moods, thereby creating the perfect ambience for your function. With the M3 just minutes away, the hotel is within easy reach of any number of major visitor attractions, from Stonehenge to Jane Austen Country, from Windsor Castle to the Watercress Steam Railway.

Just off the A30 Winchester Road route into Basingstoke, on the ancient Harrow Way, is **Viables Craft Centre**. Situated in an attractive Victorian farm setting with resident craft workshops, it has been in existence for over twenty years. Recently, Viables Craft Centre has been the focus of artistic activity to develop it as a centre for design-led contemporary and traditional craft. Partially grant-aided by the local authority, Viables Craft Centre has made significant steps towards achieving charitable status and introducing craft education as an integral part of the Centre's activities. As part of this development, a Ceramics Residency has been established and an expanding craft educational programme has also been launched. The Granary has been converted into a summer gallery and has been used by the Southern Arts Touring Service, as well as for local arts exhibitions. Community-based projects, in partnership with professional designers, are creating unique and exciting site features. Two such projects have resulted in the new entrance to the Centre, and also a fun "crocodile" bench, both of which were designed and made in co-operation with local schools and groups. **Viables Craft Centre, The Harrow Way, Basingstoke, Hampshire, RG22 4BJ. Tel: 01256 473634**

Just to the east of Basingstoke, **Basing House** was once one of the grandest residences in the realm. Built during the reign of Henry VIII, it rivalled even the king's extravagant mansions. Less than a hundred years later, during the Civil War, Cromwell's troops besieged the house for an incredible three years, one of them reporting that the mansion was 'as large as the Tower of London'. When Basing House was finally captured the victorious New Army burnt it to the ground, but a magnificent 16th century barn survived, its timber roof a marvel of the carpenter's craft.

The Vyne (National Trust), 4 miles north of Basingstoke, has enjoyed a much happier history. Built in the early 1500s for Lord Sandys, Lord Chamberlain to Henry VIII, the house enjoys an idyllic setting with lawns sweeping down to a

The Vyne, Nr Basingstoke

shimmering lake. A classical portico was added in 1654, the first of its kind in England. The Vyne's treasures include a fascinating Tudor chapel with Renaissance glass, a Palladian staircase, and a wealth of old panelling and fine furniture. Tel: 01256 881337.

BAUGHURST
MAP 5 REF N2

6 miles N of Basingstoke, on minor road off the A340

Collectors of unusual pubs should certainly seek out **The Wellington Arms** in Baughurst. It is believed to be one of the smallest hostelries in Hampshire. There's just one small, cosy bar with an open log fire and lots of brasses, the walls hung with plates, prints and paintings, including one of the village poacher! The Wellington is housed in a Grade II listed building which was once a shooting lodge owned by the Duke of Wellington's estate at Stratfield Saye nearby, hence

**The Wellington Arms, Baughurst Road, Baughurst, Hampshire RG26 5LD
Tel: 0118 981 4330**

the name. This charming inn is run by Jean Harrison-Lethaby who offers visitors an excellent choice of superb home-cooked food at remarkable value-for-money prices. It's served at lunchtime from Monday to Saturday and the menu features popular favourites along with dishes such as home-made Barley and Lentil soup or Wild Rabbit Stew. Jacket potatoes and filled baguettes are also available and if you arrive on a Friday evening you can savour tasty sausages cooked on the open fire. Outside, there's a large garden in rural surroundings and, a special attraction, a Petanque piste. And if you want further entertainment, try to arrive when the people of Baughurst hold their annual Ferret Race!

Collectors of curiosities might like to make a short excursion to the little town of **Kingsclere**, about 5 miles southwest of Baughurst, where the weather-vane on top of the parish church has baffled many visitors. With its six outstretched legs and squat body, the figure on the vane has been compared to a skate-boarding terrapin. Local historians, however, assert that it actually represents a bed bug and was placed here by the command of King John. The king had been hunting in the area when a thick fog descended and he was forced to spend the night at the Crown Hotel in Kingsclere. Apparently, he slept badly, his slumber continually disturbed by the attentions of a bed bug. The next morning, he ordered that the townspeople should forever be reminded of his restless night in Kingsclere by erecting this curious memorial to his tormentor.

PAMBER HEATH   MAP 5 REF N1
8 miles N of Basingstoke, on minor road off the A340

There are three 'Pambers' set in the countryside along the A340. At **Pamber End** stand the picturesque ruins of a once-magnificent 12th/13th century Priory Church, idyllically sited in sylvan surroundings. Set apart from the village, they invite repose and meditation. **Pamber Green**, as you might expect, is a leafy enclave; but for anyone in search of a good country pub, the Pamber to make for is Pamber Heath.

Lots of pubs have a few pots scattered around, but the collection at **The Pelican** in Pamber Heath is something else. There are hundreds of them hang-

The Pelican, Silchester Road, Pamber Heath, Tadley, Basingstoke
Hampshire RG26 3EA Tel: 0118 970 0286

ing from the ceiling beams, in every shape and colour you can imagine, some pewter and some ceramic. They've been amassed over the years by Liz Saunders who together with her husband Danny runs this lively and sociable pub. From time to time the collection receives additions from 'locals' who return from holidays abroad or at home with yet another remarkable specimen. Liz and Danny have been in the licensed trade for many years now so they certainly know how to make visitors welcome.

Good food is definitely part of The Pelican's appeal. Liz looks after the cooking and her menu offers an excellent choice of wholesome fare. In addition to the daily special, there are hearty main meals ranging from Sirloin Steak to home-cooked Ham Salad; with jacket potatoes, baguettes (served with Spicy Spirals), and well-filled sandwiches for lighter appetites. Liz's Sunday Roasts are particularly popular as is her catering for functions and special occasions, and her culinary skills are also much in demand for outside catering. A visit to The Pelican is strongly recommended and if you arrive on a sunny day, you can enjoy your refreshment outside in the pleasant Beer Garden.

HOOK   Map 5 ref O2
5 miles NE of Basingstoke, on the A30

Conveniently located at the crossroads of the A30 and the A287, **The Dorchester Arms** is just a mile from junction 5 of the M3 and about the same distance from the centre of Hook. This welcoming and family-oriented pub is housed in a substantial Victorian building with bay windows and an atmospheric interior of pretty wallpaper and curtains with prints, photographs and porcelain plates

The Dorchester Arms, Hook Common, Hook, Hampshire RG27 9JJ
Tel: 01256 762690 Fax: 01256 767006

lining the walls. The Dorchester has been run since 1987 by Bernie and Sharon Mullin and during that time they have established an extensive reputation for their excellent food. Sharon is the cook and her weekday menu offers a wide choice of main dishes, including fish dishes, omelettes, home-made pies, and ploughman's, along with vegetarian options, an All Day Breakfast, and a hearty 'Dorchester Grill'. Daily Specials and a children's menu are also available and the desserts include a melt in the mouth home-made Apple Crumble with Custard. At Sunday lunch-time there's a special Roast of the Day (meat or vegetable), as well as dishes such as Lemon Sole or Beef, Ale & Mushroom Pie. If you enjoy good, wholesome food, well-prepared and well-presented, you should certainly make your way to the Dorchester Arms.

ODIHAM   Map 5 ref O3
8 miles E of Basingstoke, on the A327

Odiham Castle must have a very good claim to being one of the least picturesque ruins in the country. It looks like something rescued from a giant dentist's tray, with gaping window holes and jagged, crumbling towers. Back in 1215, though, Odiham Castle was a state-of-the-art royal residence. Great pomp and circumstance attended King John's stay at the castle, then just seven years old, the night before he set off to an important meeting. The following day, in a meadow beside the River Thames called Runnymede, John reluctantly ascribed his name to a bill of rights. That document, known as Magna Carta, proved to be the embryo of democracy in western Europe.

The town itself has a handsome High Street and a 15th century church, the largest in Hampshire, in which collectors of curiosities will be pleased to find a rather rare item, a hudd. A portable wooden frame covered with cloth, the hudd provided Odiham's rector with graveside shelter when he was conducting burials in inclement weather. In a corner of the graveyard stands the **Pest House**, built around 1625 as an isolation ward for patients with infectious diseases. From 1780 until 1950, it served as an almshouse and is now open to visitors on most weekends.

Close to the church, and reputed to be one of the oldest licensed houses in Hampshire, **The Bell** stands in the heart of this beguiling old market town, with ancient stocks and a whipping post just across the road. For centuries, The Bell has been at the centre of the town's regular celebrations - the annual fairs, Bonfire Night, and the Christmas festivities. Until well into the 20th century, farm workers and their wives from the surrounding area would walk into town each Saturday evening to shop for the following week and spend their remaining coppers in hostelries such as The Bell. Sadly, by the early 1990s The Bell had fallen on hard times and when Bob and Sue Porter, together with their daughter Mandy, took over here the building was in a sorry state. It's hard to believe that now as you enter this charming old inn with its original beams, log fire and exposed brick-work. Gleaming horse brasses adorn the walls and, (a more re-

The Bell, The Bury, Odiham, Hook, Hampshire RG29 1LY
Tel: 01256 702282

cent addition), coins from all around the world are dotted across the ceiling. RAF pilots from the Odiham Air Base, a mile or so away, have added their own touch to the inn's decor by sending postcards to their friendly 'local' from their far-flung postings. At lunch-time, The Bell offers a good choice of traditional, wholesome fare. Main courses include such favourites as Steak & Kidney Pie, Breaded Plaice and vegetarian Chilli & Rice. For smaller appetites, there's a range of Jacket Potatoes, Ploughmans, sandwiches and toasties to choose from. And if you enjoy a game of darts or cribbage, those are both available, but beware of taking on the pub's own teams - they have a formidable reputation!

HARTLEY WINTNEY   MAP 5 REF P2
9 miles NE of Basingstoke, on the A30

Riding through Hartley Wintney in 1821, William Cobbett, the author of *Rural Rides* and a conservationist long before anyone had thought of such a creature, was delighted to see young oaks being planted on the large village green. They were the gift of Hartley Wintney's lady of the manor, Lady Mildmay, whose far-sighted benevolence now provides the village centre with a uniquely sylvan setting of majestic oak trees.

Mighty oaks may not be the most appropriate plants for your own garden but you will find the ones that are, in abundance, at **The Coach House Garden Centre**, conveniently located on the A30 London Road between Hartley Wintney

The Coach House Garden Centre, London Road (A30), Hartley Wintney, Hook, Hampshire RG27 8HY Tel: 01252 842400 Fax: 01252 842675

and Hook. Whatever the season, the Coach House has a huge range of plants to make your garden beautiful. Friendly knowledgeable staff are ready to help with your choice of quality nursery-fresh plants or with any of the other hundreds of gardening items they stock. You'll find just about everything you could ever need, from fencing to fertilisers, pots to swimming pools, turf to garden tools. The Coach House can even supply you with gas, coal and logs and will deliver free in the local area.

Even if you're not planning to improve your garden right now, it's still worth visiting to sample the fare on offer in the lovely Coffee Shop with its friendly atmosphere. The home-made food includes a 5-item Breakfast Special, hot lunches, cream teas, and an excellent choice of snacks, sandwiches and sweets. On Sundays, the Coffee Shop serves a hearty Roast Lunch; children have their own menu; and all the prices represent extremely good value for money. There's also a children's play area and an in-house well-stocked florist's shop, "Green Fingers".

A visit to the Coach House Garden Centre is an outing in itself but keen gardeners might also like to take a look at the magnificent gardens of **West Green House**, about a mile to the west of Hartley Wintney. Owned by the National Trust, the pretty early-18th century house is surrounded by lovely gardens planted with a dazzling variety of trees, shrubs and plants. One of its interesting features is a stone column surmounted by an elaborate finial which was erected in 1976. It bears a Latin inscription which declares that a large sum of money was needed to put the column in place, money "which would otherwise have fallen, sooner or later, into the hands of the Inland Revenue".

While you are in Hartley Wintney a visit to the **Old Church**, south of the village, is well worth while. Parts of the building date back to medieval times, but the fascination of old St Mary's lies in the fact that, after being completely renovated in 1834, it has remained almost totally unaltered ever since. High-sided box pews line the main aisle, there are elegant Galleries for choir and congregation spanning the nave and both transepts, and colourful funeral hatchments add to St Mary's time-warp atmosphere.

EVERSLEY   MAP 5 REF P2
10 miles NE of Basingstoke, on the A327

Despite the current infatuation of breweries with creating "themed" pubs, ("cloned" might be a better word), the traditional English tavern is happily still very much alive and well: nowhere more so than at **The Golden Pot** in Eversley. The interior of this 200-year-old building displays all the authentic credentials: low-beamed ceilings, small-pane leaded windows, darkwood and pine furni-ture, a large collection of modern and old Teddy Bears, copper and brasses, even an open fire. This appealing old inn, with a separate restaurant, is owned and run by Justin and Antoinette Winstanley. Justin, who has a background of ca-

The Golden Pot, Reading Road, Eversley, Hampshire RG27 0NB
Tel: 0118 973 2104

tering and management experience with the Forte group, ensures the smooth running of the pub: Antoinette, who is Swiss-born, brings a tantalising Conti-nental flavour to the menu on offer, (a menu which changes 3 times a year, incidentally). How many other Hampshire hostelries, one wonders, include amongst their starters Wild Mushroom & Truffle Tortellini served with a light cream sauce, or Thai Fish Cakes with a Mango & Chilli Salsa? Main courses are equally tempting, (how about Saffron Risotto with Mushrooms, sprinkled with Gruyere cheese?), and diners are really spoilt with a choice of around a dozen different desserts. The Golden Pot is certainly the best reason for visiting this unassuming village which just stops short of wandering over the county boundary into Berkshire, but Eversley can also boast an important literary connection. Charles Kingsley, author of such immensely popular Victorian novels as *The Water Babies* and *Westward Ho!*, was Rector of the village for 33 years from 1842 until his death in 1875 and is buried in the churchyard here. Kingsley was an attractive character with a burning passion for social justice, but modern readers don't seem to share the Victorian enthusiasm for his works. It's a sad fate for a prolific man of letters, although perhaps not quite so dispiriting as that met by one of Kingsley's predecessors as preacher at Eversley. He was hanged as a highwayman.

STRATFIELD SAYE   MAP 5 REF O2
7 miles NE of Basingstoke, off the A33

About 4 miles west of Eversley, **Stratfield Saye House** was just one of many rewards a grateful nation showered on the Duke of Wellington after his decisive defeat of Napoleon at Waterloo. The Duke himself doesn't seem to have been reciprocally grateful: only lack of funds frustrated his plans to demolish the gracious 17th century house and replace it with an even more impressive mansion which he intended to call Waterloo Palace. Quite modest in scale, Stratfield Saye fascinates visitors with its collection of the Duke's own furniture and personal items such as his spectacles, handkerchiefs and carpet slippers. More questionable are the priceless books in the library, many of them looted from Napoleon's own bibliotheque. A good number of the fine Spanish and Portuguese paintings on display share an equally dubious provenance, "relieved" during the Duke's campaign in those countries as "spoils of war". That was accepted military practice at the time and, these quibbles apart, Stratfield Saye House is certainly one of the county's "must-see" attractions.

ALDERSHOT   MAP 5 REF P3
15 miles E of Basingstoke, on the A331

Back in 1854, Aldershot was a village of some 800 inhabitants. Then the Army decided to build a major camp here and the population has grown steadily ever since to its present tally of around 55,000. The story of how Aldershot became the home of the British Army is vividly recounted at the **Aldershot Military Museum** which stands in the middle of the camp and is a must for anyone with an interest in military history. Housed in the last two surviving Victorian barrack blocks, its tiny appearance from the outside belies the wealth of fascinating information contained inside. For example, there's a detailed cutaway model of a cavalry barracks showing how the soldiers' rooms were placed above the stables, an economic form of central heating described as "warm, but aromatic".

It was the army at Aldershot who became the first aviators in Britain, using Farnborough Common for their flying, and building their aircraft sheds where the Royal Aircraft Establishment stands today. The **Airborne Forces Museum** has many interesting exhibits illustrating the part these pioneers played during the early days of the 20th century and during two World Wars. In memory of those who lost their lives in these conflicts, **The Heroes Shrine** in Manor Park, commemorates the dead of World War I, while the nearby walled and sunken garden, shaded by a huge deodar tree, honours the fallen of World War II.

Another celebrated military figure, the Duke of Wellington, is celebrated by an imposing bronze statue on Round Hill. It originally stood in London on top of the Triumphal Arch at Hyde Park Corner and was removed to Aldershot in 1885.

ALTON   Map 5 ref O4
13 miles S of Basingstoke, off the A31

Surrounded by hop-fields and some of Hampshire's loveliest countryside, Alton is an appealing market town with a history stretching back far beyond Roman times. (The name actually means "Old Town"). Alton boasts a large number of old coaching inns, and the impressive, partly-Norman **St. Lawrence's Church** which was the setting for a dramatic episode during the Civil War. A large force of Roundheads drove some eighty Royalists into the church where 60 of them were killed. The Royalist commander, Colonel Boles, made a last stand from the splendid Jacobean pulpit, firing repeatedly at his attackers before succumbing to their bullets. The church door and several of the Norman pillars are still pock-marked with bullet holes fired off during this close-combat conflict. More cheerful are the comical carvings on these pillars of animals and birds, amongst them a wolf gnawing a bone and two donkeys kicking their heels in the air.

Nearby is the old cemetery and the well-tended Grave of Fanny Adams. The expression "Sweet Fanny Adams" arose from the revolting murder in 1867 of a young girl in the town who was hacked into pieces by her assassin. With macabre humour, sailors used the phrase "Sweet Fanny Adams" to describe the recently-issued tinned mutton for which they had a certain mistrust. Over the years, the saying became accepted as a contemptuous description for anything considered valueless. A poor memorial for an innocent girl.

There's a different sort of monument in Amery Street, a narrow lane leading off the market place. On a small brick house is a plaque commemorating the Elizabethan poet Edmund Spenser who came to Alton around 1590 to enjoy its "sweet delicate air".

Also in Amery Street, in the heart of this very English town, is a little corner of Italy, the **Osteria Antica** or "Old Hostelry", an outstanding restaurant owned and run by Margarette Wells and Tiziano Tesolin. When they arrived here in 1996 the building was certainly old and also very much in need of attention. In a labour of love they have transformed it into an attractive eating-place by retaining the 15th century exposed beams, restoring the latticed windows, and installing high quality furnishings and fittings. The cane-backed chairs, crisp

Osteria Antica, 16 Amery Street, Alton, Hampshire GU34 1HN
Tel: 01420 88988 Fax: 01420 549417

table cloths, flowers on each table and the open fire in the ground floor restaurant all add to the appeal. The menu, naturally, concentrates on top-quality Italian cuisine with Calamari Mafiosa (fresh squid poached with tomatoes, white wine, chili and garlic) amongst the starters; a tasty selection of pasta dishes, available in full or half portions and including a succulent Pennette di Salmone Affumicato (tubes of pasta coated in a creamy sauce of smoked salmon, vermouth, cream and tomato); and main courses of fish, meat, poultry or vegetarian dishes. All the food is freshly prepared so at busy periods it may take a little while to be served, but, as a note on the menu says the restaurant has "a plentiful supply of diversions at the bar to reward your patience". Tiziano and Maggie are always delighted to cater for private parties, weddings, birthdays and other special occasions: just ask them for sample menus and further information. Osteria Antica's central location in the town means that it is within easy reach of Alton's Allen Gallery, Curtis Museum, the railway station on the popular Watercress Line with its steam locomotives, and just a short distance outside the town, at Chawton, the charming 17th century house where Jane Austen wrote or revised her six famous novels.

Well worth a visit while you are in Alton is the **Allen Gallery** in Church Street (free), home to an outstanding collection of English, Continental and Far Eastern pottery, porcelain and tiles. Housed in a group of attractive 16th and 18th century buildings the Gallery's other attractions include the unique Elizabethan Tichborne Spoons, delightful watercolours and oil paintings by local artist William Herbert Allen and a comfortable Coffee Lounge. Across the road, the Curtis Museum (free) concentrates on exploring 100 million years of local history with displays devoted to the "shocking tale of Sweet Fanny Adams", other local celebrities such as Jane Austen and Lord Baden Powell, and a colourful Gallery of Childhood with exhibits thoughtfully displayed in miniature cases at an ideal height for children.

A good time to visit the town is mid-July when the **Alton Show** takes place. Established in 1840, this is one of southern England's most important agricultural gatherings with a wide range of events featuring such attractions as Heavy Horses, llamas, beagles, gun dogs and birds of prey.

CHAWTON MAP 5 REF O4
2 miles S of Alton, off the A31

From the outside, the home in which Jane Austen spent the last eight years of her life, **Chawton House**, and where she wrote three of her most popular novels *(Mansfield Park, Emma* and *Persuasion)*, is a disappointingly dull, blank-faced building. Sadly, once you step inside, the interior is equally dispiriting. You can

Chawton House

see the sitting-room in which she penned those cleverly-crafted novels, the bedroom to which she retired, but the house is curiously empty, as elusive as the author herself. Unless you are a really dedicated Jane-ite, this is a literary shrine which radiates only a minimum charge of magic.

The Wakes, the home of Gilbert White in **Selborne**, about 3 miles south of Chawton, is quite different. A humble curate of the parish from 1784 until his death in 1793, Gilbert spent his spare hours meticulously recording observations on the weather, wild-life and geology of the area. Astonishingly, a percipient

The Wakes, Selborne

publisher to whom Gilbert submitted his notes recognised the appeal of his humdrum, day-to-day accounts of life in what was then a remote corner of England. *The Natural History and Antiquities of Selborne* was first published in 1788, has never been out of print, and still provides what is perhaps the most entertaining and direct access to late-18th century life, seen through the eyes of an intelligent, sceptical mind.

ALRESFORD
MAP 5 REF N4
10 miles SW of Alton, off the A31

Pronounced Allsford, Alresford was created around 1200 by a Bishop of Winchester, Geoffrey de Lucy, as part of his grand plan to build a waterway from Winchester to Southampton. Where the river Arle flows into the Itchen, he constructed a huge reservoir covering 200 acres, its waters controlled to keep the Itchen navigable at all seasons. The **Bishop's Reservoir** is now reduced to some 60 acres but it's still home to countless wildfowl and many otters. Known today as Old Alresford Pond, it's one of the most charming features of this dignified Georgian town. Alresford can also boast one of the county's most beautiful streets, historic **Broad Street**, lined with elegant, colour-washed Georgian houses interspersed with specialist shops and inviting hostelries.

Most notable of the hostelries is **The Horse and Groom Inn**, a charming old half-timbered building parts of which date back to the 1600s. The large bay windows look out from an interior of ancient beams, open fires, interesting nooks and crannies everywhere with old pictures and vintage photographs lining the walls. Gerry and Phil Budge took over here in 1996 when Phil retired

The Horse and Groom Inn, Broad Street, Alresford, nr Winchester
Hampshire SO24 9AQ Tel: 01962 734809

from the Army after 26 years service with REME. A rugby devotee, Phil now officiates as a referee within the county of Hampshire. Top quality food is the watchword at The Horse and Groom. The lunchtime bar menu offers a huge choice of tempting dishes ranging from a succulent 10oz Ribeye Steak, through traditional favourites such as Country Sausages with Bubble & Squeak, to Ploughman's Lunches, jacket potatoes, and sandwiches. And since we're in the heart of Britain's most productive watercress-growing area, there is of course an Egg Mayonnaise and Watercress sandwich on the menu. There are also daily specials, a children's menu and in good weather you can enjoy your food either out front, overlooking the street, or in the spacious courtyard and beer garden at the rear. In the evenings, (except on Sundays), dinner is available from 6.30pm with last orders taken at 9.30pm and offers an equally inviting choice of dishes, including a Chef's home-made Soup of the Day, and a Fresh Catch of the Day which is detailed on the blackboard. Sunday Lunch at The Horse and Groom is also rather special with a selection of 5 main courses at prices which represent real value for money. If you are planning to visit for Sunday lunch, it's strongly recommended that you book ahead to avoid disappointment.

Alresford's most famous son was Admiral Lord Rodney, a contemporary of Lord Nelson, who built the grand Manor House near the parish church, but the town can also boast two famous daughters. One was Mary Sumner, wife of the Rector of Alresford, who founded the Mother's Union here in 1876. The other was Mary Russell Mitford, author of the fascinating collection of sketches of 18th century life, *Our Village,* published in 5 volumes between 1824-1832. Mary's prolific literary output was partly spurred on by the need to repay the debts of her spendthrift father. Dr Mitford managed to dissipate his own inherited fortune of many thousands of pounds; his wife's lavish dowry which almost doubled that income disappeared equally quickly, and when Mary at the age of ten won the huge sum of £20,000 in a lottery, the good doctor squandered that as well. Mary's classic book tells the story

One of Alresford's attractions that should not be missed is the **Watercress Line**, Hampshire's only preserved steam railway, so named because it was once used to transport watercress from the beds around Alresford to London and beyond. The line runs through 10 miles of beautiful countryside to Alton where

Watercress Line, Alresford

it links up with main line services to London. Vintage steam locomotives make the 35-minute journey up to 8 times a day, and there are regular dining trains as well as frequent special events throughout the year. More details on 01962 733810.

OVERTON   Map 5 ref M3
8 miles W of Basingstoke, on the B3400

A large village near the source of the River Test, Overton has a broad main street lined with handsome houses. During the stage coach era, it was an important staging post on the London to Winchester route and the annual sheep fair was one of the largest in the county selling at its peak up to 150,000 lambs and sheep. The fair flourished for centuries only coming to an end in the early 1930s.

"Great food, great wine, great time....and at sensible prices" is the inviting motto of **Farley's Restaurant**. The restaurant is owned and run by award-win-

Farleys, 19 Winchester Street, Overton, Hampshire RG25 3HR
Tel: 01256 771771 Website: www.farleysrestaurant.freeserve.co.uk

ning local chef Stephen Farley, a young college-trained chef who offers a good choice of exciting and interesting dishes prepared with care and attention to detail. Starters, for example, include Grilled Leeks over a feta cheese & pancetta salad, or Crab and Ginger ravioli with a lemon grass & chilli vinaigrette. Among the main courses you'll find Braised side of local rabbit flavoured with celery & thyme, and chick pea & basil dumplings bound in a ratatouille sauce. Desserts are equally inventive, ranging from Cinnamon coated apple beignets with a calvados sorbet to British cheeses served with celery, a plum compote and walnut bread. All dishes are prepared using top quality fresh ingredients obtained where possible from local producers and suppliers.

If you are planning a private party or special event, Farleys has a 40-cover function room and Stephen will be delighted to prepare a special menu to meet your dietary and budgetary requirements. His restaurant is housed in a turn of the century Victorian building, double-fronted with diamond leaded light windows, high, beamed ceilings and fireplaces at both ends of the dining room. Crisp linen cloths drape the tables, the old cast iron chairs provide an interesting talking point, and around the walls hang accomplished paintings by local artist Rosemary Trollope. Lunch is served daily except Mondays and Saturdays, with special roasts on Sundays; dinner is served each evening from Tuesday to Saturday.

Overton itself was once an important staging post for coaches travelling to and from the south-west and its wide main street is still lined with attractive houses. Other places of interest within easy reach include the **Silk Mill** at Whitchurch; the grand 17th century house called The Vyne, north of Basingstoke, and, a few miles to the north-west, the flamboyant Victorian extravaganza of Highclere Castle.

An attractive building in the half-timbered style, **The Old House at Home** is an inviting traditional village inn standing in the centre of the village. It's run by Joe and Edel Cotter, both of them from Cork in southern Ireland and both blessed with more than their fair share of Irish charm. Joe is a motor racing fanatic as well as being a computer addict, never happier than when he is creating 'copy'. He has even established a web site where you can call up the menu

The Old House at Home, Station Road, Overton, Hampshire RG25 3DO
Tel: 01256 770335 E-mail: jcotter@ohah.freeserve.co.uk

details if you wish. The Old House at Home offers a good choice of bar snacks and restaurant meals, all freshly prepared. The specials on the blackboard are changed daily and youngsters can either choose one of the special children dishes or a children's portion from the main menu. There's a large selection of wines, beers and spirits to complement your meal and, of course, Irish Coffee to round it off. Food is served daily from 11am to 2.30pm, from 5pm to 11pm, and on Sundays from 12 noon right through until 10.30pm. Take out food is also available and there are Marquee facilities available for weddings and small functions. Families are very welcome at The Old House which has a secure, fenced garden area where children can play in safety. This is a lively, sociable inn with its own pool, darts and quiz teams, and the Cotters also provide live music entertainment at weekends. If there's anything more you'd like to know about The Old House at Home, why not contact Joe's web site or send him an E-mail: he'll be delighted!

PETERSFIELD

An appealing market town, Petersfield is dominated by the bulk of **Butser Hill**, 900ft high and the highest point of the South Downs offering grand panoramic views over the town and even, on a clear day, to the spire of Salisbury Cathedral, some 40 miles distant. In the 1660s, Samuel Pepys noted his stay in Petersfield, at a hotel in which Charles II had slept before him. Another king is commemorated in the Square where William III sits on horseback, incongruously dressed in Roman costume. Unusually, the statue is made of lead.

Most of the elegant buildings around the Square are Georgian, but the **Church of St Peter** is much older, dating back to Norman times and with a fine north aisle to prove it. Just off the Square, the **Flora Twort Gallery** was once the home and studio of the accomplished artist of that name who moved to Petersfield at the end of World War I. Her delightful paintings and drawings capture life in the town over some 40 years - "reminders of some of the things we have lost" as she put it shortly before her death at the age of 91 in 1985.

From the Gallery, a short walk along Sheep Street, (which has some striking timber-framed 16th century houses and Georgian cottages), brings you to **The Spain**, a pleasant green surrounded by some of the town's oldest houses. It apparently acquired its rather unusual name because dealers in Spanish wool used to hold markets there.

Although it stands only half a mile from the centre of Petersfield, **Heath Farmhouse** is surrounded by peaceful countryside and enjoys wonderful views across the Downs. "All our guests remark how quiet it is" says Prue Scurfield who, together with her husband David, owns and runs this exceptionally inviting guesthouse. It was originally built as a farmhouse around 1820, (a few years after Jane Austen had completed her final novels at nearby Chawton), and is now a Grade II listed building. The Scurfields offer visitors a double, twin or family room, one of which has an en suite bathroom. All the bedrooms are spacious and comfortable, enjoy pleasant outlooks, and are provided with television and tea/coffee-making facilities. Bathrooms are equipped with both bath and shower. A full traditional English breakfast is included, if required, and special diets can be catered for. There's also a sitting room available for guests to use. Prue and David have been running their guest house for some eight years and lived in Petersfield for many more years before that.

A former printer, David now runs a glass engraving business, working mainly on commissioned items. If you enjoy classical music, do ask him about his

**Heath Farmhouse, Heath Road East, Petersfield, Hampshire GU31 4HU
Tel: 01730 264709**

collection of LPs. He's been acquiring them since his teens and now has more than a thousand recordings. Prue's passion is gardening, as the well-tended grounds of the farmhouse bear witness. Visitors who share her interest in gardening will want to visit the interesting Physic Garden in the centre of the town. Set in an ancient walled plot, the garden has been planted in a style and with plants that would have been familiar to the distinguished 17th century botanist, John Goodyer, who lived in Petersfield. Other attractions close by include a pay & play Golf Course (a mere 100 yards away), and a public heath which provides pleasant walks around a large lake where rowing boats are available for hire in summer. And of course there's Jane Austen's house at Chawton, Gilbert White's home at Selborne, and the stately National Trust property of Uppark, all within easy reach.

RAKE   Map 5 ref P5
6 miles NE of Petersfield, on the B2070

Rake is the only village in England bearing this curious name which derives from an Old English word meaning a "throat" or "pass" and Rake does indeed lie in a pass that separates Hampshire from West Sussex. On the edge of the village and surrounded by superb countryside, The Sun Inn dates back to the time when the present B2070 was a major coaching route from London to the southwest. No doubt **The Sun** was just as hospitable a place of refreshment then as it certainly is today with its open fires, outstanding selection of food and drink, and welcoming hosts, Patrick and Sally Mohan. The lunch menu is available every day, with orders taken between 12 noon and 2pm, and it offers a generous range of options from sandwiches and baguettes, (brie, mango & mushroom, for example), through omelettes, salads, jacket potatoes and veg-

The Sun Inn, Rake, nr Liss, Hampshire GU33 7PQ
Tel: 01730 892115 Fax: 01730 894104

etarian choices to tasty fish dishes or a challenging 12oz Ribeye Steak. In the evening, orders for dinner are taken between 7pm and 9.30pm, weekdays; 7pm and 9pm, Sundays. Sandwiches and lighter meals are not featured on the dinner menu which instead adds further choices of main meals with a special emphasis on daily specials of fish dishes. Everything is freshly prepared, beautifully presented and served with a smile. The Sun has a well-selected wine list presenting a choice that ranges from house wines by the glass or bottle to a Chablis Premier Cru. On fairweather days, guests can also enjoy their meal on the vine-covered sun terrace overlooking the tranquil wooded countryside. The inn has ample parking but please note that children under 14 cannot be accommodated. If you are travelling anywhere in the East Hampshire/West Sussex area, The Sun Inn is one Hidden Place you should certainly seek out.

MILLAND

MAP 5 REF P5

5 miles NE of Petersfield, on minor road off the B2070

Pots have been made in this village for more than 50 years. Jane Hawkins built the **Milland Pottery** in 1947 along with two partners. Restricted by post-war shortages and a limited budget, the building was constructed using local timbers, wattle and daub. These materials give the appearance of antiquity, the draughts in winter much the same! Visitors are frequently taken aback when they discover the relative youth of the building. Over the years, the partnerships have changed. For 23 years Jane ran the pottery with her husband George.

**Milland Pottery, Milland, nr Liphook, Hampshire GU30 7JP
Tel: 01428 741530**

After George's death, Jane let Angela Carter come and work with her and, as Angela says, "some 20 years later I seem to have become part of the fixtures". The pots they make are both decorative and functional, using bright-coloured slips on an earthenware clay. The small showroom has a wide selection of ware for sale but many pots are made to commission. There's a steady demand for commemorative wares made to celebrate weddings, births, anniversaries and other events.

In recent years, the Milland Pottery has been offering various activities for children. Courses are run for under-12s in the holidays, at half-terms and on term-time Saturday mornings. Angela can also help out with the annual children's birthday party dilemma - just bring them along to the Pottery for an hour of mucky fun. Decorating plates and mugs is another activity which proves very popular with everyone. The pot is provided and you specialise it with your own design, a great idea for an original present. The Pottery, which you may have seen on the BBC-TV series *Country Ways*, is just one mile off the B2070 between Liphook and Rake and signposted from the main road. It's open from 10am-4.30pm, Monday to Friday, 10am-1pm on Saturdays, and also on some weekends in summer.

BURITON   MAP 5 REF O6
3 miles S of Petersfield, on minor road off the A3

An old church surrounded by trees and overlooking a large pond is flanked by an appealing early-18th century **Manor House** (private) built by the father of Edward Gibbon, the celebrated historian. He wrote much of his magnum opus *Decline and Fall of the Roman Empire* in his study here. Gibbon was critical of the house's position, "at the end of the village and the bottom of the hill", but was highly appreciative of the view over the Downs: "the long hanging woods in sight of the house could not perhaps have been improved by art or expense".

Named after the five bells of Buriton church, **The Five Bells** inn is on record as far back as 1639. Much of the building dates back to that era, as witnessed by the low-beamed ceilings and the large inglenook fireplace with its roaring log fires. The present kitchens and restaurant were added in the 18th century with the restaurant at that time serving as a farrier's. Later, it became a small factory

The Five Bells, High Street, Buriton, nr Petersfield,
Hampshire GU31 5RX Tel: 01730 263584

producing clay pipes and it's said that a number of pipes have been left under the restaurant floor for future generations to uncover. Prior to its final use as a restaurant, the building was used as the village morgue, a service fairly common to inns in the 19th and early 20th century. That use may explain why the inn is haunted by a small lady dressed in grey peasant clothes who appears occasionally at night, but more often in the morning. Mine host at this charming old inn is Bridget Slocombe, a lady with a very welcoming smile and a friendly, infectiously happy personality. Bridget also has an obvious flair for producing tasty food. Her extensive menu covers fish, game, meat and vegetarian dishes as well as a large selection of curries and an excellent choice of home-made sweets. Also on offer at lunchtime is a range of appetising snacks. In good weather, these can be enjoyed in the pleasant garden to the rear or on the sheltered outside patio. The Five Bells lays on live music, ranging from pop to jazz, on Mondays and Wednesdays, and if you are planning to stay in the area offers 2 self-catering units, both with en suite double bedrooms.

About 3 miles south-east of Buriton, **Uppark** (National Trust), is a handsome Wren-style mansion built around 1690 and most notable for its interior. Uppark was completely redecorated and refurnished in the 1750s by the Fetherstonhaugh family and their work has remained almost entirely unchanged - not only their furniture but even some of the fabrics and wallpapers remaining in excellent condition. The house has an intriguing connection with the author H.G. Wells. Sir Harry Fetherstonhaugh was married late in life to his dairymaid. They had no children and after his death she lived on at Uppark with her sister. It was her sister who employed Wells' mother as a housekeeper and the boy's recollections of life at Uppark are fondly recorded in his autobiography.

EAST MEON   Map 5 ref O5
5 miles W of Petersfield, on minor road off the A3 or A272

Tucked away in the lovely valley of the River Meon and surrounded by high downs East Meon has been described as "the most unspoilt of Hampshire villages and the nicest". As if that weren't enough, the village also boasts one of the finest and most **venerable churches** in the county. The central tower, with walls 4ft thick, dates back to the 12th century, and is a stunning example of Norman architecture at its best. Inside, the church's greatest treasure is its remarkable 12th century Tournai font of black marble, exquisitely carved with scenes depicting the fall of Adam and Eve. Only four of these wonderful fonts are known to exist in England and East Meon's is generally regarded as the most magnificent of them.

Just across the road is the 15th century **Courthouse** which also has walls 4ft thick. It's a lovely medieval manor house where for generations the Bishops of Winchester, as Lords of the Manor, held their courts. It would have been a familiar sight to the "compleat angler" Izaac Walton who spent many happy hours fishing in the River Meon nearby.

There always seems to be something rather special about staying at a genuine old farmhouse for bed and breakfast and **Oxenbourne Farm** near East Meon is no exception. Marjorie Greenwood has been running this small farm since 1984, looking after the sheep, free range hens and horses at livery. The farmhouse itself is some 200 years old and has a wonderfully welcoming atmosphere. There are 2 letting rooms, with a shared bathroom, and also standings for 5 caravans in an adjoining field. Families are welcome and walkers will particularly appreciate the superb walking country all around, with an abundance of Green Lanes and the South Downs Way also within easy reach. The bustling little town of Petersfield is just a few miles to the east; the historic cathedral city of Winchester a little further to the west. If you prefer the urban attractions of

Oxenbourne Farm, East Meon, Petersfield, Hampshire GU32 1QL
Tel: 01730 823239

Portsmouth and Southampton, there are excellent motorway links to both those cities and also to the rural attractions of the New Forest.

Set in 10 acres of its own grounds, **Coombe Cross House** is a lovely early Georgian house surrounded by lawns, shrubs and trees, with a sunny patio for fairweather days, and superb views over the South Downs. This stylish, beautifully decorated and appealingly furnished house provides an ideal location for anyone seeking relaxed bed & breakfast accommodation - especially if they have an interest in horses and riding. Rozanne Bulmer, the owner of Coombe Cross

Coombe Cross House, East Meon, nr Petersfield, Hampshire GU32 1HQ
Tel: 01730 823298 Fax: 01730 823515

House, is an enthusiastic equestrian who is currently Secretary of the Hursley Hambledon Hunt. Guest who bring their own horses to Coombe Cross will find a full livery service available. The house has 4 twin or double rooms, one on the ground floor, and all with their own private bathroom. Each attractively appointed room is supplied with television, tea and coffee-making facilities, as well as an iron and hair-drier. Full traditional English, or a Continental, breakfast is available and visitors can also have packed lunches and/or evening meals by arrangement. And if you are a keen rider, why not check ahead to see what equestrian events are in the offing around the time you plan to stay?

LANGRISH
Map 5 ref O5
3 miles W of Petersfield, on the A272

Home to the Talbot-Ponsonby family for 7 generations, **Langrish House** is set in 14 acres of rolling Hampshire countryside, its grounds complete with lawns, woodland, lake and formal garden. This stylish hotel was originally a small 17th century Manor House used by sheep farmers, but it has been extended over the years, with major additions in 1842. Langrish House is owned and run by Nigel and Robina Talbot-Ponsonby who aim to combine the advantages of a modern hotel with the comforts of a family home. The 14 guest rooms are well-appointed: all with ensuite bathrooms, television, central heating and IDD telephones and each room enjoys views over the extensive grounds. For those who prefer a quiet, relaxing time, there are the gardens and the lake to enjoy, wildlife to watch, silence to revel in. In summer there are shady trees to read under: in winter, settle down in front of log fires crackling in the grate. Visitors to Langrish House have the choice of two restaurants. The Garden Restaurant

Langrish House, Langrish, nr Petersfield, Hampshire GU32 1RN
Tel: 01730 266941

enjoys tranquil views out and across the lawns to the woodland beyond: The Cromwellian Restaurant sits cosily in the old dungeons and owes its name to an incident that occurred during the Civil War. It appears that after the Battle of Cheriton in 1644, Royalist prisoners were brought here, compelled to dig the cellars, and were then imprisoned in them. There's a much more cheerful atmosphere nowadays, with a Roux Diners Club Scholarship 'Chef of the year' finalist as resident Head Chef who offers a menu based on fresh, locally-bought ingredients and providing a choice of English or Continental dishes. This outstanding hotel is also a superb venue for any event. The Great Hall with its Minstrel's Gallery Bar has its own separate entrance and the lovely gardens and historic setting make Langrish House an ideal setting for weddings. "We love weddings here" Robina says, "and will enjoy helping you plan your important day".

2 Northwest Hampshire

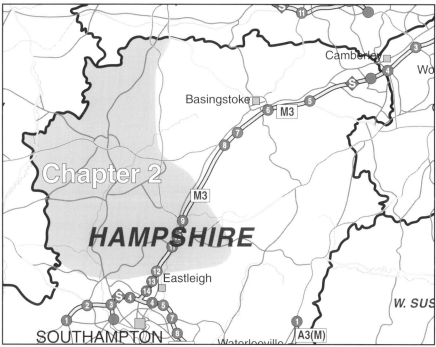

© MAPS IN MINUTES ™ (1998)

Some of Hampshire's grandest scenery lies in this part of the county as the North Downs roll westwards towards Salisbury Plain. There's just one sizeable town, Andover, and one major city, Winchester: the rest of the region is quite sparsely populated (for southern England) with scattered villages bearing evocative names such as Hurstbourne Tarrant and Nether Wallop. Winchester is of course in a class of its own with its dazzling Cathedral, but there are many other attractions in this area, ranging in time from the Iron Age Danebury Hill Fort, through the Victorian extravaganza of Highclere Castle, to Stanley Spencer's extraordinary murals in the Sandham Memorial Chapel at Burghclere.

ANDOVER

Andover has expanded greatly since the 1960s when it was selected as a "spillover" town to relieve the pressure on London's crowded population. But the core of this ancient town, which was already important in Saxon times, retains much of interest. One outstanding landmark is St Mary's Church, completely rebuilt in the 1840s at the expense of a former headmaster of Winchester College. The interior is said to have been modelled on Salisbury Cathedral and if it doesn't quite match up to that sublime building, St Mary's is still well worth a visit.

Equally striking is the **Guildhall** of 1825, built in classical style, which stands alone in the Market Place where markets are still held every Tuesday and Saturday. Andover has also managed to retain half a dozen of the 16 coaching inns that serviced 18th century travellers at a time when the fastest stage coaches took a mere 9 hours to travel here from London. As many as 50 coaches a day stopped at these inns to change horses and allow the passengers to take refreshments.

For a fascinating insight into the town's long history, do pay a visit to the **Andover Museum** (free) in Church Close. There are actually two museums here, both of them housed in buildings which began life as an elegant Georgian town house in 1750 and were later extended to serve as Andover's Grammar School from the 1840s to 1925. The Andover Museum traces the story of the town

Andover Museum, 6 Church Close, Andover, Hampshire SP10 1DP
Tel: 01264 366283 Fax: 01264 339152

from Saxon times to the present day with a range of colourful exhibits which include a 19th century Period Room and a display evoking Victorian Andover and a workhouse scandal of the time. The Museum also hosts an exciting programme of temporary exhibitions with subjects including art, craft, photography, history and much more. Former classrooms of the grammar school now house the Museum of the Iron Age (small charge) which tells the story of Danebury, an Iron Age hillfort that lies 6 miles southwest of Andover. The displays provide a vivid impression of what life was like for our prehistoric ancestors who farmed, fought, worshipped and died in Wessex seventy generations ago. The Andover Museum complex also incorporates a smart new coffee shop.

Another good way of getting to know the town is to join one of the guided tours along the **Andover Heritage Trail**. Scheduled tours, lasting about 90 minutes, take place on Tuesday and Saturday afternoons but can also be arranged for groups at other times. For more details telephone 01264 324068.

Two miles east of Andover, **Finkley Down Farm Park** provides a satisfying day out for families with young children. Youngsters can feed and handle the animals, groom a pony, ride on a mini-tractor, and expend any excess energy in the well-equipped playground. Romany caravans and farming bygones are on display and other attractions include a tea room, gift shop and picnic area. Tel: 01264 352195.

Another good family day out can be enjoyed at **The Hawk Conservancy**, 4 miles west of the town. With more than 200 birds to see in 22 acres of grounds, the Hawk Conservancy is one of the largest collections of raptors in the world. Flying demonstrations take place three times daily and include species such as owls, eagles, vultures and condors, falcons, kites, hawks and secretary birds. More details on 01264 772252.

LONGPARISH
MAP 4 REF L3

5 miles E of Andover, on the B3048

Living up to its name, Longparish village straggles alongside the River Test for more than two miles. This stretch of the river is famously full of trout but no one has yet beaten the record catch of Col. Peter Hawker who lived at Longparish House in the early 1800s. According to his diary for 1818, in that year this dedicated angler relieved the river of no less than one ton's weight of the succulent fish. A previous owner of the colonel's house had actually captured double that haul in one year, but the bounder had cheated by dragging the river.

With its creeper-clad walls, **The Plough Inn** is an appealing sight in this village of attractive cottages. Along with its "olde worlde" charm, this fine old country inn also boasts a large garden which has twice won the "Test Valley in Bloom" competition. Pauline Dale has been here since 1994 and has firmly established The Plough's reputation for good food and drink. On offer is a range

The Plough Inn, Longparish, Hampshire SP11 6PB
Tel: 01264 720358 Fax: 01264 720377

of traditional real ales and bottled continental beers, as well as a fine selection of wines from vineyards across the world. The inn's chef brings a wealth of experience which is reflected in an impressive menu choice and the presentation of classic dishes such as Lobster Thermidor, and the Chef's Specialities of Shoulder of Lamb Kleftico and Chicken Lobster. The Plough also offers an extensive traditional bar menu, an ever-changing daily specials board, a vegetarian dish of the day, and children have the choice of their own menu or half-portions of some dishes from the main menu. Food is available at lunchtime and in the evening every day and The Plough even provides a swift service luncheon menu which can be ordered by fax or telephone.

Set in the heart of this quiet and picturesque village is **The Cricketers Inn** which lives up to its name with lots of old pictures and prints of the game and colourful caricatures of local cricketers proudly displayed around the walls. After all, the village team has played at Lords in the Village Cricket Competition and the inn can even boast that David Gower has been here to preside over a "cricketathon" in aid of charity. Alison Woodford - young, enthusiastic and welcoming, runs this friendly pub where you'll find traditional games such as shove-halfpenny and darts, and a good choice of wholesome, home-made food. The menu includes simple dishes such as jacket potatoes and Chinese spring rolls, along with vegetarian options and hearty traditional dishes like Steak & Kidney Pie. Outside, there's an attractive Beer Garden, its lawn surrounded by

**The Cricketers Inn, Longparish, Hampshire SP11 6PZ
Tel: 01264 720335**

trees, shrubs and flower borders. You might well want to stay longer at such a pleasant place: if so, the Cricketers Inn has a double room to let, comfortable, well-appointed and en suite.

PENTON MEWSEY   Map 4 ref K3
2 miles NW of Andover, on minor road off the A342 or A343

For those who enjoy deciphering the cryptic place-names of English villages, Penton Mewsey offers a satisfying challenge. The answer goes like this: Penton was a 'tun' (enclosure or farm) paying a 'pen' (penny) as annual rent. That's the Saxon part. Later, in the early 1200s, Penton was owned by Robert de Meisy so his surname provided the second part of the village's name.

APPLESHAW   Map 4 ref K3
4 miles NW of Andover, off the A342

The houses in the village of Appleshaw sit comfortably along both sides of its broad, single street. Many of them are thatched and a useful, century-old clock in the middle of the street, placed here to celebrate Queen Victoria's Jubilee, adds to the time-defying atmosphere. The former **Vicarage**, built in Georgian times, is as gracious as you would expect of that era, and the neo-Gothic architecture of the parish church, rebuilt in 1830, is in entire harmony with its earlier neighbours.

Appleshaw nowadays is perhaps best known for its ancient pub, **The Walnut Tree**. Standing in the centre of the village, it's the only hostelry within a radius of 4 miles or so. The inn dates back to the 15th century and its antiquity is evident in the beams, low ceilings, small-paned windows, old planked bar and open fires. Old-fashioned settle benches add to the atmosphere, one of them bearing the inscription:

"Not a place for dogs or feet,
But just a place to put your seat".

Sean and Jean McDermott arrived here in 1998 after many years in the catering trade and quickly established The Walnut Tree as a lively and sociable centre of village life. Three different cricket teams have made the pub their base and have their own special 5-pint white enamel jug to cope with their need for liquid refreshment. At one end of the bar, there's a piano, paperbacks are ranged along a shelf, and a gallery of motor racing photographs going back many years

The Walnut Tree, Appleshaw, Andover, Hampshire SP11 9BN
Tel: 01264 772626

adorn the walls along with framed prints and old photographs. The wholesome food on offer here, cooked by Sean, includes an extensive range of English traditional fare as well as French and Chinese dishes. The Sunday roasts are particularly popular, so do book ahead if you can. During the summer, visitors can enjoy their refreshments at benches and tables out front, or on the terraced, lawned garden to the rear. And if you enjoy walking, there are literally hundreds of miles of footpaths to be explored, either in the vicinity of Appleshaw or in the great open spaces of Salisbury Plain, a few miles to the west.

TANGLEY
MAP 4 REF K3
6 miles NW of Andover, on minor road off the A342 or A343

For the best views, approach Tangley from the east, along the country lane from Hurstbourne Tarrant. Its mostly Victorian church is notable for its rare font, one of only 38 in the whole country made of lead and the only one in Hampshire. Dating back to the early 1600s, it is decorated with Tudor roses, crowned thistles, and fleur-de-lys.

Tangley sits amongst woods on the hill-top high above Tangley Bottom, the low-lying ground which forms the county boundary with Wiltshire. The village is surrounded by some of the best scenery in Hampshire and another attraction of this isolated spot is **The Cricketers Arms**, a former drovers' inn dating back to 1770. The Cricketers is owned and run by Edward Simpson. His inn has an appealing traditional atmosphere, with low-beamed ceilings, a huge open fire, latticed windows and floors part wood, part flagstones. Old cricketing prints and photographs adorn the walls and barrels of Real Ale are displayed behind the bar. The Cricketers has been recommended in the *Good Beer Guide* but also offers a good choice of wines. The food here is highly praised, whether it's just a bar snack - a filled baguette or Greek salad for example, or main dishes which

**The Cricketers Arms, Tangley, nr Andover, Hampshire SP11 0SH
Tel: 01264 730283**

include fish, game and rather unusual options such as Wild Boar, followed by an abundant choice of desserts. Very popular are the home-made pizzas which are also available to take away. In good weather, visitors can enjoy their refreshments at picnic tables in the peaceful Beer Garden. Definitely worth exploring the Hampshire by-ways to find this outstanding hostelry.

FACCOMBE   MAP 4 REF L2

12 miles N of Andover, on minor road off the A343

Faccombe is tucked away in the Hampshire countryside close to the Berkshire border, set on chalk Downs some 750ft above sea level, with the highest points of the North Downs, **Pilot Hill** and **Inkpen Beacon**, both nearby. Hidden away in this appealing little village which is owned by the Faccombe Estate, **The Jack Russell Inn & Restaurant**, dating back to the 1800s, is well worth seeking out for its exceptional food and excellent accommodation. Mine host, Alan Precious, offers his guests an outstanding menu that ranges from hearty snacks such as Steak, Kidney & Ale Pie to main dishes which include a Whole Pot Roasted Partridge, a "Catch of the Day", and steaks, followed by some interest-

**The Jack Russell Inn & Restaurant, Faccombe, nr Andover
Hampshire SP11 0DS Tel: 01264 737315**

ing desserts - Dark Chocolate Marquise, for example, with warm spiced blackcurrants. Meals are served in the non-smoking conservatory restaurant which enjoys superb views over farmland and hills. Outside, there's a secluded Beer Garden, children's play area and the Chef's very own Herb Garden. If you are planning to stay in this peaceful area, the inn has 3 superbly equipped and furnished rooms, all en suite and with amenities such as satellite TV. An extra attraction for walkers is the Test Way, a long-distance footpath which runs from Inkpen Beacon to the south coast following the track of the disused "Sprat & Winkle" railway.

HIGHCLERE   MAP 4 REF L2

14 miles N of Andover on the A343

About 5 miles east of Faccombe, **Highclere Castle** is an example of Victorian neo-Gothic architecture at its most exuberant. If the central tower reminds you of another well-known building, that may be because the Castle was designed by Sir Charles Barry, architect of the Houses of Parliament. It stands on the site of a former Palace of the Bishops of Winchester, overlooking an incomparably lovely park, one of Capability' Brown's greatest creations. The ornate architecture and furnishings of the Castle interior delights many, others feel somewhat queasy at its unrelenting richness. Highclere is the family home of the 7th Earl and Countess of Carnavon and it was the present Earl's grandfather who in 1922 was with Howard Carter at the opening of Tutankhamun's tomb. A small museum in the basement of the Castle recalls that breath-taking moment. Another display reflects the family's interest in horse racing. For more than a century, Earls of Carnavon have owned, bred and raced horses, and the present Earl is racing manager to the Queen. In addition to the superb parkland, there's also a Walled Garden, planted entirely with white blooms, a gift shop, restaurant and tea rooms. More details on 01635 253204.

A couple of miles northeast of Highclere Castle, at **Burghclere**, the **Sandham Memorial Chapel** (National Trust) is, from the outside, a rather unappealing construction, erected in 1926 by Mr and Mrs J.L. Behrend in memory of a relation who died in World War I. Their building may be uninspired but the Behrends can't be faulted on their choice of artist to cover the walls with a series of 19 murals. Stanley Spencer had served during the war as a hospital orderly and 18 of his murals represent the day-to-day life of a British Tommy in wartime. The 19th, covering the east wall of the Chapel, depicts the Day of Resurrection with the fallen men and their horses rising up. The foreground is dominated by a pile of white wooden crosses the soldiers have cast aside. The whole series is enormously moving, undoubtedly one of the masterpieces of 20th century British art. Tel: 01635 278394

NETHER WALLOP   Map 4 ref K4
8 miles SW of Andover, on minor road off the A343

The names of the three Wallops, (Over, Middle and Nether), have provided a good deal of amusement to visitors over the centuries, so it's slightly disappointing to discover that Wallop is just a corruption of the Old English word *waell-hop*, meaning a valley with a stream. At Nether Wallop the stream is picturesquely lined with willow trees, while the village itself is equally attractive with many thatched or timbered houses. The most notable building in Nether Wallop though is **St Andrew's Church**, partly because of its Norman features and handsome West Tower of 1704, but also because of its striking medieval wall paintings which provide an interesting contrast with Stanley Spencer's at Burghclere. Some 500 years old, these lay hidden for generations under layers of plaster and were only rediscovered in the 1950s. The most impressive of them shows St George slaying the dragon. Outside St Andrew's stands an item of great interest for collectors of churchyard oddities. It's a dark grey stone pyramid, 15ft high, with red stone flames rising from its tip. This daunting monument was erected at his own expense and in memory of himself by Francis Douce,

'Doctor of Physick', who died in 1760. Dr Douce also left an endowment to build a village school on condition that the parishioners would properly maintain the pyramid.

Situated about a mile to the east of the village, **Danebury Vineyards** welcomes groups of visitors by arrangement for a guided tour of the 6 acres of vines and winery. Tastings and dinners can also be arranged. The vineyard was planted in 1988 on south facing slopes of free draining chalk, an excellent siting for the varieties of grape grown here. The British climate generally results in a late-ripening crop producing grapes which are most suitable for the white wines with which Danebury Vineyards has made its name. Inspired by its connection with Danebury Racecourse, (which was often faviured with the public presence of Queen Victoria's heir, the Prince of Wales, and the slightly less public presence of

**Danebury Vineyards, Danebury House
Nether Wallop, Stockbridge, Hampshire SO20 6JX
Tel: 01264 781851 Fax: 01264 782212**

his mistress, Lily Langtry), Danebury wines are named after former winners of the Derby and each bottle label carries a colourful racing scene, linocuts created by Katie Clemson. *Pyrrhus*, for example, is a fine dry white wine full of aromatic perfumes and made from a single grape variety, Schonburger. An especially popular product is a fine dry sparkling wine called *Cossack* made by the traditional method from a blend of two grapes, Auxerrois and Rülander. Both are available at extremely competitive prices. Established for little over a decade, Danebury Vineyards have proved to be a worthy successor in a tradition of English viticulture that goes back to Roman times and, although wine-making virtually died out in England during the early 1900s, is now flourishing once again.

MIDDLE WALLOP

MAP 4 REF K4

7 miles SW of Andover on the A343

A mile or so to the northwest, the village of Middle Wallop became famous during the Battle of Britain when the nearby airfield was the base for squadrons of Spitfires and Hurricanes. Many of the old buildings have been incorporated into the **Museum of Army Flying** which traces the development of Army Flying from the balloons and kites of pre-World War I years, through various imaginative dioramas, to a helicopter flight simulator in which visitors can test their own skills of 'hand and eye' co-ordination. Other attractions include a Museum Shop, licensed café & restaurant, and a grassed picnic area. More details on 01980 674421.

About 3 miles east of Middle Wallop, **Danebury Ring** is Hampshire's largest Iron Age hill fort. Intensively occupied from about 550 BC until the arrival of the Romans, the site has been meticulously excavated over the last 30 years and the finds are now displayed at the Museum of the Iron Age in Andover. Visitors can wander the 13 acre site and with the help of explanatory boards, reconstruct the once-bustling community with its clearly defined roads, shops, houses and what were probably temples.

WINCHESTER

One of the country's most historic cities, Winchester was adopted by King Alfred as the capital of his kingdom of Wessex, a realm which then included most of southern England. There had been a settlement here since the Iron Age and in Roman times, as Venta Belgarum, it became an important military base. **The Brooks Experience**, located within the modern Brooks Shopping Centre, has

Winchester Cathedral

displays based on excavated Roman remains with its star exhibit a reconstructed room from an early-4th century town-house.

When the Imperial Legions returned to Rome, the town declined until it was refounded by Alfred in the late 800s. His street plan still provides the basic outline of the city centre. A Saxon cathedral had been built in the 7th century but the present magnificent **Cathedral**, easily the most imposing and interesting building in Hampshire, dates back to 1079. It's impossible in a few words to do justice to this glorious building and its countless treasures such as the famous Winchester Bible. Winchester Cathedral boasts the longest nave in Europe, a dazzling 14th century masterpiece in the Perpendicular style, a wealth of fine wooden carvings, and gems within a gem such as the richly decorated Bishop Waynflete's Chantry of 1486. Sumptuous medieval monuments, like the effigy of William of Wykeham, founder of Winchester College, provide a striking contrast to the simple black stone floorslabs which separately mark the graves of Izaak Walton and Jane Austen.

Just south of the Cathedral, on College Street, are two other buildings of outstanding interest. No. 8, College Street, a rather austere Georgian house with a first-floor bay window, is **Jane Austen's House** in which she spent the last six weeks of her life in 1817. The house is private but a slate plaque above the front door records her residence here. Right next door stands **Winchester College** the oldest school in England, founded in 1382 by Bishop William of Wykeham to provide education for seventy 'poor and needy scholars'. Substantial parts of the 14th century buildings still stand, including the beautiful Chapel. The Chapel is always open to visitors and there are guided tours around the other parts of the College from April to September. If you can time your visit during the school holidays, more of the College is available to view.

Two years after Jane Austen was buried in the Cathedral, the poet John Keats stayed in Winchester and it was here that he wrote his timeless *Ode to Autumn - 'Season of mists and mellow fruitfulness'*. His inspiration was a daily walk past the Cathedral and College and through the Water Meadows beside the River Itchen. A detailed step-by-step guide to Keats' Walk is available from the Tourist Information Centre.

The city's other attractions are so numerous one can only mention a few of the most important. **The Great Hall**, (free), off the High Street, is the only surviving part of the medieval Castle rebuilt by Henry III between 1222 and 1236. Nikolaus Pevsner considered it "the finest medieval hall in England after Westminster Hall". Other buildings of interest include the early-14th century **Pilgrim Hall** (free), part of the Pilgrim School, and originally used as lodgings for pilgrims to the shrine of St Swithun, and **Wolvesey Castle** (English Heritage), the residence of the Bishops of Winchester since 963. The present palace is a gracious, classical building erected in the 1680s, flanked by the imposing ruins of its 14th century predecessor which was one of the grandest buildings in medieval England. Also well worth a visit is the 15th century **Hospital of St**

Cross, England's oldest almshouse. Founded in 1132 by Henri du Blois, grandson of William the Conqueror, it was extended in 1446 by Cardinal Beaufort, son of John of Gaunt. It is still home to 25 Brothers and maintains its long tradition of hospitality by dispensing the traditional Wayfarer's Dole to any traveller who requests it.

Historic surroundings and fine cuisine blend perfectly at the **Old Chesil Rectory** which is both the oldest house in the city, dating back to 1459, and also one of Winchester's most outstanding restaurants. At the time it was built, this lovely old house which is now one of the city's best loved landmarks stood outside the city walls in an area known as the Soke and marked on early maps as the village of Chesil. The name Chesil is probably a corruption of the old English word *chisol*, meaning a beach or bank, since in medieval times the river here was much wider than it is now and Chesil village would have been right on its eastern bank. Originally built as a merchant's house, it became a Rectory in the 1500s then reverted to being a private house. By the late 1700s the house was divided into a number of separate tenements and towards the end of the 19th century the fabric had deteriorated so badly that it only narrowly escaped demolition. The Rectory is now owned by Winchester City Council who, in co-operation with its tenants, take great care to maintain the house and retain its early-Tudor character and charm. All the old beams are still in place, and so too is the original oak flooring, a feature it would be impossible to re-create nowadays. Philip and Catherine Storey took over here in 1998 and they provide their

Old Chesil Rectory, 1 Chesil Street, Winchester, Hampshire SO23 0HU
Tel: 01962 851555

guests with a dining experience truly worthy of such a grand old building. Philip is the chef and his inventive menus, which change daily, offer a choice of dishes designed to delight the most discriminating gourmet. In addition there's an extensive, and informatively annotated, wine list which, together with the outstanding cuisine, should ensure that a meal at the Old Chesil Rectory will be a special event you will remember for a long time.

Collectors of unique pub interiors should definitely make their way to the **Black Boy** on Wharf Hill where they'll find a welcoming pub and also a fascinating display of unusual objects of every kind. David Nicholson arrived at this ancient hostelry in 1995 after world-wide experience in the catering and pub trade and, with the help of his wife, has created an interior decor quite unlike any other pub in the country. There's not enough space here to give a complete account of the incredible collection of paraphernalia which smother the walls, ceiling and floors of the Black Boy. Where else would you find a collection of

The Black Boy, 1 Wharf Hill, Winchester, Hampshire SO23 9NQ
Tel: 01962 861754

watch faces hanging from the ceiling, a bar counter made from bottle tops, or old printing plates mounted as wall tiles? There are thousands of hanging keys, and a range of old pub games, including one with a chain with a ring at the end. The object is to swing the chain so that the ring catches onto a hook in the wall. Not so easy as it sounds. And watch out for the two pump handles which, when they are pulled, squirt the customer with water. Modern pub games are also available and although the Black Boy's speciality is its well-maintained beers there's also a good choice of quality, home-made food. Along with jacket pota-toes, offered with a wide range of fillings, the menu also includes dishes such as breaded mushrooms with a garlic dip, chilli on rice, and beef & hash. In good weather you can enjoy a barbecue in the peaceful Beer Garden at the rear. Win-chester, of course, can boast scores of tourist attractions but after a visit here you may well find that what remains most vivid about the city in your memory is the one and only Black Boy.

CRAWLEY
MAP 4 REF L4

7 miles NW of Winchester, on minor road off the B3049

Crawley is a possibly unique example of an early-20th century model village. The estate was bought by the Philippi family in 1900 who enthusiastically set about adding to the village's store of genuine traditional cottages with faithful fakes built in the same style. (They also provided their tenants with a state-of-the-art bath house and a roller skating rink). Sensitive to tradition and history, they did nothing to blemish the partly Norman church, leaving its unusual interior intact. Instead of stone pillars, **St Mary's** has mighty wooden columns supporting its roof, still effective more than 500 years after they were first hoisted into place.

This sizeable village in the heart of the Hampshire countryside is also well worth seeking out in order to visit the **Rack and Manger**, run by Jane and Alan Standring. They are both members of the Zabadac Gourmet Club, which is one good sign, and their hostelry has appeared in the Good Pub Guide, which is another. The Rack and Manger began as a brewery back in the mid-1700s, served

Rack & Manger, Stockbridge Road, Crawley, nr Winchester Hampshire SO21 2PH Tel: 01962 776281

for a spell as stables, but has now settled down as an atmospheric pub with panelled walls, open fires, low-beamed ceilings, and an interesting decor of old photographs, prints, half barrels mounted on the ceiling labelled with the names of various wines - and fishing rods. Alan, it turns out, is an enthusiastic fisherman who takes part whenever he can in angling competitions. So it's not surprising to find that the house specialities are fresh fish and seafood, marked up daily on the "Tote Board". The Board's name fits in with the amusing "horse race" theme running through the whole of the menu. "Under Starters Orders" offers a dozen different starters, ranging from home-made soup of the day to mini Lobster Tails; main meals are listed under "Grand International", (Peking style Chicken Stir Fry, or Cajun Spiced Poussin, for example); "Round the Course" is devoted to substantial dishes such as a 24oz Mixed Grill, Venison Steak, or a Whole Duck Breast; while "The Final Furlong" offers a good choice of vegetarian options. Children's portions are available on request for most meals and priced accordingly. The final page of the Rack and Manger's menu is headed "The Winners Enclosure (If You Can Make It!)" and invites diners to inspect the wide selection of fresh handmade Cheesecakes and Gâteaux in the display cabinet. This outstanding hostelry also has an inviting Beer Garden, complete with wishing well, and its own ample parking. Definitely a Hidden Place not to be missed.

TWYFORD
Map 4 ref M5

5 miles S of Winchester, on the B3335

Hampshire churchyards are celebrated for their ancient yew trees, but the one at Twyford is exceptional. A visitor in 1819 described the clipped tree as resembling "the top of a considerable green hillock, elevated on a stump". The grand old yew is still in apparently good health and provides a dark green foil to the trim Victorian church of striped brick and flint which was designed by Alfred Waterhouse, architect of the Natural History Museum in London.

Three well-known historical figures have strong associations with the village. Benjamin Franklin wrote much of his autobiography while staying at Twyford House, Alexander Pope attended school here until he was expelled for writing a lampoon on the Master, and it was at the old Brambridge House that Mrs Fitzherbert was secretly married to the Prince Regent, later George IV, in 1785.

LONGWOOD DEAN
Map 4 ref M5

5 miles SE of Winchester off the A272

In the small village of Longwood Dean, lying on a quiet country lane between Twyford and Alresford, **Mays Farm** offers first class bed & breakfast accommodation in a charming old building surrounded by terraced lawns and well-maintained gardens. The house dates back to the 1600s and twenty years

Mays Farm, Longwood Dean, Nr Winchester, Hampshire SO21 1JS
Tel: 01962 777486 Fax: 01962 777747

ago it was in a sadly dilapidated state. James and Rosalie Ashby came to the rescue, completely renovating and refurbishing the ancient building while preserving its original exposed ceiling beams and wall timbers as well as the open fireplace with its substantial lintel of English oak. There are 3 double or twin rooms available, all well-equipped and enjoying superb views over the Hampshire countryside. A traditional hearty English breakfast is included in the tariff and served in the dining room with its splendid old oak furniture. Outside, there's an interesting menagerie of farmyard animals, (all well-behaved and managed by the gardener!), and walkers will be pleased to know that the South Downs Way long distance footpath is just a mile or so away. Anyone looking for peace and tranquillity will surely find it here.

ROMSEY   Map 4 ref K5
10 miles SE of Winchester, on the A27/A3090

"Music in stone", and "the second finest Norman building in England" are just two responses to **Romsey Abbey**, a majestic building containing some of the best 12th and 13th century architecture to have survived. Built between 1120 and 1230, the Abbey is remarkably complete. Unlike so many monastic buildings which were destroyed or fell into ruin after the Dissolution, the Abbey was fortunate in being bought by the town in 1544 for £100. Subsequent generations of townspeople have carefully maintained their bargain purchase. The Abbey's most spectacular feature is the soaring Nave which rises more than 70ft and extends for more than 76ft. Amongst the Abbey's many treasures is the Romsey Rood which shows Christ on the cross with the hand of God descending from the clouds.

Romsey Abbey

Just across from the Abbey, in Church Court, stands the town's oldest dwelling, **King John's House**, built around 1240 for a merchant. It has served as a royal residence but not, curiously, for King John who died some 14 years before it was built. He may though have had a hunting lodge on the site. The house is now a museum and centre for cultural activities.

Romsey's most famous son was undoubtedly the flamboyant politician Lord Palmerston, three times Prime Minister during the 1850s and 1860s. Palmerston lived at Broadlands, just south of the town, and is commemorated by a bronze statue in the town's small triangular Market Place.

On the southern outskirts of the town, close to the Test Way and the Broadlands estate of the Mountbatten family, **The Old Horse & Jockey** offers visitors excellent food, fine ales and comfortable accommodation. It's owned and run by Nick and Sue Emberley who have spent many years dispensing hospitality at quality hostelries in and around the New Forest. They took over here in 1996 and their local reputation as warm and welcoming hosts offering wholesome fare at value for money prices has received an international seal of approval from Les Routiers, as well as from Egon Ronay, the AA, and most recently, Michelin 1999. The regular menu includes a wide selection of meal, poultry and fish dishes, with daily specials adding to the choice.

The pub's inviting interior with its many nooks and crannies is attractively furnished with stripped pine and darkwood tables, the walls smothered with prints and photographs. Outside, there's a large mature garden with lawns, shrubs and trees, a children's play area and an extensive car park. If you are planning to stay in the area, do try to snap up one of the Old Horse & Jockey's two bed & breakfast rooms, both of them well-appointed with television, refreshment tray and en suite facilities. Within easy reach are the unspoilt acres of the New For-

**The Old Horse & Jockey, Mainstone, Romsey, Hampshire SO51 8HG
Tel: 01794 519515**

est, the urban attractions of Southampton, peaceful stretches of the Test Valley, and the historic cathedral cities of Winchester and Salisbury.

In addition to its Abbey, Romsey also boasts one of the finest Stately Homes in the county, **Broadlands**, a gracious Palladian mansion built by Lord Palmerston's father in the mid-1700s. The architect was Henry Holland, the landscape was modelled by the ubiquitous 'Capability' Brown. The important collections of furniture, porcelain and sculpture were acquired by the 2nd Viscount Palmerston. The house passed to the Mountbatten family and it was Lord Louis Mountbatten who first opened Broadlands to the public shortly before he

Broadlands, Nr Romsey

was killed in 1979. The present owner, Lord Romsey, has established the Mountbatten Exhibition in tribute to his grandfather's remarkable career as naval commander, diplomat, and last Viceroy of India. An audio-visual film provides an overall picture of the Earl's life and exhibits include his dazzling uniforms, the numerous decorations he was awarded, and an astonishing collection of the trophies, mementoes and gifts he received in his many rôles.

SUTTON SCOTNEY
8 miles N of Winchester, on the A34

Map 4 ref M4

Standing at a crossroads, Sutton Scotney was once a busy little place. Today, it is by-passed by the A34 so visitors can peacefully explore its picturesque side streets lined with thatched cottages and Georgian houses. Unusually, the village has no church but the clock tower of the Jubilee Hall, erected in 1897, has a distinctly ecclesiastical air about it.

Conveniently located on the edge of the village near the junction of the A303 and A34, the **Bullington Cross Inn** enjoys an excellent reputation for its home cooked meals and Real Ales. John Jefford is the cook and he offers a menu of traditional dishes such as Steak & Kidney Pie, fish and chips, and of course a good old-fashioned Sunday roast. His co-host, Natasha Shearwood, looks after the customers in this welcoming hostelry which dates back some 250 years. "Tash", incidentally, is an enthusiast for animal welfare, the devoted owner of 4 goats, 2 Rottweilers, and a pig! The inn's attractive L-shaped bar has an open fire and low-beamed ceilings and is decorated with an interesting array of brasses, prints and old photographs. Another feature in the bar which provides a good conversation piece is a tank of colourful tropical fish. Outside, there's a Beer Garden, childrens' play area and ample parking space.

Bullington Cross Inn, Sutton Scotney, nr Winchester
Hampshire SO21 3QG Tel: 01962 760285

3 Southeast Hampshire

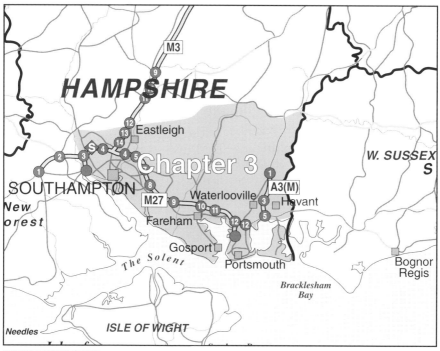

© MAPS IN MINUTES ™ (1998)

With a population of 1.2 million, Hampshire is the 5th most populous county in England. A goodly proportion of those 1.2 million people live along the coastal crescent that stretches from Southampton through Farcham and Portsmouth to Havant. Inland, though, there are parts of the South Downs as peaceful and scenic as anywhere in the county.

Southampton boasts one of the finest natural harbours in the world and has been the leading British deep-sea port since the days of the Norman Conquest. Portsmouth did not develop as a port until the 16th century but makes up for its shorter history by its romantic associations with such legendary ships as *HMS Victory,* the *Mary Rose,* and *HMS Warrior.* Portsmouth is also a popular seaside resort providing, together with its neighbour, Hayling Island, some seven miles of sandy beaches. Southsea Castle and the massive Portchester Castle have interesting historical associations, and the ruins of Netley Abbey and the Bishop's Palace at Bishop's Waltham are both outstandingly picturesque.

Like most major ports, Southampton and Portsmouth have something of a cosmopolitan air about them, making an intriguing contrast with the rural charms of the inland villages.

SOUTHAMPTON

From this historic port, Henry V set sail for Agincourt in 1415, the Pilgrim Fathers embarked on their perilous journey to the New World in 1620, and, on April 10th, 1912, the *Titanic* set off on its maiden voyage, steaming majestically into the Solent. The city's sea-faring heritage is vividly recalled at the excellent **Maritime Museum** (free), housed in the 14th century **Wool House**. The museum tells the story of the port from the age of sail to the heyday of the great ocean liners.

As a major sea-port, Southampton was a prime target for air raids during World War II and suffered grievously. But the city can still boast a surprising number of ancient buildings. Substantial stretches of the medieval Town Walls have miraculously survived, its ramparts interspersed with fortifications such as the oddly-named 15th century **Catchcold Tower** and **God's House Gate and Tower**, which now houses the city's archaeological museum. Perhaps the most impressive feature of the walls is **Bargate**, one of the finest medieval city gates in the country. From its construction around 1200 until the 1930s, Bargate remained the principal entrance to the city. Its narrow archway is so low that Southampton Corporation's trams had to be specially modified for them to pass through. Inside the arch stands a statue of George III, cross-dressing as a Roman Emperor. Bargate now stands in its own pe-

Bargate, Southampton

destrianised area, its upper floor, the former Guildhall, now a Museum of local history and folklore.

Another remarkable survivor is the **Medieval Merchant's House** in French Street which has been expertly restored and authentically furnished, now appearing just as it was when it was built around 1290. One of the most popular visitor attractions in Southampton is the **Tudor House Museum & Garden**, a lovely 15th century house with an award-winning Tudor Garden complete with fountain, bee skeps and 16th century herbs and flowers.

There's so much history to savour in the city, but Southampton has also pro-

Tudor House Museum, Southampton

claimed itself "A City for the New Millennium". West Quay, one of the largest City Centre developments in Europe, is scheduled to open in 2000; a £3.4m injection from the Heritage Lottery Fund will enhance Southampton's already highly acclaimed central parks; the £27m Leisure World offers a wide range of leisure activities; and the new, state-of-the-art Swimming & Diving Complex incorporates separate championship, diving and fun pools.

Another major development is **Ocean Village**, an imaginatively conceived waterfront complex with its own 450-berth marina, undercover shopping, excellent restaurants, a multi-screen cinema, and, occupying a stylish building on the water's edge near the Pier, **Harry Ramsden's** fish and chip restaurant. Here you'll find the same legendary quality that has made Harry Ramsden's name a by-word for lovers of Britain's national dish.

The Southampton restaurant is a far cry from the white-painted hut, 10ft by 6ft, which Harry opened up at Guiseley, near Leeds, back in 1928. This modern building is air conditioned, with lofty, arched windows overlooking the marina, and with a decor that includes cut glass chandeliers, oak panelling, stained glass panels, and wall to wall carpeting. There's a licensed bar with spectacular views and amongst other amenities are free car parking, good disabled access, baby-changing facilities, braille menus, high chairs, and even left-handed fishknives! The extensive menu, in addition to the classic fish dishes cooked in Harry Ramsden's traditional and unique batter, also offers alternative dishes such as chicken fillets,

Harry Ramsden's, Ocean Village, Canute Road, Southampton Tel: 01703 230678 Fax: 236345

Steak & Harry's Ale Pudding, a vegetarian dish of the day, and two separate children's menus. (For more information, see the entry for the Harry Ramsden's restaurant in Bournemouth).

As you'd expect in a city with such a glorious maritime heritage, there's a huge choice of boat excursions, whether along the River Hamble, around the Solent, or over to the Isle of Wight. Blue Funnel Cruises operate from Ocean Village; Solent Cruises from Town Quay.

The city also occupies an important place in aviation history. A short step from Ocean Village, the **Hall of Aviation** presents the story of aviation in the Solent and incorporates the **R.J. Mitchell Memorial Museum**. Mitchell lived and worked in Southampton in the 1930s and not only designed the Spitfire but also the S6 Seaplane which won the coveted Scheider Trophy. The centrepiece of the Hall of Aviation is the spectacular Sandringham Flying Boat which you can board and sample the luxury of air travel in the past - very different from the Cattle Class standards of today's mass travel. Tel: 01703 635830.

WEST END   MAP 6 REF M6
3 miles NE of Southampton, on minor road off the A27

An ideal destination for a family outing is **Itchen Valley Country Park** on the outskirts of Southampton. Its 440 acres of water meadows, ancient woodland, conifer plantations and grazing pasture lie either side of the meandering River Itchen, famous for its clear waters and excellent fishing. The Park is managed by Eastleigh Borough Council's Countryside Service to provide informal recreation, enhance and conserve wildlife habitats and as an educational resource. The best place to begin your visit is the **High Wood Barn Visitor Centre**, an

Itchen Valley Country Park, Allington Lane, West End
Southampton SO30 3HQ Tel: 01703 466091

attractive timber structure built in the style of a 17th century Hampshire Aisle Barn. Inside, you'll find information, interactive exhibits, a freshwater aquarium, a shop selling countryside gifts and publications, and the Woodland Cafe which provides a range of refreshments. (You are also welcome to make use of the various picnic sites in the Park and there are two permanent barbecues behind the Centre which are available to hire). From the Visitor Centre, waymarked trails help you to discover the different areas of the Park and an informative leaflet reveals the history and wildlife of a landscape shaped by hundreds of years of traditional farming and woodland management. Children are well-provided for at the Park. In High Hill Field there's an adventure play area for the under-12s that includes an aerial runway, and behind the Visitor Centre a play area for the under-5s has giant woodland animals designed by local schoolchildren and built by sculptor Andy Frost. A full programme of events and activities is run throughout the year - phone for details. Wheelchair users (and pushchair pushers) will find part of the Forest Trail easily accessible and this stretch also has a tapping rail to assist those with visual impairments. A manual wheel-chair and a motorized buggy are available to borrow from the Visitor Centre (deposit £5). Cyclists are provided with their own off-road cycle route and there's also a Bridle Route reserved for horse-riders who have paid the annual licence fee. In fact, within its spacious environs the Park seems to provide something to enjoy for just about everybody.

HORTON HEATH
Map 6 ref M6

5 miles N of Southampton, on the B3354

A couple of miles north-east of Itchen Valley Country Park, Horton Heath is a sizeable village which rather surprisingly has no church but can boast a rather special pub. Located on the edge of the village, **The Lapstone** has established a superb reputation for quality food and ales and for the warm and friendly welcome from "mine hosts" Mike and Iris Gillett. All the food is home-cooked and, along with the regular menu of home-made soup, pies, pasties, and sandwiches, the daily specials include traditional style dishes with game specialities as Rabbit or Game, Beer & Ale. Vegetarian options are available and there's also a

The Lapstone, Botley Road, Horton Heath, Southampton SO50 7AN
Tel: 01703 601659

selection of Children's Choices. Meals can be enjoyed either in the cosy bar or, in good weather in the large, secluded flower garden at the rear where there are also swings and slides for the children. The Lapstone also offers its patrons pool, and a separate darts area, but this is primarily a 'talk bar' where people come to talk. Mike and Iris are both dog lovers with an Alsatian and a spaniel, so dog lovers are definitely welcome. They also seem to have a lively interest in pigs. There's a collection of flying pigs in all guises around the bar area and even a mobile of a flying pig which, Iris says, is her response to anyone telling "tall stories"! The Lapstone lays on live music every other weekend and also a very popular speciality night for food once a month - perhaps Chinese, or Irish, according to the occasion. The inn is also biker-friendly and twice a year there are competitions for the best vintage or modern bike. If you need any further recommendation of The Lapstone, have a word with regular patron Roy who has been coming to the pub every day for the past 50 years.

BISHOP'S WALTHAM

MAP 6 REF M6

10 miles NE of Southampton, on the B2177/B3035

A few miles east of Horton Heath, Bishop's Waltham is a charming and historic small town. It was the country residence of the Bishops of Winchester for centuries and through the portals of their sumptuous **Palace** have passed at least 12 reigning monarchs. Amongst them were Richard the Lionheart returning from the Crusades, Henry V mustering his army before setting off for Agincourt, and Henry VIII entertaining Charles V of Spain (then the most powerful monarch in Europe) to a lavish banquet. The Palace's days of glory came to a violent end during the Civil War when Cromwell's troops battered most of it to the ground. The last resident Bishop was forced to flee, concealing himself beneath a load of manure. The ruins remain impressive, especially the Great Hall with its 3-storey tower and soaring windows. The Palace is now in the care of English Heritage and entrance is free.

The town itself offers visitors a good choice of traditional and specialist shops, amongst them a renowned fishmonger, butcher, baker - even a candle-maker. And just north of the town you can visit one of the country's leading vineyards.

With global warming apparently well under way, it may not be too long before the south of England becomes once again as prolific a producer of wine as it was in Roman times. In those days, the English climate was much more benign than it is now and virtually every Roman encampment had its own flourishing vineyard, the wine it produced highly esteemed for both its festive and medicinal properties. Almost two thousand years later, **Northbrook Springs Vineyard** selected their site to the north of Bishop's Waltham, 15 acres of well-drained downland soil over chalk, sloping gently to the south and south-east. A perfect micro-climate for vine-growing. The resulting wines wonderfully reflect the clear, fresh days of an English summer. Visitors to Northbrook Springs are offered a tour of the vineyard which explains the complex, labour-intensive process of planting, growing, pruning and harvesting the vines and a free tasting in the Vineyard Shop

Northbrook Springs Vineyard, Beeches Hill
Bishop's Waltham, Hampshire SO32 1FB
Tel/Fax: 01489 892659

(open Tuesday to Sunday) of a selection of crisp, clear, flavourful wines amongst which you can find the ideal accompaniment to a June picnic out of doors, or a seasonal dinner in December.

South of Bishop's Waltham, at Waltham Chase, **Jhansi Farm Rare Breed Centre** is dedicated to the conservation of rare breed farm animals, some of them critically endangered. The Farm has a pets' corner housing a large variety of pure bred rabbits, guinea pigs, chipmunks and birds, a souvenir and pet shop, tea room, picnic and play area, nursery and water gardens, with events such as sheep shearing and hand spinning taking place throughout the season. Tel: 01489 894200.

HAMBLE
Map 6 ref M7
6 miles SE of Southampton, on the B3397

Famous throughout the world as a yachting centre, Hamble takes its name from the river, a mere 10 miles long, that flows past the village into **Southampton Water**. Some 3,000 vessels have berths in the **Hamble Estuary** so there's an incredible variety of boats thronging the river during the season, anything from vintage barges to the sleekest of modern craft.

Ask any yachting enthusiast to recommend a pub in the Southampton Water/River Hamble area and the answer will almost certainly be the **King and Queen** tavern in the High Street of this ancient village. Standing in the heart of Hamble, it's an attractive Victorian building with a garden that provides a superb setting for admiring the day to day activity on the cobbled High Street. This celebrated pub is run by Stephen Hodges and Kelly Smith, a young enthu-

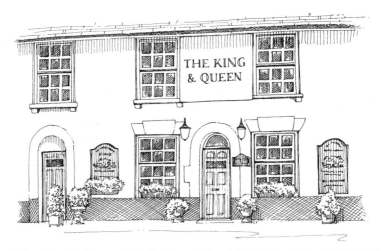

The King & Queen, High Street, Hamble, Hampshire SO31 4HA
Tel: 01703 454247 Fax: 01703 452134 e-mail: KingQueen7@aol.com

siastic pair who share a passionate interest in yachting. As you might expect, there's a strong nautical flavour to the decor inside their hostelry - many striking photographs of yachts in various weather conditions and, above the bar, a strip of old Admiralty charts, those masterpieces of marine surveying and meticulous draughtsmanship. The food and drink on offer at the King & Queen are equally impressive. There's an extensive and varied Bar Menu ranging from home-made soup of the day or Chicken Liver Pâté to Marinated Prawn & Cucumber Salad or a Hot Thai Chicken Curry. The main menu, served in the evening, is a temptation from beginning to end, offering an excellent selection of meat, fish and vegetarian dishes. And amongst the desserts, some difficult choices have to be made: home-made Autumn Fruit Pudding or Creme Brulée, for example, cooling sorbets or a cheese board arrayed with fresh, prime quality cheeses.

Situated amongst green fields on the edge of this picturesque village, **Riverside Holiday Park** overlooks the Mercury Marina and Hamble River and will strongly appeal to visitors or holiday-makers who enjoy fishing, sailing and walking in the countryside. The 8-acre site has 50 touring pitches and is very well-equipped with electric hook-ups, free showers and toilet facilities, together with a laundry room and enclosed wash-up area. The Marina with its restaurant and bar is only 2 minutes walk away and also located there is a sailing centre. In addition, the Park has 8 pine lodges and 5 static caravans to rent, all of them offering an exceptionally comfortable holiday life-style. Colour TV, kitchen with microwave, bed linen and duvets are all provided along with free gas and electricity. Cots are available to hire. The Park is open from March to October for caravanners but the pine lodges can be rented throughout the year, including Christmas and New Year. It's well worth asking about the various special offers which include Spring Break deals, mini Easter breaks, senior citizens' savings, infant offers and discounts on fortnight bookings. Riverside's convenient location provides easy access to the New Forest and other attractions not far away

Riverside Holiday Park, Satchell Lane, Hamble, Hampshire SO31 4HR
Tel: 01703 453220

include Paulton's Park, Beaulieu Motor Museum, and the historic cities of Portsmouth and Winchester.

Anyone interested in England's industrial heritage should travel a couple of miles north from Hamble to **Bursledon**. Ships have been built here since medieval times, the most famous being the *Elephant*, Nelson's flagship at the Battle of Copenhagen. The yard where it was built, now renamed the Elephant Boatyard is still in business. On a rise to the north of the village stands **Bursledon Windmill**, the only working windmill in Hampshire. Built in 1814 at a cost of £800, its vanes ground to a halt during the great agricultural depression of the 1880s. Happily, all the machinery remained intact and after a lengthy restoration between 1976 and 1991, the sails are revolving once again whenever a good northerly or southerly wind is blowing, producing stoneground flour for sale. The windmill is open to visitors at weekends, or whenever the sails are turning! Tel: 01703 404999.

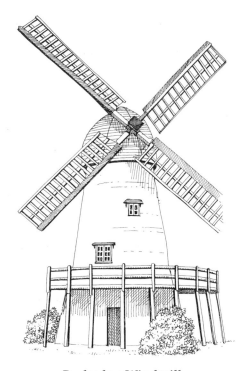

The village can boast yet another unique industrial site. When **Bursledon Brickworks** was established in 1897 the machinery installed was at the very

Burlesdon Windmill

forefront of brickmaking technology. The works closed in 1974 but a Charitable Trust has now restored its gargantuan machines, thus preserving the last surviving example of a steam-driven brickworks in the country. More details on 01489 576248.

Heritage of a different kind can be found a couple of miles northwest of Hamble, at ruined **Netley Abbey** (English Heritage), a wonderfully serene spot surrounded by noble trees. "These are not the ruins of Netley" declared Horace Walpole in the mid-1700s, "but of Paradise". Jane Austen was equally entranced by the Abbey's romantic charm and she made many visits. Dating back to 1300, the extensive ruins provide a spectacular backdrop for open air theatre performances during the summer.

PARK GATE
MAP 6 REF M7

8 miles SE of Southampton, on the A27

Back in the days when strawberries still had real taste and texture, Park Gate was the main distribution centre for the produce of the extensive strawberry farms all around. During the season, scores of special trains were contracted to transport the succulent fruit to London, some 3,000 tons of it in 1913 alone. By the 1960s, housing had taken priority over fruit farms and today the M27 marks a very clear division between the built up areas to the south, and the unspoilt acres of countryside to the north.

Less than a mile from Junction 9 on the M27 and with the Solent coastline a few miles to the south, **Little Park Lodge** offers visitors an ideal base for exploring south-east Hampshire. The market town of Fareham is a five minute drive away; Southampton and the historic city of Portsmouth can both be reached in about 20 minutes. A warm and friendly welcome can be found at this family run bed and breakfast, and it will be Julie or Mike Slamaker who greets you on

**Little Park Lodge, 5 Bridge Road, Park Gate, Southampton
Hampshire SO31 7GD Tel: 01489 600500**

arrival. Their attractive modern house has two guest rooms, pleasantly furnished, provided with colour television and refreshment tray, hot and cold water basins and a shared shower room and toilet. The excellent breakfasts, served in the conservatory, offer a good range of choices, including a vegetarian option, and any reasonable dietary request will be met. Julie and Mike have children of their own so young guests are very welcome and there's a safe and secure garden for them to play in, complete with Wendy House. Please note that guests are asked not to smoke inside the house.

PORTSMOUTH

Currently, any brochure promoting Portsmouth always adds the words "Flagship City". With good reason, since the port is home to the most famous flagship in naval history, **HMS Victory**. From the outside it's a majestic, three-masted ship: inside it's creepily claustrophobic, except for the Admiral's and Captain's spacious, mahogany-panelled quarters. Visitors can pace the very same deck from which Nelson master-minded the decisive encounter with the French navy

HMS Victory, Portsmouth

off Cape Trafalgar in 1805. Standing on this deck, ostentatiously arrayed in the gorgeous uniform of a British Admiral of the Fleet, Nelson presented a clear target to a sharp-sighted French sniper. The precise spot where Nelson fell and the place on the sheltered orlop (lowest) deck where he died are both marked by plaques.

The death of Nelson was a tragedy softened by a halo of victory: the loss of the **Mary Rose**, some 260 years earlier was an unmitigated disaster. Henry VIII had ordered the ship, the second largest in his fleet, to be built. He was standing on Southsea Common above Portsmouth in 1545, watching the Mary Rose manoeuvre, when it suddenly heeled over and sank. All seven hundred men on board drowned. "And the King he screeched right out like any maid, 'Oh, my gentlemen! Oh, my gallant men!'" More than four centuries later, in 1982, the hulk of the *Mary Rose* was carefully raised from the seabed where it had lain for so long. Some seventeen years after that recovery, its oak frame is still drying out, the impressive remains now housed in the timber-clad **Mary Rose Museum** and open to visitors.

Another ship you can see at Portsmouth doesn't possess the same historical glamour as the *Victory* or the *Mary Rose,* but **HMS Warrior** merits a visit because when this mighty craft was commissioned in 1860, she was the Navy's first ironclad warship. A great advance in technology, but the distinctions between the officers' and crew accommodation show little difference from those obtaining in Nelson's day.

Like Southampton, Portsmouth suffered badly during World War II, losing most of its 17th and 18th century buildings. **St George's Church**, a handsome Georgian building of 1754 with large galleries, was damaged by a bomb but has been fully restored, and just to the north of the church, the barn-like **Beneficial Boy's School**, built in 1784, is another survivor. One of the most interesting buildings is to be found in **Southsea**, the city's resort area. **Southsea Castle** was built in 1544 as one of Henry VIII's series of forts protecting the south coast from French attacks. It has been modified several times since then but the original Keep is still intact and there are good views across the Solent from the gun platforms.

Portsmouth also offers visitors a wealth of varied museums, three of which deserve special mention. **The Royal Armouries**, housed in the huge Victorian Fort Nelson, claims to be 'Britain's Loudest Museum', with live firings every day; the **Charles Dickens Birthplace Museum** at 393, Old Commercial Road, has been restored and furnished to show how the house looked when the great novelist was born here in 1812; and the **D-Day Museum** in Southsea commemorating the Allied invasion of Europe in 1944 and most notable for the 83 metre long Overlord Tapestry, a 20th century equivalent of the Bayeux Tapestry which is well worth seeing.

About ten minutes from 'Pompey' dockyard **The Old Canal Inn** in Shirley Avenue enjoys a convenient corner location and a reputation for good food, ales and entertainment. This sociable local is run by Barry and Julie Martin who arrived here in August 1998 after more than a decade in the trade managing other pubs in the area. The Old Canal is a lively place with its own darts and pool teams and entertainment at weekends. A Social Club and coach trips are organised from the pub as well as raffles, and Barry also runs a mobile disco. Children are welcome and have their own "Disney Room" where the popular cartoon characters adorn the walls and there are plenty of games to keep them amused. The inn was purpose-built in 1931 and still retains the green tile bricks that were the trademark of United Brewer, a local Hampshire brewery. The original brewery glass windows, decorated with the United logo, are also still in place, as is the original 'Key Stone', embedded in the pavement outside the front door. High ceilings and the L-shaped bar all add to the atmosphere. Additional attrac-

**The Old Canal Inn, 2 Shirley Avenue, Milton, Portsmouth PO4 8HE
Tel: 01705 825750**

tions at the Old Canal are its regular 'Theme Nights' when the food and entertainment are linked to that night's theme. If you enjoy friendly traditional pubs,
then you should certainly seek out the Old Canal.

Standing at the head of Portsmouth Harbour, **Portchester Castle** is not only
the grandest medieval castle in the county but also stands within the best-preserved site of a Roman fort in northern Europe. Sometime around 280 AD, the
Romans enclosed 8 acres of this strategic headland and used it as a base for their
ships clearing the Channel of pirates. The original walls of the fort were 20ft
high and 10ft thick, their depth much reduced by local people pillaging the
stone for their own buildings.

The medieval castle dates back to 1120 although the most substantial ruins
are those of the royal palace built for Richard II between 1396 and 1399. Richard was murdered in 1399 and never saw his magnificent castle. Also within the
walls of the Roman enclosure is **Portchester Church**, a superb Norman construction built between 1133 and 1150 as part of an Augustinian Priory. For
some reason, the Priors moved inland to Southwick, and the church remained
disused for more than five and a half centuries until Queen Anne personally
donated £400 for its restoration. Apart from the east end, the church is entirely
Norman and, remarkably, its 12th century font of wondrously carved Caen stone
has also survived the centuries.

HAYLING ISLAND
MAP 6 REF O8

4 miles S of Havant, on the A3023

A traditional family resort for more than a century, Hayling Island manages to provide all the usual seaside facilities without losing its rural character. Much of the foreshore is still open ground with wandering sand dunes stretching well back from the 4-mile long shingle beach. Bathing is safe here and West Beachlands even boasts a European Blue Flag which is only awarded to beaches meeting 26 environmental criteria. One of Hayling's more unusual beach facilities is the line of old-fashioned beach huts all of which are available to rent.

Hayling is something of a Mecca for board sailors. Not only does it provide the best sailing in the UK for beginners and experts alike, it is also the place where board-sailing was invented. Many places claim that honour but Peter Chilvers has a High Court ruling to prove it. In 1982 a Judge decided that Mr Chilvers had indeed invented the sailboard at Hayling in 1958. As a boy of ten, he used a sheet of plywood, a tent fly-sheet, a pole and some curtain rings to sail up an island creek.

The rural nature of much of the island has also made it popular with campers. Only a few minutes from the M27 and the A3(M) motorways, the three camp sites operated by Zita Good and her sons on Hayling Island provide ideal locations for a peaceful family holiday. **The Oven, Fleet Farm**, and **Lower Tye Farm Camp Sites** are all set in attractive countryside with level, sheltered and marked pitches and an excellent range of amenities. There's a shop, snack bar, electric hook-ups, and children's play area at each site and all three are near family pubs that cater for children. In addition, there's a heated swimming pool at the Oven site, (small charge per session), a plunge pool at Lower Tye, and the Fleet site is on the creek. Toilets and hot water are included in the price at the

The Oven Camp Site, Manor Road, Hayling Island PO11 0QX
Tel: 01705 464695.
Lower Tye Farm Camp Site, Copse Lane, Hayling Island PO11 0QB
Tel: 01705 462479
Fleet Farm Camp Site, Yew Tree Road, Hayling Island PO11 0QF
Tel: 01705 463684

Oven and Lower Tye sites, while the Oven site also provides toilet facilities for the disabled and a boat washing area for campers. Oven, incidentally, takes its name from the fact that it was surrounded by trees and therefore a very 'warm' environment, while the Fleet name refers to the many days when the Royal Navy could be seen from the site. All three sites have facilities for long term touring caravan parking and also for caravan storage. A basic unit for two people costs just £8. Hayling Island, of course, is perfect for children with its safe beaches which have won the Blue Flag for cleanliness many years running, while adults will find ample facilities for wind-surfing, sailing, horse riding, golf, tennis and walking.

4 The Isle of Wight

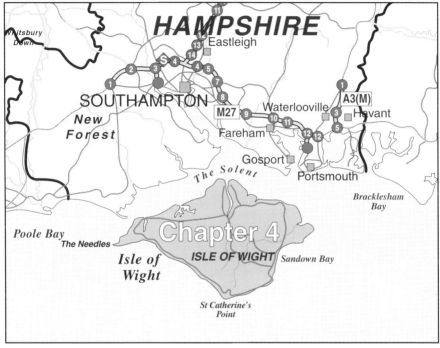

© MAPS IN MINUTES ™ (1998)

The Isle of Wight has adopted a motto which declares: "All this beauty is of God". It echoes the poet John Keats' "A thing of beauty is a joy for ever", the first line of his poem *Endymion* which he wrote while staying on the island in the hope that its crisp country air would improve his health.

Other distinguished visitors have described Wight as "The Garden Isle", and "England's Madeira" but it was quite late in the day before the island became popular as a resort. This was partly because for centuries, right up until the 1600s, the island was a first port of call for pestiferous French raiders who made the islanders' lives a misery with their constant incursions.

The turning point came in the 1840s when Queen Victoria and Prince Albert bought an estate near East Cowes, demolished an existing house, and Albert designed and built an Italianate mansion he named Osborne House. A few years later, the Poet Laureate, Alfred, Lord Tennyson, bought Farringford on the eastern side of the island. Socially, the Isle of Wight had arrived.

Most of the island's 125,000 residents, (the town of Peterborough outnumbers all of them by about 10,000), live in the northeast quadrant of the island, with its main resort towns of Sandown and Shanklin strung along the east coast. The rest of Wight is wonderfully peaceful with a quiet, unassertive charm all of its own.

We begin our tour of the island at its capital, Newport, and then make a clockwise circuit of the island starting at Cowes and ending up at Yarmouth.

NEWPORT

Set around the River Medina, Newport has a history going back to Roman times. Excavations in 1926 uncovered the well-preserved remains of a **Roman Villa**, a 3rd century farmhouse in which one side of the building was given over entirely to baths. Visitors can follow the bather's progress through changing room, cold room, warm and hot rooms with underfloor heating systems, and integral cold and hot plunge baths. A Roman style garden has been re-created in the grounds and provides an interesting insight into the wealth of new plants the Romans introduced into Britain.

Newport received its first charter back in 1190 but the growth of the small town received a severe setback in 1377 when it was completely burnt to the ground by the French. Recovery was slow and it wasn't until the 17th century that Newport really prospered again. Indirectly, this was also due to the French since the island was heavily garrisoned during the Anglo-French wars of that period. Supplying the troops with provisions and goods brought great wealth to the town.

Some striking buildings have survived, amongst them **God's Providence House**, built in 1701 and now a tea room; John Nash's elegant **Town Hall** of 1816; an 18th century brewers warehouse near the harbour which now houses the **Quay Arts Centre**, incorporating a theatre, two galleries, a craft shop, café and bar; and a charming **Tudor Old Grammar School**.

Just around the corner from the Old Grammar School, **The George Inn** is a conveniently located town centre hostelry, its Victorian frontage colourful in summer with hanging baskets of flowers. Inside, the decor and furnishings are in the best traditional style, with beamed ceilings, open fires and upholstered benches around the walls. The olde-worlde atmosphere is enhanced further by Victorian paintings and vintage photographs of local scenes, lots of pewter and copper, and a large collection of old plumbers' blow lamps hanging from one of the ceilings. Dawn and Andrew Webster run this welcoming inn and take great pride in offering tasty, wholesome food, all of it freshly prepared to order. Their comprehensive menu ranges from substantial grills to home-made 'George Specials', from fish dishes to salads, sandwiches or filled rolls, ploughmans and baked potatoes. Daily specials and home-made sweets of the day are detailed on a blackboard, and the wine list offers a good choice of value-for-money wines.

The George Inn, 92 St James' Street, Newport, Isle of Wight PO30 1LB
Tel: 01983 522557

Meals are served daily from 10.30am to 10.30pm, (Sunday, 12 noon to 10pm), while the inn itself is open daily from 10.30am to 11.00pm (Sunday, 12 noon to 10.30pm). Outside, there's a large paved patio to the rear, complete with barbecue. The George's central position means that Newport's many places of interest are all within easy reach. Notable amongst them are the remains of a 3rd century Roman villa mentioned earlier, the parish Church of St Thomas whose foundation stone was laid by Queen Victoria's consort, Prince Albert, and the Museum of Island History, housed in the former Town Hall designed by John Nash. Church Litten Park, on the site of an old churchyard whose Tudor Gateway still remains, is a peaceful spot and interesting for its memorial to Valentine Gray, a 9-year-old chimney sweep whose death in 1822 as a result of ill-usage by his master caused a national outcry.

To the northwest of Newport, **Parkhurst Forest** offers miles of woodland walks, while over to the northeast, at **Wootton, Butterfly World and Fountain World** is home to hundreds of exotic butterflies flying free inside a beautifully landscaped indoor garden with ponds, streams, fountains and waterfalls. Other attractions include an Italian water garden, a Japanese water garden with Koi Carp, a restaurant, garden centre and shop. Tel: 01983 883430.

CARISBROOKE   MAP 6 REF M9
1 mile SW of Newport, on the B3323/B3401

Another quote from John Keats: *"I do not think I shall ever see a ruin to surpass Carisbrooke Castle"*. The **castle** is set dramatically on a sweeping ridge and it's

Carisbrooke Castle

quite a steep climb up from the picturesque village to the massive Gatehouse. This was built in 1598 but the oldest parts of the castle date back to Norman times, most notably the mighty Keep which, apart from Windsor, is the most perfect specimen of Norman architecture in Britain. Archaeologists believe that the Castle stands on the site a Roman fort built some thousand years earlier.

During the season costumed guides, or storytellers as English Heritage prefers to call them, conduct visitors around the noble ruins. The most poignant of their stories concern Charles I and his youngest daughter, Elizabeth. Charles was imprisoned here in the months before his trial and the guides will point out the mullioned window through which he unsuccessfully attempted to escape. After the King's execution, Cromwell's Council of State ordered that his daughter Elizabeth, 'for her own safety', should also be incarcerated at Carisbrooke. The 14 year old implored them not to send her to her father's former prison, but they were adamant. Elizabeth was a sickly child and less than a week after her arrival at the Castle she 'was stricken by fever and passed away, a broken-hearted child of fourteen'. The story touched the heart of Queen Victoria who set up a monument in Newport church where the Princess was buried. The effigy, in pure white Carrara marble, bears an inscription stating that it had been erected "as a token of respect for her virtues, and of sympathy for her misfortunes by Victoria R 1856".

More cheerful aspects of a visit to the Castle include the Donkey Centre. Donkeys walking a treadmill were once used to turn the huge 16th century wheel in the Wellhouse to draw water from a well 161ft deep. A light at the bottom of the well gives some idea of its depth. Before donkeys were trained to raise the water, the task was performed by prisoners and nowadays visitors are invited to have a go at walking the treadmill themselves.

Also within the Castle grounds are a **Coach House Exhibition** and **Victorian Island Exhibition**, the **Isle of Wight Museum** and a tea room. More details on 01983 522107.

If you have children under 14, give them (and yourself) a treat by visiting **The Eight Bells** in Carisbrooke High Street. Sisters Dawn Webster and Sharon Read, who own and run this inviting hostelry, have created what must surely be the most extensive Kid's Menu in the country. The choice of starters, main courses (including Cheesy Chicken Feet), jacket potatoes, sandwiches, desserts such as Mr Jelly Belly, should entice the most picky of your offspring. There are even Cocktails for Kids, although nothing stronger than a Blackcurrant Bomb or an Orange Whizzer. Parents are also well-provided for. They are offered a wide choice of tasty, wholesome dishes: steaks and grills, 'Home Kitchen' meals like the Spicy Chicken coated in the Eight Bells' own spicy marinade, fish and

The Eight Bells, 31 High Street, Carisbrooke, Nr Newport
Isle of Wight PO30 1NR Tel: 01983 825501

vegetarian options, House Specials such as Cheese & Pineapple Melt, as well as baked potatoes, ploughman's and salads. And if that isn't enough choice, there are also daily specials listed on the blackboard. Food is served throughout the day until 10.30pm every day, with special roast meals at Sunday lunch-time. The Eight Bells is housed in an attractive Grade II listed building, traditionally furnished and with separate smoking and non-smoking dining areas. Outside, there's a pleasant Beer Garden with a large ornamental pond, and ample car parking. Historic Carisbrooke Castle is just a short walk away and the many other attractions of this small island never more than a few miles distant.

COWES
MAP 6 REF M8

5 miles N of Newport, on the A3020

Cowes' origins as the most famous yachting resort in the world go back to the early 1800s. It was then a rather shabby port whose main business was shipbuilding. In 1811, the Duke of Gloucester came to stay and as part of the rather limited entertainment on offer watched sailing matches between local fishermen. The Duke's patronage led to amateur gentlemen running their own race and founding a club. The Prince Regent joined in 1817 and on his accession as George IV it was first re-christened the **Royal Yacht Club**, and then the **Royal Yacht Squadron**. Nowadays, **Cowes Week** has become the premier yachting event of the year and also a fixture in the aristocratic social calendar.

Any visit to Cowes would be incomplete without calling in at **Galerias Segui** and the Restaurant above. Located in the High Street, as its name suggests, it is both a restaurant and a gallery displaying paintings, famous Isle of Wight Studio glass and Chessell pottery, home furnishings, other high class giftware and much more. Visitors pass through the gallery to reach the attractive restaurant with its Mexican pine furniture and Spanish decor.

These continental influences are explained by the fact that Galerias is owned and run by Jose Miguel (Andy) Segui, who is Spanish, and his wife Julia (who is English). They met in Majorca, married, and moved to Cowes in 1979 where they have built up their business from scratch.

Their menu has a strong Mexican and Spanish flavour with a good choice of tapas and Mexican dishes. Lighter options include Provencettes, (hot grilled and filled baguettes with savouries such as sun-dried tomatoes and mozarella), very popular savoury crepes with tempting fillings,—Turkish lamb, chicken & almonds, oriental and fresh crab to name but a few. The evening menu includes Paella and

**Galerias Segui, 75 High Street, Cowes
Isle of Wight PO31 7AJ
Tel: 01983 292148 Fax: 01983 280174**

there is a good wine list with many carefully selected Spanish wines. House wine is served by the glass.

If you are planning to stay in Cowes, the Seguis may be able to help you. They have a large, well decorated, self-contained apartment to sleep four. If you would like a really unique view, their mini-apartment on the ground floor could be what you are looking for. It has two twin bedrooms, large shower-room, well-equiped kitchen, separate WC and wonderful views of Cowes Harbour from both bedrooms.

Only a 3 minute walk from the Red Funnel High Speed Ferry Terminal, **Rawlings Hotel & Restaurant** displays all the style and elegance of the Georgian age in which it was built. Despite its town centre location, Rawlings is a wonderfully peaceful retreat, even boasting its own long, secluded garden complete with heated swimming pool. Owner David Crowther, a former lawyer who took over here in 1992, describes Rawlings as an hotel and Member' Club

**Rawlings Hotel & Restaurant, 30 Sun Hill, Cowes
Isle of Wight PO31 7HY Tel: 01983 297507 Fax: 01983 281701**

incorporating a fully licensed restaurant which is open to non-members and offers à la carte and table d'hôte menus to suit all tastes and pockets. The restaurant uses the best of local produce and hosts speciality evenings featuring world wide cuisine. It serves full English breakfast for non-members as well as residents and is open for luncheon and dinner. Coffee and tea are always available and, when the restaurant is closed, food is generally available from the Bar.

Here, you'll find a range of interesting snack which in fair weather can also be enjoyed on the Patio by the pool. Rawlings has 14 comfortable, well appointed rooms, all with en suite bathrooms. Coffee and tea-making facilities, clock radio and colour television are standard. Residents, including non-members, are invited to use all the Club facilities, including the Bar and Pool. For devotees of golf, fishing, sailing or rambling, special breaks are available. The hotel also offers a fully equipped business meeting centre, complete with fax and telephone facilities, giant screen television and video, and a comfortable ambiance which also makes it ideal for private parties, gatherings and receptions. If you'd like to know more about Rawlings, you're welcome to just pop in. You're assured of a warm welcome and they will be pleased to show you around this outstanding hotel which is popular with the yachting fraternity and has also been featured in *Marie Claire* magazine.

Lovers of antiques who are planning to stay on the island won't find a more congenial place for bed and breakfast than **Royal Standard Antiques** in Park Road. Built in 1852 as two dwellings and a shop, the building became a pub 3 years later and took the name 'The Royal Standard'. When Dennis and Caroline Bradbury opened their antiques shop and bed & breakfast here in 1994 they decided to keep the name by which it had been known for so long. They're a versatile couple. Caroline has been an amateur operatic singer, now she only sings in the bath! Dennis is musical too, playing the trumpet in the Bob Howarth Big Band. He's also responsible for repairing and refurbishing antiques and

Royal Standard Antiques, 70-72 Park Road, Cowes
Isle of Wight PO31 7LY Tel: 01983 281672

takes particular pleasure in working with glass. Caroline, on the other hand, is a keen upholsterer who enjoys producing new items from old. Their shop is chock-a-block with lovely antiques which might include at any one time such pieces as spinning wheels, an old chapel organ or a pianola awaiting renovation. Visitors are invited to browse amongst the varied stock of Victorian and Edwardian bottles and pots, old tools, rural and domestic bygones, furniture, pictures and prints, pub and restaurant decor items, architectural antiques, commemoratives and general antiques. Dennis is also an avid collector of ornamental plates, some of which are displayed to good effect around the walls of the upstairs dining room. This is where the guest rooms are, 3 of them in all: a double with bathroom, one twin and one single. The rooms are comfortable and full of character, while outside there's a charming enclosed courtyard with climbing clematis and lots of potted plants. Devotees of antiques may find it hard to tear themselves away from such a cornucopia of collectables but when they do, the town centre and busy harbour are just a short walk away, with Northwood Park virtually on the doorstep.

Just 50 yards from the sea front at Cowes and facing directly down the High Street, **Watchhouse Barn Coffee Shop & Restaurant** catches the eye for a couple of reasons. Firstly, there are the colourful hanging baskets and window boxes, and secondly there is an unusual window display which invariably attracts the

**Watchhouse Barn Coffee Shop & Restaurant, 31 Bath Road, Cowes
Isle of Wight PO31 7RH Tel: 01983 293093**

attention of passers-by. It's a nearly life-sized carved wooden model of an Australian aborigine which says Barry Grazier 'is always noticed by the ladies due to his dress!' Together with his wife Tracey, Barry owns and runs this friendly and cheerful eating place and the aborigine model is a reminder of the days when he worked as a prisoners' escort in the Australian prison service. He has also travelled the world in the catering business. A trained chef, Barry has chefed at such upmarket venues in London as Marlborough House, Lancaster House and the Guildhall, and now teaches catering on a part time basis. Tracey and Barry serve food throughout the day, with a separate menu for the evening. During the daytime, there's a wide choice of light meals, (including an All Day Breakfast), jacket potatoes, ploughman's, sandwiches and filled baguettes, along with specials of the day, Cream Teas and a tempting selection of cream cakes and delicious gâteaux.

The Graziers have children of their own, so youngsters are welcome here (they have their own menu), as are pets 'with well behaved owners'. For fairweather days, there's a patio to the rear for open air eating. The Watchhouse Barn's evening menu offers a comprehensive choice of dishes with the emphasis on fresh, local produce, including locally-caught lobsters when available. The restaurant does not have a liquor licence but diners are free to bring their own wines, beers or spirits - and there's no corkage charge. The Watchhouse also has a take-away service and telephone orders are welcome.

Linga Longa must be one of the most inspired names for a gift shop from which most visitors will find it difficult to drag themselves away. There are no mass-produced souvenirs or tacky, over-priced franchised products on sale here. Pauline Hart, who also runs the well-known Cottage Gift Shop in Shanklin on the east coast, has travelled widely and, when selecting items for her gift shop, chosen wisely. Pauline hails from South Africa, so it's not surprising that prime place in her gift shop is devoted to a vibrant selection of crafts from that region: artefacts full of energy and exuberantly colourful. But you will also find a wide variety of unique gifts from around the world such as hand-decorated Ostrich Eggs, meticulously-

Linga Longa, 13 Bath Road, Cowes
Isle of Wight PO31 7QN
Tel: 01983 296347 Fax: 01983 867512

carved hardwood figures, beaded decorative knives, or skin-friendly mohair knitwear. A word of advice: if you buy one of Linga Longa's soft mohair blankets, chilly nights will be just a thing of the past.

Across the River Medina, **East Cowes** is most famous for **Osborne House**, a clean-cut, Italianate mansion designed and built by Prince Albert in 1846. Queen Victoria loved "dear beautiful Osborne" and so did her young children. They had their very own house in its grounds, a full-size Swiss Cottage, where they played at house-keeping, cooking meals for their parents, and tending its vegetable gardens using scaled-down gardening tools. In the main house itself, visitors can wander through both the State and private apartments which are crammed with paintings, furniture, ornaments, statuary and the random bric-à-brac that provided such an essential element in the decor of any upper-class Victorian home. Osborne House possessed a special place in the Queen's affec-

Osborne House, East Cowes

tions. It had been built by the husband she adored with an almost adolescent infatuation: together they had spent many happy family days here. After Albert's premature death from typhoid in 1861, she often returned to Osborne, her staff instructed to lay out the Prince's clothes in his dressing-room each night, and the Queen herself retiring to bed with his nightshirt clasped in her arms. In 1901 she returned to Osborne for the last time, dying here in her 83rd year, her death co-incidentally signalling the beginning of the slow decline of the British Empire over which she had presided as Queen-Empress. Tel: 01983 200022.

WOOTTON CREEK

MAP 6 REF M8

4 miles NE of Newport, off the A3054

About 4 miles southeast of East Cowes, Wootton is notable for its ancient bridge and mill-pond. A pleasant place to stay and if you are looking for bed and break-fast accommodation on the island, it would be difficult to find a more picturesque location than **Ashlake Farmhouse**. The house itself is a long, low building which obeys its own architectural rules. Windows erupt at unexpected levels and the weathered red-tiled roof dips and rises in response to the irregularly-shaped rooms it covers. The walls of this lovely 17th century farmhouse are built with glowing stone pillaged from nearby Quarr Abbey. The builders of Ashlake Farm-house did a pretty thorough job of pillage: all that remains of Quarr Abbey now is a rather sad, grey wall. But they also knew exactly the right place to use the stones they had cannibalised. The farmhouse they built with the Abbey stones enjoys lovely views, standing on ground that slopes down to Wootton Creek where, from the long jetty, you can rent a dinghy, spend a few hours fishing, enjoy the wildlife, or just sit in the evening sun and watch the boats go by. Carol Pearce, who hosts this exceptional B & B, provides her guests with a su-perb English breakfast, served in a beamed dining room or on a terrace overlooking the Creek. (All diets are catered for). Once you've enjoyed that, the

Ashlake Farmhouse, Ashlake Farm Lane, Wootton Creek, Nr Ryde Isle of Wight PO33 4LF Tel: 01983 882124

idea of having your evening meal here as well will seem very appealing. Feel free: anything from a simple barbeque to the grandest of banquets can be provided by prior arrangement. Located alongside Ashlake Farmhouse is Smugglers Barn, a lovely old property dating from 1620. Carol describes it as 'tiny, but beautiful'. The old barn has been imaginatively converted to provide very comfortable self-catering accommodation. Well-equipped with a microwave, refrigerator and television, pretty bathroom, and appealing features like the spiral staircase and wrought-iron balcony, Smugglers Barn provides just about everything a family on holiday could be looking for.

RYDE

MAP 6 REF N8

9 miles NE of Newport, on the A3054

About 4 miles east of Wootton the largest town on the island, Ryde, offers visitors a huge expanse of sandy beach and a half-mile long pier, one of the first to be built in Britain. Passenger ferries from Portsmouth dock here, the hovercraft service settles nearby, and the car ferry from the mainland disgorges its cargo a couple of miles to the west. The town is essentially Victorian, a popular resort in those days for affluent middle-class families. Then, as now, visitors enjoyed strolling along the elegant Esplanade with its sea views across Spithead Sound to Portsmouth.

Just a few yards from the Esplanade, in Castle Street, the **Blue Moon Restaurant** is housed in a charming Victorian building decorated in Regency-style with interior decor to match. Its youthful owner, Carol Hole, studied hotel and catering administration at Huddersfield University and her inviting restaurant combines the serving of well-prepared, attractively presented food with unobtrusive efficiency and genuine friendliness. The lunch time menu, available between 11.30 am and 3 pm, offers a wide choice of light meals, jacket potatoes, salads and sandwiches, as well as more substantial main meals and a children's menu. (If they prefer, they can choose half portions of any of the menu items). Carol's à la carte menu

**Blue Moon Restaurant, 2 Castle St
Ryde, Isle of Wight PO33 2ED
Tel: 01983 612010**

is available between noon and 3pm, and from 6.30pm to 10pm all year. There's a particularly good range of fish dishes, but meat, poultry and vegetarian options are all available as well. And if you don't see what you would like listed, a note on the menu invites you to ask and 'if it is possible our chef will prepare it for you'. The Blue Moon's desserts also deserve a special mention. All are home-made and range from traditional favourites such as bread & butter pudding, or Spotted Dick, to fresh fruit or cheese & biscuits. The restaurant is not licensed but you are invited to bring along your own wine - and there's no corkage fee. With its outstanding food and service, this is definitely a restaurant to be visited more than once in a blue moon. (Please note that the establishment operates a non-smoking policy).

SEAVIEW   MAP 6 REF N8
2 miles SE of Ryde, on the B3330/B3340

To the east of Ryde, the aptly named resort of Seaview has a good beach with clean firm sand, ideal for making sandcastles. There are little rock pools where small children can play in safety while trying to catch the abundant crabs and shrimps. Lines of clinker-built wooden dinghies bob about on the waves, and out to sea rise two of "Palmerston's Follies" - forts constructed in the 1850s as a warning signal to the French to keep away. This charming little place also boasts an outstanding hotel. The island offers an excellent choice of good hotels but **The Priory Bay Hotel** is truly in a class of its own, a unique property with a history stretching back more than a thousand years. Long before the Domesday Book was written, there was a Cluniac monastery here, occupying a breathtaking site commanding views over the Solent and Spithead. A splendidly decorated

The Priory Bay Hotel, Priory Drive, Seaview, Isle of Wight PO34 5BU
Tel: 01983 613146 Fax: 01983 616539

15th century portal now provides an imposing entrance to the hotel, although the oldest surviving building is an attractive thatched barn of around 1100AD which is believed to have been part of the original Priory Farm. Medieval monks, Tudor farmers and Georgian gentry have all added to this charming medley of beautiful buildings. The Priory, under whose magnificent magnolias Queen Victoria sat, has been a silent witness to our nation's history as Ships of the Realm passed out of their Portsmouth base on their way to serve around the world.

Although only a couple of miles from Ryde, the hotel is wonderfully secluded, set in 70 acres of peaceful woodland, lawns and terraced gardens that were reputedly designed by Gertrude Jekyll. In addition to its privately-owned beach, The Priory Bay Hotel offers residents the use of a 9-hole golf course (par 3), an outdoor swimming pool and tennis courts, with sailing, riding, walking and other amenities all available locally. The food served at the Priory Bay is also notable. Using local produce where possible, the hotel offers creative menus specialising in fresh, local seafood, and a high standard of cuisine. To inspire the Chef further, Andrew Palmer who owns and runs this exceptional hotel, has begun the restoration of the estate's own herb and vegetable gardens. In addition to the inspiring fare available in the main restaurant, during the season the Beach Restaurant is open for breakfast, lunch and dinner, serving the best of local seafood, mainly grilled or barbecued, as well as simple salad and pasta dishes.

The Priory's buildings have developed over the centuries creating a unique architectural experience. As a result, each bedroom has its own individual character, allowing regular guests to enjoy a different atmosphere with each visit. Sympathetically restored and redecorated in 1998, the rooms are superbly furnished and appointed. And, if you prefer, self-catering, accommodation is available in either the historic Tithe Cottages or in attractive modern cottages.

ST HELENS
MAP 6 REF N9

4 miles SE of Ryde, on the B3330

Famed for its magnificent village green, St Helen's straggles down the hillside above the mouth of the River Yar, a quiet spot beloved by yachtsmen. It must be the only village to be named after a Roman Emperor's wife - the Helen who was the wife of Constantine and in whose honour a church was erected here in 704. Another "royal" figure, the Queen of Chantilly was actually born in the village, and if the name is unfamiliar to you, seek out Sophie Dawes' Cottage which bears a wall plaque stating that "Sophie Dawes, Madame de Fouchères, Daughter of Richard Dawes, Fisherman and Smuggler, known as the Queen of Chantilly, was born here in 1792". As a young girl, Sophie left St Helens to seek her fortune in London where she worked (non-professionally) in a Piccadilly brothel for a while before ensnaring the exiled Duc de Bourbon and becoming his mistress. The duke paid for her education and when he was able to return to France, took her with him, marrying her off to a compliant Baron. Eventually, she married her duke, now Prince de Condé and having made sure that his will was in order, contrived his murder. Although she was tried for the crime, political considerations led to the case being quietly dropped. Sophie returned to England with her ill-gotten gains but in her last years she seems to have been stricken with remorse and gave lavishly to charity.

Just half a mile from St Helen's picturesque little harbour, and less than a mile from the nearest beach, **Field Lane Holiday Park** is a great place for a family holiday. Owned and run by June and Bob Ennis for the past 25 years, the park is home to 33 modern mobile homes, all equipped with the latest, up to the minute conveniences. The 6-acre site is beautifully landscaped with plenty of trees to provide shade, and the homes are attractively grouped together rather than laid out in regimented rows. The park environment is particularly well-suited to children: no cars are permitted in the park, it is totally enclosed and the children's play area provides a good social centre for youngsters to make friends. Since they took over the running of Field Lane in 1974, June and Bob have carried out a continuing programme of improvements and the high standards they've achieved reflect their total commitment to the holiday industry on the Isle of Wight. A friendly atmosphere, coupled with a personal service, are at the top of their priorities. A large number of their guests return year after year knowing that they will be staying with friends. Each time they come back, it seems that something new will have been added to the amenities. Recent additional features include a 2½ acre games field, a 9-hole putting course, and facilities for playing cricket, football, badminton and basket ball. Inside the impressive, purpose-built service building is a well-stocked shop and off-licence furnished

Field Lane Holiday Park, Field Lane, St Helens, Isle of Wight PO33 1UX
Tel: 01983 872779

with all your holiday requirements. There's a separate telephone kiosk and a launderette with ironing facilities, washing machine and tumble drier. The tumble drier might be rather redundant: as June and Bob point out, you will probably find more occasions to use the clothes lines provided around the park since this area enjoys the best sunshine record in the British Isles!

BEMBRIDGE   MAP 6 REF N9
5 miles SE of Ryde, on the B3350

The most easterly point of the island, Bembridge was itself an island until the reclamation of the huge inland harbour of Brading Haven in the 1880s. The story of that major work is one of many aspects of the town's history featured in the **Bembridge Maritime Museum** which also displays ship models, artefacts from shipwrecks, and diving equipment, as well as action videos of underwater footage and lifeboat rescues. A fascinating exhibition of life in Bembridge, past and present, is portrayed in photographs and artefacts at the **Bembridge Roy Baker Heritage Centre** in Church Road. Also well worth a visit is the **Bembridge Windmill** (National Trust). Dating from around 1700, it is the only windmill to have survived on the island, with much of its wooden machinery still intact.

BRADING   MAP 6 REF N9
3 miles S of Ryde, on the A3055

For what is little more than a large village, Brading is remarkably well-stocked with visitor attractions, amongst them a diminutive **Town Hall** with whipping post and stocks outside, and a fine church housing some striking tombs of the Oglander family. The most ancient of the village's sights is the **Brading Roman Villa** which in the 3rd century was the centre of a rich and prosperous farming estate. It covers some 300 square feet and has fine mosaic floors with a represen-tation of that master-musician, Orpheus, charming wild animals with his lyre.

The oldest surviving house on the island is now home to the **Isle of Wight Waxworks**, an all-weather family attraction displaying scenes and characters from Island history. Naturally, there's a Chamber of Horrors, as well as a World of Nature Exhibition, Professor Copperthwaites Extraordinary Exhibition of Oddities, some delightful gardens, and a shop. Close by, **The Lilliput Antique Doll & Toy Museum** exhibits more than 2000 dolls and toys, ranging across the centuries from around 2000 BC to 1945. The collection also includes dolls' houses, tinplate toys, trains, rocking horses, and many unusual and rare playthings.

On the edge of the village stands **Morton Manor**, a lovely old house, dating back to 1249, largely rebuilt in 1680, set amidst one of the finest gardens in England. The landscaped grounds feature rose and Elizabethan sunken gardens, ponds and cascades, and many mature specimen trees including the largest Lon-don Plane you're ever likely to see. Other attractions include the Stable Shop, licensed tearooms, a safe children's Play Area with a traditional Elizabethan Turf

Maze, and even a Vineyard. In fact, Brading has two vineyards. The other is the well-known Adgestone Vineyard, planted in 1968 and the oldest on the island. Entry is free, as is the wine tasting. There are pony trap rides around the vineyard during the season, a gift shop and café.

A mile or so northwest of the village, **Nunwell House & Gardens** should definitely not be missed. The picturesque house has been a family home since 1522 and is of great historic and architectural interest. It was here that Sir John Oglander, an ancestor of the present owner, was host to Charles I on his last night of freedom and modern day visitors can still see the Parlour Chamber in which they met. The house is beautifully furnished, there are exhibits recalling the family's military connections, and Nunwell is surrounded by 5 acres of tranquil gardens enjoying views across the Solent.

Back in Brading High Street, **The Wheatsheaf Inn** has been trading since it was built in 1768. The present 'mine hosts', Brian and Kay Wallace who arrived here in September 1996 have thoroughly researched their predecessors, uncovering the fact that one landlord, Harry Garland Duffett, ran the inn for 38 years

The Wheatsheaf Inn, High Street, Brading, Isle of Wight PO36 0DQ
Tel: 01983 408824

from 1915 to 1953. Today, this grand old hostelry offers visitors a good choice of basket meals, toasties, baguettes, ploughman's and sandwiches as well as main meals and daily specials. Food is served daily from 12 noon until 2.30pm, while the inn itself is open from 11am until 4pm, and again from 7.00pm until

11pm. Outside, there's an attractive patio and beer garden, and a vast area for parking. This is a sociable pub with its own pool and darts teams and the community spirit is encouraged further by annual trips abroad organised by Brian and Kay. Recent destinations have included the island of Rhodes and a cruise to Bilbao.

Some of the grandest views on the island can be enjoyed from **Brading Down**, just west of the village on the minor road that leads to Downend. From Downend, it's less than a mile to **Arreton Manor** which claims, with some justification, to be "the most beautiful and intriguing house on the Isle of Wight". There was a house on this site long before Alfred the Great mentioned Arreton in his will of 885 AD and the manor was owned by successive monarchs from Henry VIII to Charles I. The present house was built during the reigns of Elizabeth and James I and it's a superb example of the architecture of that period, with mellow stone walls and Jacobean panelling complemented by furniture from the same era. Perhaps the most appealing aspect of Arreton is that indefinable atmosphere of a house that has been lived in for centuries. Other attractions include a **Museum of Childhood, Lace Museum, National Wireless Museum**, gift shop, tea-rooms and picnic area. Tel: 01983 528134.

A mile or so southwest of Arreton Manor stands another grand old house, **Haseley Manor**. In the mid-1970s, it was a deserted and decaying shell but in a heroic work of restoration has been saved by Raymond and Krystyna Young. They have furnished and decorated the rooms in period, adding audio-visual tableaux explaining the different eras. Visitors can also watch a film showing how the mammoth task of restoration was carried out. Inside the house, there's an indoor play area for small children, a working pottery where children can try their hand at the slippery craft, tea-room and gift shop. Outside, the attractions include magnificent herb, flower and water gardens; a Children's Farm and Adventure Playground, and a picnic area. Tel: 01983 865420.

ALVERSTONE
MAP 6 REF N9

2 miles NW of Sandown, on minor road off the A3055

A couple of miles west of Haseley Manor, the secluded and picturesque village of Alverstone sits beside the tiny River Yar. It has everything you expect of an English village - except for a pub. The deeds of the estate's owner, Lord Alverstone, specifically forbid the sale of intoxicating liquor within the village.

About ¾ of a mile north of Alverstone village is historic **Kern Farm**, once owned by the Knights Templar. Farmhouse holidays are becoming increasingly popular and Kern Farm, offers visitors an excellent choice of either bed & breakfast or self-catering accommodation. Kern is a 250-acre working farm, (sheep, horses and arable), enjoying a superb position commanding magnificent views of the downs and surrounding countryside. It's ideal for walkers since it lies on the Bembridge Trail and is just 3 miles from the sandy beaches at Sandown. The

Kern Farm, Alverstone, Sandown, Isle of Wight PO36 0EY
Tel: 01983 403721

location has been accorded all sorts of official recommendations: it's designated as an Area of Outstanding Beauty; the farm has won a Conservation Award; its southern end is a Site of Special Scientific Interest, and the farmhouse itself was listed in 1992 as a building of 'special architectural interest'. It dates back to the 1500s and offers two pretty bedrooms for bed & breakfast guests, both rooms en suite and one with a four-poster bed. Self-catering accommodation is provided in the 16th century West Wing, adjoining the main farmhouse. This stone-built listed cottage has been tastefully refurbished, creating a unique atmosphere and wonderful views for those seeking a break away from it all, yet within a 10-minute drive to shops, pubs and restaurants. Children over 12 years old are welcome but the owners regret that pets are not permitted and no smoking is allowed within this historic cottage. The owner of Kern Farm, Gaynor Oliver, also offers visitors another self-catering option. Combe View is a spacious, four-bedroom bungalow which sleeps 7 people plus baby. The accommodation is excellent throughout with carpeted bedrooms and sitting room with colour television, gas fire and sliding doors onto the sun terrace. The bungalow is extremely well-equipped: there's a washing machine, tumble drier, refrigerator, deep freeze, electric cooker, microwave, and even a payphone. If you are planning to stay on the island, you should certainly send off for Mrs Oliver's brochures which provide full details of these outstanding properties.

SANDOWN

MAP 6 REF N9

6 miles S of Ryde, on the A3055

"A village by a sandy shore" was how a guide-book described Sandown in the 1870s. Since then, its superb position on sweeping Sandown Bay has transformed that village into the island's premier resort. Now a lively town, Sandown offers its visitors every kind of seaside attraction. There are miles of flat, safe sands where a Kidzone safety scheme operates during the season, a traditional Pier complete with theatre, colourful gardens, a Sunday market, abundant sporting facilities, and even pleasure flights from the nearby airfield. On the edge of the town, the **Isle of Wight Zoological Gardens** specialises in breeding severely endangered exotic species and is home to the UK's largest variety of Royal Bengal, Siberian and Chinese tigers. The Zoo is also a World Health Organisation centre for venomous snakes, their venom extracted for use in antidotes for snake bites. You may well see TV "Snake Man" Jack Corney handling these lethal reptiles and children who are photographed with a small harmless snake are presented with a handling certificate to prove it! There are all-weather snake and parrot shows, a kiddies' play area and Pets' Corner, a seafront pub and café, the Zoofari Gift Shop, and a snack bar. A Road-Runner Train operates frequent services between the Zoo and the town centre. More details on: 01983 403883.

In Sandown's High Street, the **Museum of Isle of Wight Geology** is especially popular with children who love its life-sized dinosaurs - the Isle of Wight is renowned for the number and quality of the dinosaur remains that have been discovered here. The museum, "120 million years in the making", has excellent displays on all aspects of the island's geology. As part of its educational programme, museum staff will advise you on the best places to look for fossils and, when you return with your discoveries, will identify them for you. Tel: 01983 404344.

Conveniently located just a short distance from the popular safe sandy beaches of Sandown Bay, the **Westfield Hotel** is also just a few minutes walk from the Pier, Theatre, High Street shops and the railway station. Resident proprietors Diane and Peter Bass take pride in providing a homely and happy atmosphere and make every effort to ensure that your holiday will be one of comfort, relaxation and enjoyment. An attractive bay-fronted building, the Westfield also has a light and airy conservatory, a cosy television lounge, a beautiful front garden which has won many awards and a large, lawned garden to the rear. In the sunny dining room, the menu offers a varied choice, with the accent on plentiful home-cooked English food served in the traditional way. Guests are very welcome to enjoy the atmosphere of the friendly licensed bar and are free to invite their friends for a quiet drink or a game of pool, darts, cards, or even shove ha'penny. All 14 guest bedrooms are en suite with toilet and showers, comfortably furnished, and provided with tea-making facilities and colour TV. For the comfort, health and safety of all guests, the dining room

**Westfield Hotel, 17 Broadway, Sandown, Isle of Wight PO36 9BY
Tel: 01983 403802 Fax: 01983 406404**

and bedrooms are non-smoking areas. The hotel enjoys a 3-Crowns listing, welcomes children and has ample parking for guests. Close by is The Heights Health and Leisure Centre, perfect for family leisure activities and the many coastal footpaths and the island's frequent bus services make Sandown the perfect base from which to explore this beautiful island. And throughout the season, the Sandown Bay area hosts a wide range of special events - from the Regatta in August to Sunday markets, from the Isle of Wight Power Boat Festival in May to the National Strong Man finals in September.

Enjoying a superb seafront location on the island's sandiest beach and with beautiful views of the Culver Cliffs, **Fort Spinney Holiday Centre** offers visitors an excellent choice of self-catering holiday chalets and apartments. The Centre caters for families and couples looking for a truly relaxing holiday, providing a range of holiday units in a variety of sizes and prices to suit all requirements. All accommodation is single storey and set in large lawned gardens, (dogs, incidentally are not permitted). The modern two berth self-contained apartments each consists of a bedroom, (with a choice of double or two single beds), bathroom with toilet, bath and shower, lounge, kitchen and diner. Larger apartments are also available which can accommodate up to 4 people. The Centre's chalets are ideal for 4 people, although they will sleep up to a maximum of 6 people, including children of any age. For larger groups of up to 8 people, there are two bungalows and a large apartment for rent. All the accommodation at Fort Spinney is extremely well appointed, with gas and electricity included in the rental, and there's a laundry room on site with washing machine and dryer. There's no shop on the site but advance groceries for the day of your arrival, together with daily milk and a newspaper service can all be arranged. Sandown's splendid beach is virtually on your doorstep, and when you fancy a change from the

**Fort Spinney Holiday Centre, Yaverland Road, Sandown
Isle of Wight PO36 8QB Tel: 01983 402360**

beach, it's but a short, level walking distance to the town's shops, theatre, sea-front entertainments and the Tiger Sanctuary. If you want to roam further afield, the island has an excellent bus service and you'll find a bus stop just 50 metres from the Centre. Some of Fort Spinney's top quality accommodation is available all year round, providing the opportunity for a really peaceful out of season holiday.

Kathleen and Roger Clemens, who own and run Fort Spinney Holiday Centre, offer similar high quality accommodation at **Sandown Holiday Chalets** off Avenue Road. The spacious, 2-acre site, surrounded by trees, is well laid out with plenty of open space and colourful flower beds. The chalets are in reality small bungalows, built of local stone and fully equipped for up to 6 people. Each chalet has two double bedrooms, one containing a double bed and the other with 2 single beds. There's a lounge/diner/kitchen with the kitchen area containing a full size gas cooker and electric fridge. Within the lounge area are 2 single sofa beds providing sleeping accommodation for two. A colour television is provided for your enjoyment and there's an electric fire. The private bathroom contains bath, wc and hand basin. Each unit is fully equipped except for towels and tea towels, and all gas and electricity is included in the rental. (Please note that no pets are allowed). The site also has a launderette and there's ample free parking at the front entrance. All the amenities and entertainments the town has to offer, and the beach itself, are just ten minutes' walk from Sandown Holiday Chalets. In addition, the main Ryde to Sandown bus route has a stop

Sandown Holiday Chalets, Avenue Road, Sandown
Isle of Wight PO36 9AP Tel: 01983 404025

fifty metres from the site entrance. Long acclaimed by the public as the premier holiday centre of the south coast, Sandown offers safe swimming along four miles of beach as well as boating and fishing. This, and other attractions the town has to offer, together with a chalet at Sandown Holiday Chalets should make your holiday complete in every way. And if you schedule a holiday here in the less busy months, there are specially reduced terms available for 2 or 3 people staying here in either early or late season.

SHANKLIN
12 miles SE of Newport, on the A3055

MAP 6 REF N9

Like Sandown, Shanklin was just a small village a century or so ago. The old village has survived intact, a charming little complex of thatched houses standing at the head of the **Shanklin Chine**. The famous Chine is a spectacular ravine some 300ft deep, 180ft wide, noted for its waterfalls and rare flora. There's a Nature Trail to follow or you can join a guided tour. **The Heritage Centre** includes an interesting exhibit on PLUTO (the PipeLine Under The Ocean) secretively constructed during World War II to transport fuel from the island to the Continent during the D-Day landings. There's also a memorial to the soldiers of 40 Commando who trained in this area for the disastrous assault on Dieppe in 1942.

The old village stands on a 150ft-high cliff from which the ground slopes gently down to the safe, sheltered beach, with its long, seafront esplanade. With its scenic setting, many public gardens, and healthy climate, Shanklin has appealed to many celebrities. Charles Darwin was particularly fond of the town, the American poet Longfellow fell in love with it, and John Keats was a familiar figure in Sandown throughout the summer of 1818. The grassy open space known as Keats Green commemorates his stay here during which he wrote some of his best-known poems.

The **Cottage Restaurant** is set in the heart of the unbelievably picturesque old village, one of the most photographed corners of Olde Englande. Standing in a quiet cul-de-sac, The Cottage was originally *several* cottages, all built in the early 1800s, which is why there are intriguing differences in level between the different parts of the restaurant. Nooks and crannies abound and sumptuous furnishings create the appealing atmosphere of a very stylish and tasteful private house, decorated with great flair and panache. Owners Mike and Pauline Hart, respectively from South Africa and the former Northern Rhodesia, have also lived in Australia and New Zealand so they bring a distinctly cosmopolitan flavour to their unique restaurant. The menu offers an extensive choice of dishes reflecting the very best of international cuisine. Amongst the starters, for example, there's a Butternut & Coconut Soup and a creamy Seafood Crepe, while the main courses range from a classic Dover Sole Meunière to Braised Guinea Fowl served with an apricot and liqueur sauce; from Monk Fish Thermidor to succulent Ostrich Steaks, pan fried and dressed with a fruity pepper sauce. Your choice of dessert, a memorable Pavlova or Tipsy Cake perhaps, will be followed by a complimentary pot of coffee accompanied by truffles. As a final grace note to your meal, you should seriously consider sampling the house speciality, "Dom Pedro", a wondrous confection of ice cream and liqueur cocktail. The Cottage Restaurant's regular menu is supplemented by daily specials, (genuine Scampi for example, or a tasty vegetarian Mushroom

Cottage Restaurant, 8 Eastcliffe Road, Shanklin, Isle of Wight PO37 6AA
Tel: 01983 862504 Fax: 01983 867512

Risotto), and in good weather you can enjoy the superlative food in an enclosed and secluded Summer Garden. A visit to Old Shanklin village is an experience that will surely linger in your memory; combine it with a meal at The Cottage Restaurant and you have something really unforgettable.

Right next door to The Cottage Restaurant, Pauline Hart has opened the very distinctive **Cottage Gift Shop**, an attractive old building made even more appealing during the season with hanging baskets and window boxes of colourful flowers. Pauline herself has considerable experience as an artist and potter so

**Cottage Gift Shop, 4 Eastcliffe Road, Shanklin, Isle of Wight PO37 6AA
Tel: 01983 862504 Fax: 01983 867512.**

she brings a very critical eye to bear on anything she decides to include amongst the quality gifts on offer here. She also observes another criterion: everything in her unique gift shop has been sourced in South Africa. Nowhere else on the island, (or on the mainland, for that matter), will you find such a remarkable range of beautifully produced artefacts: contemporary pieces which continue an age-old tradition of superb craftsmanship. There's no space here to detail the dazzling variety of the items on display, but special mention should be given to the wondrously-carved hardwood pieces and the ostrich eggs inventively-decorated in flamboyant colour.

Nowadays, you'll find **The Plough & Barleycorn** in the heart of Sandown. When it was built around 1800, though, it was surrounded by an extensive orchard. The orchard has gone but the inn still boasts a large and secluded

**The Plough & Barleycorn, North Road, Shanklin, Isle of Wight PO37 6DB
Tel: 01983 862882**

lawned garden to the rear, a secure place for children, complete with swings and a sizeable Wendy House. There's more outside seating on the patio at the front, a pretty spot with masses of shrubs and vines and hanging baskets of flowers. Ted and Linda Sutton, who run this inviting inn, bring years of experience in the licensed trade during which time they have managed pubs from Gosport to Edinburgh, and even in Spain. The Plough is a lively hostelry with regular week-end live entertainment, pub quizzes and Scrabble contests, as well as traditional games such as pool and darts. There's even a dance floor in the L-shaped Lounge Bar. The food on offer is traditional home-cooked English fare with a good choice of main meals including vegetarian options, salads, bar snacks, sandwiches and baguettes. Children are also well catered for: they have their own menu and most adult meals are also available as children's portions. From time to time, Ted and Linda arrange theme nights devoted to a particular cuisine, Chinese perhaps, or Indian. The interior of The Plough has been recently refurbished to a high standard and an interesting feature is Linda's extensive collection of tea-pots of all shapes and sizes. One regular patron who comes in daily is in his nineties but the pub has an even older patron. According to the *Isle of Wight Ghost Book* there's a resident ghost at The Plough, a rather shy old fisherman who only manifests himself to those who believe!

VENTNOR

MAP 6 REF M10

11 miles S of Newport, on the A3055

Along the south-eastern corner of the island stretches a 6-mile length of ragged cliffs known as Undercliffe. Clinging to the slopes at its eastern end, Ventnor has been described as "an alpinist's town" and as "a steeply raked auditorium with the sea as the stage". Promoted as a spa town in the 1830s, its distinguished visitors have included a young Winston Churchill and an elderly Karl Marx.

Ventnor Heritage Museum houses a fascinating collection of old prints, photographs and working models relating to the town's history, while **Ventnor Botanical Gardens** shelters some 10,000 plants in 22 acres of grounds, amongst them many rare and exotic trees, shrubs, alpines, perennials, succulents and conifers. There's a picnic area and children's playground, and during August the Gardens host open-air performances of Shakespeare plays. Above the town, **St Boniface Down** (National Trust), at 785ft the highest point on the island, provides some dizzying views across coast and countryside.

A mile or so to the west, in neighbouring St Lawrence, **The Isle of Wight Rare Breeds and Waterfowl Park**, set in 30 acres of coastal farmland, operates as a survival centre for more than 40 breeds of rare farm animals. The Park is also home to over 100 species of waterfowl and poultry, there's a guinea pig "village" and chipmunk "mansion", special children's areas, a unique temperate waterfall house, lakeside cafeteria and gift shop. Tel: 01983 852582.

About 3 miles inland from Ventnor, **Appuldurcombe House** (English Heritage) is a sad shell of a once-imposing 18th century mansion, but the ornamental grounds landscaped by 'Capability' Brown provide an enchanting setting for walks and picnics.

SHORWELL   Map 3 ref L9
7 miles SW of Newport, on the B3323

Pronounced 'Shorell' by Caulkheads, as Isle of Wight natives are known, the village of Shorwell has no fewer than three venerable manor houses within its boundaries. **West Court**, **Wolverton**, and **North Court** were built respectively during the reigns of Henry VIII, Elizabeth I, and James I. They possess all the charm you would expect from that glorious age of English architecture but sadly none of them is open to the public. However, you can visit St Peter's Church to gaze on its mesmerisingly beautiful 15th century wall-painting and admire its 500-year-old stone pulpit covered by an elaborate wooden canopy of 1620.

This small village has yet another attraction. **Yafford Mill** is an 18th century water mill in full working order. It's surrounded by ponds and streams where you'll find Sophie, the resident seal, and within the grounds there are paddocks which are home to rare cattle, sheep and pigs, a collection of antique farm machinery, a steam engine and narrow-gauge railway. There are also waymarked nature walks, a playground, picnic area, gift shop, tea gardens and licensed bar. Tel: 01983 740610.

About a mile to the southeast of Shorwell and situated in an area of outstanding natural beauty, **Bucks Farm** is the home of the Jones family, Carol and

Bucks Farm Holiday Cottages, Shorwell, Newport
Isle of Wight PO30 3LP Tel: 01983 551206

Edwin, and their two young sons. It's a working farm of about 500 acres but the Jones have converted some of the handsome stone farm buildings to form Bucks Farm Holiday Cottages. Carol and Edwin live in the Tythe Barn adjoining the holiday cottages and a small cluster of further dwellings make up the community of Bucks Heath, beautifully set in the superb open countryside between Shorwell and Kingston, just one and a half miles from the coast.

Cleverly using the name Bucks Farm as an acronym, the Jones' promise: Brilliant Value, all linen supplied; Unforgettable hospitality and bikes to borrow; Cots for babies, extra bed, listening service; Kids toy boxes for inside, and an outdoor play area; Stocked store cupboard and complimentary bottle of Island Wine; Favoured area, excellent walks, (the Shepherd's Trail passes nearby), maps provided; All central heating and electricity included; Ready made beds and towels for your convenience; Menus from local restaurants and information pack. Even that list isn't exhaustive. It doesn't mention the fresh fruit and flowers awaiting your arrival, the maid or laundry service, picnic hampers or catering for a dinner party that Carol also offers, or the lovely views across Freshwater Bay. Or additional attractions such as the Cleveland Bay horses which Carol has at stud here, and the largest plantation of sunflowers on the island.

There are two properties, Rose Cottage, (which accomodates up to 6 + 2 and a baby), and Byre Cottage, (sleeping 4 + 2 and a baby), both attractively furnished and outstandingly well-appointed. Children 'with well behaved parents' are welcomed, but the nature of the Farm which combines arable, sheep and horses does not allow for pets to be brought. The cottages are self-catering, but Carol and Edwin also offer bed & breakfast accommodation in the Tythe Barn itself, with a 'huge' English, vegetarian or continental breakfast included in the price. As many guests at Bucks Farm have found, it's a good idea to heed Carol's advice to 'Keep up with the Jones' and holiday with us!'

FRESHWATER   MAP 3 REF K9

11 miles W of Newport, on the A3055

Freshwater and the surrounding area are inextricably linked with the memory of Alfred, Lord Tennyson. In 1850, he succeeded Wordsworth as Poet Laureate, married Emily Sellwood, and shortly afterwards moved to **Farringford**, just outside Freshwater. The house, set in 33 acres of parkland, is now a hotel where visitors can relax in the luxuriously appointed drawing room with its delightful terrace and views across the downs. Tennyson was an indefatigable walker and however foul the weather would pace along nearby High Down dramatically arrayed in a billowing cloak and a black, broad-brimmed sombrero. After his death, the area was re-named Tennyson Down and a cross erected high on the cliffs in his memory. There are more remembrances of the great poet in the Church of All Saints in Freshwater town where Lady Tennyson is buried in the churchyard and a touching memorial inside commemorates their son Lionel, "an affectionate boy", who died at the age of 32 while returning from India.

As Tennyson grew older, he became increasingly impatient with sightseers flocking to Farringford hoping to catch sight of the now-legendary figure. He moved to his other home at Blackdown in Sussex where he died in 1892.

If you are looking for a gift or memento of your visit to the island, you had best get yourself to the **Yarmouth Gift & Craft Shop** on the outskirts of Freshwater. Brian and Nancy Coombs who own and run this outstanding establishment promise "unusual gifts for special people" and they certainly deliver on that promise. They started their business some 6 years ago in Yarmouth (hence the name) and today their shop represents a veritable fairyland of crafts and gift items. Pride of place goes to a large range of dolls house furniture and accessories. The shop's catalogue lists literally hundreds of these dainty pieces and includes everything from a miniature grandfather clock to a scullery sink. You can furnish the house from top to bottom, fill the kitchen with food and utensils, stock the bathroom with toiletries, and provide the bedroom with a brass double bed. And then you can populate the house with fine quality resin figurines. There's a wide selection to choose from, amongst them a great-grandmother asleep with a cat, a boy with a catapult, a cook with a rolling pin, and a kneeling housemaid with a brush. (All the items, incidentally, are also available by mail order). In addition to their dolls house pieces, Brian and Nancy also stock an enormous variety of other crafts, most of which are made by English craftspeople. You'll find exquisite hand-painted thimbles, glassware, and but-

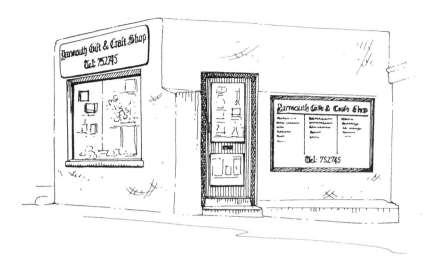

**Yarmouth Gift & Craft Shop, Shirley House, Avenue Road, Freshwater
Isle of Wight PO40 9UR Tel/Fax: 01983 752745**

terflies, knitted jumpers, Celtic T-shirts, pottery and paintings, Italian marble
statues, plus much much more. Also worth mentioning are the framed 'Verses'
which come from Cheshire: Nancy is herself an accomplished poet whose work
has appeared in various anthologies and has also been recorded on audio tape.

About a mile south of the town, Freshwater Bay was once an inaccessible
inlet, much favoured by smugglers. Quite apart from the Bay's scenic attractions, thousands of visitors flock here every year to see **Dimbola Lodge**, one of
the most important shrines in the history of early photography. It was the home
of Julia Margaret Cameron (1815-1879) who bought it in 1860 to be close to her
friend Tennyson. Three years later, she was given a camera and immediately
devoted herself with her usual energy to mastering the technical and artistic
aspects of what was then called the "Black Art". (Because handling the chemi-
cals involved usually left the photographer's hands deeply stained). The
coal-house at Dimbola Lodge was turned into a dark room and within a year,
Julia had been elected a member of the Photographic Society of London. She
photographed most of the leading lights of the artistic community of the time,
the most famous perhaps being her classic portrait of Tennyson himself, a craggy,
bearded figure with a visionary gaze. Dimbola Lodge was acquired by the Julia
Margaret Cameron Trust in 1993 and it has been converted into a museum and
galleries devoted to her photography. There's also a gift shop, antiquarian book-
shop, and vegetarian restaurant. Tel: 01983 756814.

From the Bay itself, there are regular cruises around the island's most spectacular natural feature, the dreaded **Needles**. The boat trip takes you through
the swirling waters around the lighthouse, and past the line of jagged slabs of

The Needles

gleaming chalk towering some 200ft high. The sea has gouged deep caves out of the cliffs. Two of them are known as Lord Holmes' Parlour and Kitchen, named after a 17th century Governor of the Island who once entertained his guests in the "Parlour" and kept his wines cool in the "Kitchen".

The Needles are undoubtedly at their most impressive when viewed from the sea, but they are still a grand sight from the land. There are some particularly striking vistas from the **Needles Old Battery** (National Trust), a Victorian coastal fort standing 250ft above the sea. Visitors pass through a 200ft long tunnel and emerge onto a platform with panoramic views. Alternatively, The **Needles Pleasure Park** at Alum Bay also has good views and offers a wide range of family entertainments, a chairlift from the clifftop to the beach, boat trips to the lighthouse, a glass-making studio and many other attractions. Tel: 01983 752401.

YARMOUTH
MAP 3 REF K9

10 miles W of Newport, on the A3054

A regular ferry links this picturesque little port to Lymington on the mainland. It was once the principal port on the island which was why Henry VIII ordered the building of **Yarmouth Castle** (English Heritage) in the 1540s. It was garrisoned until 1885 but is now disused, though much remains. The town also boasts a quaint old **Town Hall**, a working Pier, and a 13th century church rather unhappily restored in 1831. It's worth going inside to see the incongruous statue on the tomb of Sir Robert Holmes, Governor of the Island in the mid-17th century. During one of the endless conflicts with the French, Sir Robert had captured a ship on board which was a French sculptor with an unfinished statue of Louis XIV. He was travelling to Versailles to model the King's head from life. Sir Robert decided that the elaborate statue of the King (in full French armour) would do nicely for his own tomb. The sculptor was ordered to replace the Royal head with Sir Robert's. No doubt deliberately, the artist made a poor fist of the job and the head is decidedly inferior to the rest of the statue.

One mile west of this appealing little town, **Fort Victoria Country Park**, owned by the Isle of Wight Council, is one of the major leisure complexes on the island. Set on the Solent coastline, it offers an enormous range of attractions. There are unspoilt sandy beaches, woodland walks, and Ranger-guided tours around the Park highlighting the local and natural history of the area. (These must be booked ahead). Within the Park, you'll also find the largest model railway in Britain, a state-of-the-art Planetarium, a Marine Aquarium with some 80 different species of local and tropical fish, and a Maritime Heritage Exhibition. Speedboat trips are also available from the slipway next to the Boathouse Lunch & Tea Gardens.

5 The New Forest

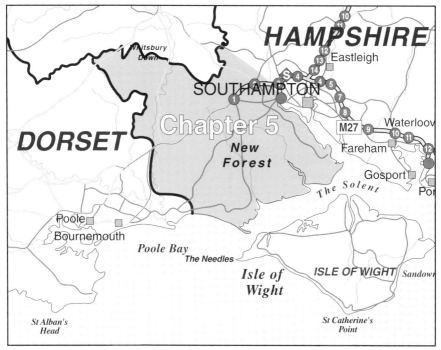

© MAPS IN MINUTES ™ (1998)

The New Forest, as is the way with English place-names, is neither New nor a Forest, although much of it is attractively wooded. Some historians believe that 'Forest' is a corruption of an ancient British word, *gores* or *gorest*, meaning waste or open ground. 'Gorse' comes from the same root word. The term New Forest came into use after William the Conqueror proclaimed the area a royal hunting ground, seized some 15,000 acres that Saxon farmers had laboriously reclaimed from the heathland, and began a programme of planting thousands of trees. To preserve wildlife for his sport, (the deer especially), William adopted all the rigorous venery laws of his Saxon royal predecessors and added some harsh measures of his own. Anyone who killed a deer would himself be killed. If he shot at the beast and missed, his hands were cut off. And, perhaps most ruthless of all, anyone who disturbed a deer during the breeding season had his eyes put out.

There are still plenty of wild deer roaming the 145 square miles of the Forest Park, confined within its boundaries by cattle grids, (known to Americans as Texas Gates). You are much more likely though to see the famous New Forest ponies, free-wandering creatures which neverthe-less are all privately owned. They are also something of a hazard for drivers, so do take care, es-pecially at night.

New Forest Ponies

The largest wild area in lowland Britain, the Forest is ideal walking country with vast tracts virtually unpopulated but criss-crossed by a cat's cradle of footpaths and bridle-ways. The Forestry Commission has also established a network of waymarked cycle routes which make the most of the scenic attractions and are also designed to help protect the special nature of the Forest. A map detailing the cycle network is available, along with a vast amount of other information about the area, from the New Forest Museum and Visitor Centre in Lyndhurst. Visitors can watch an audio visual show, see life-sized models of Forest characters, make use of its Resource Centre and Library, and explore a gift shop specialising in locally made Forest crafts. The only town of any size within the New Forest, Lyndhurst is generally regarded as its 'capi-tal', a good place then to begin a tour of the area.

LYNDHURST
MAP 3 REF K7

8 miles SW of Southampton, on the A35/A337

The most striking building in this compact little town is the **Church of St Michael**, rebuilt in mid-Victorian times in what John Betjeman described as 'the most fanciful, fantastic Gothic style that I ever have seen'. The rebuilding co-incided with the heyday of the Pre-Raphaelite movement so the church con-tains some fine stained glass by Burne-Jones, produced by the firm of William Morris, as well as a splendidly lush painting by Lord Leighton of *The Wise and Foolish Virgins*.

In St Michael's churchyard is the Grave of Alice Liddell who, as a young girl, was the inspiration for Lewis Carroll's *Alice in Wonderland*. As Mrs Reginald Hargreaves, Alice lived all her married life in Lyndhurst and was very active in local affairs.

Next to the church is the **Queen's House** which rather confusingly is re-named the King's House whenever the reigning sovereign is male. Originally built as a royal hunting lodge, its medieval and Tudor elements are still visible. Many Kings and Queens have lodged here and the last monarch to stay, George III, graciously allowed loyal villagers to watch through the window as he ate dinner. The House is now the headquarters of the Forestry Commission and is also home to the Verderer's Court, an institution dating back to Norman times which still deals with matters concerning the forest's ancient commoning rights.

This little town is noted for its variety of small shops where you can find "anything from fresh food to Ferraris!" Many are located in the High Street, an attractive thoroughfare of mostly Edwardian buildings, which gently slopes down the hill to Bolton's Bench, a tree-crowned knoll where grazing ponies can usually be found and there are excellent views over Lyndhurst and the surrounding forest. At the other end of the town, **Swan Green**, surrounded by picturesque thatched cottages, provides a much-photographed setting where cricket matches are held in summer.

Located about half a mile south of Lyndhurst on the A337, **The Crown Stirrup** has been a pub since the 15th century. Nowadays, in view of the emphasis mine hosts Mark and Kim Pycroft place on good food and wine, it might be more correct to describe The Crown Stirrup as a "restaurant with a bar". The regular menu, which includes such delicacies as Langoustines in a cream, wine, herb & garlic sauce, or a Medley of Wild Mushrooms in a Cream & Brandy Sauce served on rice, is supplemented by an extensive range of daily specials, vegetarian options, and desserts. Mark spent a year studying wine so his choices, listed on the blackboard, are carefully selected from both European and New World sources and offer excellent quality, variety and value for money. Another of Mark's interests is blues music and from time to time he arranges live entertain-

The Crown Stirrup, Clay Hill, Lyndhurst, Hampshire SO43 7DE
Tel: 01703 282272

ment. To the rear of the pub, there's half an acre of Beer Garden with a safe children's play area and a patio with a clever automatic rolling blind to provide shade on hot days. Many visitors wonder about the meaning of The Crown Stirrup's unusual name. It relates to the King's law regarding the size of dogs and goes back to medieval times when the New Forest was a Royal hunting preserve. Commoners were only allowed into the forest to hunt if their dogs were small enough to fit through the "Verderer's Stirrup". Any dog that failed this test suffered "expedition" - the removal of 3 claws from each paw so that the animal could not endanger the forest deer. The original Verderer's Stirrup still hangs in the Verderers' Hall in the 17th century Queen's House on Lyndhurst High Street.

CADNAM   MAP 3 REF K6
4 miles N of Lyndhurst, on the A335/A337

A few miles north of Lyndhurst and enjoying an ideal location on the borders of the New Forest, Cadnam is a perfect base from which to explore this attractive corner of the county. The village stands at the hub of all the major roads striking through the forest park and, very conveniently, also boasts an outstanding hostelry, **The Coach and Horses**. It's run by Andrea and Brian Morrison, a bright and friendly young couple who hail respectively from Hampshire and Perth in Scotland. The Coach and Horses is their first pub but they clearly have a natural aptitude for hospitality and a flair for creating a warm and welcoming atmosphere. If you didn't know already that Brian was an award-winning chef, a glance at his menu would give you plenty of clues. Starters include a Brie Amandine - deep fried medallions of baby brie cooked in nibbed almonds and breadcrumbs, served with salad and Cumberland sauce. Main courses offer a choice of nour-

The Coach & Horses, 11 Southampton Road, Cadnam
Southampton SO40 2NF Tel: 01703 813120

ishing steaks, chicken, fish and vegetarian dishes, along with house specialities such as Mediterranean Avocado Bake or Knuckle of Lamb braised in a tasty Madeira sauce. *And* there's also a daily specials' board offering yet more choices. For lighter appetites, the Coach and Horses provides an excellent selection of hot or cold filled baguettes, Ploughman's Lunches and salads made with seasonal ingredients. For dessert, take your pick from the superb sweet trolley or settle for a plate of fresh, prime quality cheeses. To complement your meal, there's an excellent choice of fine wines and cask ales, and, if you enjoy traditional pub games such as darts and dominoes, they are also available. (You should be careful though of challenging the Coach and Horses' own teams. They have a formidable reputation for excelling in these ancient skills!).

MINSTEAD   Map 3 ref K6
3 miles NW of Lyndhurst, off the A337

A couple of miles south-west of Cadnam, the village of Minstead offers two interesting attractions, one of which is the **Church of All Saints**. During the 18th century, the gentry and squirearchy of Minstead seem to have regarded church attendance as a necessary duty which, nevertheless, should be made as agreeable as possible. Three of the village's most affluent residents paid to have the church fabric altered so that they could each have their own entrance door leading to a private "parlour", complete with open fireplace and comfortable chairs. The squire of Minstead even installed a sofa on which he could doze during the sermon. It's easy to understand his concern since these sermons were normally expected to last for at least an hour; star preachers seem to have thought they were short-changing their flock if they didn't prate for at least twice as long. It was around this time that churches began introducing benches for the congregation.

Admirers of the creator of Sherlock Holmes, Sir Arthur Conan Doyle, will want to pay their respects at his grave in the churchyard here. A puzzle worthy of Sir Arthur's great detective is the idiosyncratic sign outside the Trusty Servant pub in the village. Instead of showing, as one might expect, a portrait of a dutiful domestic, the sign actually depicts a liveried figure with the feet of a stag and the face of a pig, its snout clamped by a padlock. A 10-line poem underneath this peculiar sign explains that the snout means the servant will eat any old scraps, the padlock that he will tell no tales about his master, and the stag's feet that he will be swift in carrying his master's messages.

Minstead's other main attraction is **Furzey Gardens**, eight acres of delightful, informal landscape with extensive views over the New Forest towards the Isle of Wight. Beautiful banks of azaleas and rhododendrons, heathers and ferns surround an attractive water garden, and amongst the notable species growing here are incandescent Chilean Fire Trees and the strange 'Bottle Brush Tree'. Tel: 01703 812464.

BEAULIEU   Map 3 ref L7

7 miles SE of Lyndhurst, on the B3056

The ruins of a 13th century Cistercian Abbey, a stately home which grew up around the Abbey's imposing gatehouse, and the **National Motor Museum** sited in its grounds are three good reasons why the village of Beaulieu has become one of the county's major visitor attractions. When Lord Montagu of Beaulieu first opened his family home to the public in the 1950s, he organised a display of a few vintage motor vehicles in homage to his father who had been

National Motor Museum, Beaulieu

a pioneer of motoring in Britain. That modest clutch of cars has now expanded to include some 250 of the oldest, newest, slowest and fastest motor-cars and bikes in British motoring history, plus some rare oddities. The motoring theme is continued in fun features such as Go Karts, Miniature Motors, and 'Fast Trax', described as the 'best in virtual racing simulators'. Tel: 01590 612123.

It was an ancestor of Lord Montagu, the 2nd Duke of Montagu, who created the picturesque riverside village of **Buckler's Hard** in the early 1700s. It was designed as an inland port to receive and refine sugar from the Duke's West Indian estates and His Grace planned his model village on a grand scale: the streets, for example, were to be 80ft wide. Unfortunately, the enterprise failed and only a single street was built. That 18th century street remains intact and unspoiled, and one of its buildings has been converted into a **Maritime Museum** reflecting the subsequent history of the village when it became a ship-building centre. More than 50 naval ships were built at Buckler's Hard, amongst them one of Nelson's favourite ships, the *Agamemnon*.

Just across the Beaulieu River from Buckler's Hard, as the crow flies, is **Exbury Gardens**. By road, that's about a 10-mile detour but one which is definitely worth making. One visitor described the Exbury Gardens as "Heaven with the gates open". Created by Lionel de Rothschild in the 1920s, Exbury is still run by his descendants, Mr & Mrs Edmund de Rothschild. They welcome visitors to share their own appreciation of these spectacular gardens where you can wander through some 200 acres of breathtakingly landscaped displays of noble trees, shrubs and botanical rarities. Tel: 01703 891203.

HOLBURY
MAP 6 REF L7
13 miles S of Southampton, on minor road off the A326

From Exbury Gardens, do find your way along the country lanes to the large village (or is it a small town?) of Holbury. Your objective should be **The Bridge Tavern** at Ipers Bridge which provides a convenient stopping-off point for any tour through this attractive area. The tavern is run by Jean and Bill Galbraith who have some 25 years experience in the trade and more than 40 years together as husband and wife.

Their 17th century pub has spacious gardens, with the little Darkwater River running alongside, and a safe children's play area. Inside, the open fire, caneback chairs and darkwood furniture provide an inviting setting in which to enjoy the Galbraiths' good, wholesome cooking. In the separate dining area, main courses include home-made Steak & Kidney Pie, a hearty Mixed Grill, a good choice of fish dishes and a tasty Nut Roast for vegetarians. There's a minimenu for younger members of the family, daily specials, and a wide selection of starters and Lite Bites - omelettes, ploughman's, jacket potatoes, and much more. Pace yourself to leave room for one of the wonderful traditional desserts such as Steam Suet Pudding, Fruit Crumbles or Strudel, all of them home-made. Traditional food again predominates at Sunday lunch-time when you would be well-advised to book ahead. The Bridge Tavern also offers an extremely well-chosen and realistically-priced wine list with European and New World vintages available either by the glass or bottle.

And if, after indulging yourself, the idea of a gentle stroll appeals, the National Trust's long distance path, the Solent Way is within easy reach of this welcoming hostelry. **The Bridge Tavern, Ipers Bridge, Holbury, Southampton, SO45 2HD. Tel: 01703 892554**

ASHLETT CREEK
MAP 6 REF M7
16 miles SE of Southampton, on minor road off the B3053

East of Holbury lie the sprawling acres of Fawley's oil refineries, but if you drive just a mile or so further along the B3053 and turn off to Ashlett Creek, you find yourself in a completely different world. Wandering creeks, mud-flats and bird-haunted marshland create a unique atmosphere. For more than 150 years **The**

The Jolly Sailor, Ashlett Creek, Fawley, Southampton SO45 1DT
Tel: 01703 891305 Fax: 01703 890700

Jolly Sailor has been welcoming visitors to this attractive village overlooking Southampton Water and the Solent. The pub began as a beerhouse in 1846 when new licensing laws allowed anyone who paid the local poor rate, plus a £2 excise fee, to sell beer. The Martin family were the first landlords of the Jolly Sailor and remained so for decades. Some local people can still recall James Martin, who was landlord here during the 1920s and '30s. A genial but fastidious man he used to follow customers with dirty shoes about with a dustpan and brush. He also had a habit of moving glasses less than six inches from the edge of the table into the middle, a practice which provoked some banter and teasing.

There's a much more relaxed atmosphere nowadays, with mine hosts Peter Murray and Ann Gray making sure that the Jolly Sailor really lives up to its name. The pub runs three darts teams, two pool teams, a go-kart team, a Golf Society, sponsors Fawley Football Club, provides many traditional pub games and, on occasions, Peter appears in his other incarnation, DJ Mad Manic Murray, to entertain regulars with special disco events. The pub was completely refurbished, inside and out, during the autumn of 1998. The exterior looks very inviting with its cream-painted clapper boarding and traditional small-paned windows, while inside there's a welcoming open log fire.

Peter and Ann also introduced a tasty new menu which offers an excellent choice of starters; home-made favourites such as Beef & Ale Pie; a new steaks and grills section (including a memorable Butterfly Cajun Chicken Breast); vegetarian and seafood dishes; as well as Daily Specials and a good selection of Light Bites. There's a separate menu for the tempting desserts and house wine is available by the glass or bottle. The Jolly Sailor is a Hidden Place that well repays a visit and, if you're a well-organised kind of person, you can even telephone or fax your food order in advance so that you can eat shortly after your arrival.

PENNINGTON
MAP 3 REF K8
9 miles S of Lyndhurst, on the A337

Returning to the coast south of Lyndhurst, we arrive at Pennington, just to the west of Lymington. **Our Bench** is the award-winning home of Mary and Roger Lewis who have been welcoming guests for bed and breakfast for some 11 years. Their large bungalow stands in this quiet village, just 2 miles from the open New Forest and a 20-minute walk from the lovely Georgian yachting town of Lymington with its Saturday market. Our Bench (which is non-smoking) is surrounded by a third of an acre of grounds and guests have the pleasure of tasting some of the home-grown fruits at breakfast, a 4-course feast served at 8.30am or earlier if required. Evening meals are also available as an optional extra and can

Our Bench, Lodge Road, Pennington, Lymington, Hampshire SO41 8HH
Tel/Fax: 01590 673141. E-mail: ourbench@newforest.demon.co.uk

be ordered at breakfast time. There are 3 double or twin rooms available, all en suite, attractively furnished, and equipped with colour television and tea/coffee-making facilities. If you really want to relax and enjoy yourself, for a small charge you can take advantage of the indoor swim/exercise pool, sauna and jacuzzi located in a chalet within the garden. Our Bench has a 3-Crown Commended rating from the English Tourist Board, holds the FHG Diploma for accommodation of the highest standard, the England for Excellence Silver Award, as well as the National Accessibility Scheme 3 rating for disabled guests. Arriving guests will find a welcoming cup of tea awaiting them, but Mary and Roger regret they have to say "no children or pets".

BOLDRE
Map 3 ref K8

7 miles S of Lyndhurst, on the A337

"The village is here, there, and everywhere" wrote Arthur Mee in the 1930s, struggling to give some literary shape to an agglomeration of hamlets - Portmore, Pilley and Sandy Down, which together make up the parish of Boldre. Mee approved of the medieval church, with its squat square tower, standing isolated on a hill-top, and also paid due tribute to its 18th century Rector, the Revd William Gilpin, whose books describing travels around Britain achieved cult status during his lifetime and even received a mention in Jane Austen's novel, *Sense and Sensibility*. Summing up his view of the village, Mee declared that "The quaint simplicity of Boldre is altogether charming". Some sixty years later, there's little reason to dispute his description.

Within this scattered parish there's "A Country House in the Forest", the words Pauline and Peter Hall use to describe their home, **Fernbrake**. It's a spacious 1920s house enjoying a lovely position in a tranquil setting with direct access to open forest and within easy reach of local beaches. A completely self-contained annexe to the house is available for quality self-catering accommodation. The annexe is like a fully-furnished home, centrally heated

Fernbrake, Coxhill, Boldre, Lymington, Hampshire SO41 8PS
Tel: 01590 622257

throughout and with a well-equipped kitchen complete with cooker, fridge/freezer, microwave and washing machine. From the lounge, French doors lead to a patio with garden furniture and a small private garden. Guests also have the use of the 1½ acres of Fernbrake's gardens where the Halls keep their ponies, goats and chickens. Upstairs are the bathroom and 2 double bedrooms, one with double bed and the other with twin beds, with room for an additional bed if necessary. Children and well-behaved dogs are welcomed. There's ample parking in the drive and the front gate opens on to the Forest where ponies, cows, donkeys and deer wander freely. The private lane leads through open Forest to a small lake about 150 yards away where there are splendid views across the Forest and spectacular sunsets. Should you fancy a change from self-catering, the nearest village, Brockenhurst, boasts 4 pubs, several very good hotels, 2 French restaurants, an Italian, an Indian, a Chinese, and an additional Chinese take-away, as well as 2 fish & chip shops. The surrounding area is dotted with very good pubs and inns, one in particular within walking distance, and Spinners, a superb woodland garden with many choice plants, trees and shrubs, is little more than a mile away. The Halls, incidentally, also do a little bed & breakfast in the main house which sometimes helps those who wish to arrive earlier or stay longer.

EVERTON   Map 3 ref K8
3 miles SW of Lymington, on the A337

"We serve seriously good food" says a signboard outside **The Crown at Everton**, a claim which is fully justified by the excellent menu on offer. This inviting pub with its old timbers and open fire is run by John and Kim Shiner, with Kim looking after the cooking. Her extensive menu includes a good mix of traditional and innovative dishes so, amongst the starters for example, you'll find a home-made soup as well as Lox (kiln-roasted and hickory smoked salmon) with herby leaf salad dressed with wild strawberry coulis. Similarly, amongst the main

**The Crown, Old Christchurch Road, Everton, nr Lymington
Hampshire SO41 0JJ Tel: 01590 642655**

dishes there's Rack of Lamb but also pan-fried venison medallions in a whisky sauce, whilst the dessert choices include a selection of British cheeses, Bramble brulee, and ice creams such as Gin & Lavender or Chestnut & Honey. John and Kim take their wine seriously too. They were the proud winners of the "Wine is Exciting...Is Your Wine List?" competition run by the trade magazine *Pub Business*. "We have spent a great deal of time creating our wine list", John says. "Sitting down with our wine merchant, tasting the wines and writing small paragraphs on why we liked each one. Our customers read our wine list just like they read the Sunday papers". Well worth visiting for its food and wine, The Crown has many interesting features and is furnished throughout with a mix of maritime memorabilia and pictures of historical interest to the area. In summer, the inn's floral displays have twice won the local award for Best Country Pub.

MILFORD-ON-SEA   MAP 3 REF K8
5 miles SW of Lymington, on the B3058

This sizeable coastal village is most notable for its fine, remarkably well-preserved 13th century **Church of All Saints**, its grand views across The Solent to the Isle of Wight, and the odd-looking construction called **Hurst Castle**. At the centre of Hurst Castle is a squat fort built by Henry VIII to guard the Solent entrance against incursions by the French. Its tower is flanked by two long low wings added in the 1860s for gun emplacements, the square openings making them look rather like shopping arcades. The Castle was used as a garrison right up until World War II but is now in the care of English Heritage which has an on-site exhibition explaining its history.

Hurst Castle stands at the tip of a long gravel spit which stretches out across the Solent to within three quarters of a mile of the Isle of Wight coast. It can only be reached by a mile and a half walk along the shingle beach, or by ferries operated by **Hurst Castle Ferry & Cruises** at Keyhaven Quay, one mile east of Milford on Sea. Manager Sean Crane runs a regular daily service during April to the end of October, with ferries departing Keyhaven on the hour from 10am and returning on the half-hour until 5.30pm. The excursion makes a pleasant day or half-day trip since in addition to the Castle itself there's safe bathing north of the lighthouse, good fishing off the southern tip of the spit, and spectacular views of The Needles as well as of huge ships making their way up The Solent. From the Spring Bank Holiday to the end of September, the company also operates afternoon cruises to The Needles. The boat leaves Keyhaven at 2pm and cruises through the busy Solent Waters to see the famous coloured cliffs and sands at Alum Bay, (the only way they can be viewed is from the sea), then on to the Needles Rocks and Lighthouse, returning around 3.30pm. There's an on-board commentary describing all the places of interest and light refreshments are available. During early and late season, the cruise is extended by half an hour since it goes via Yarmouth Pier on the Isle of Wight. Hurst Castle Ferry & Cruises also runs regular ferry services to Yarmouth during the season with

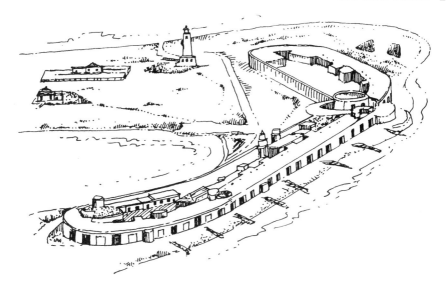

**Hurst Castle Ferry & Cruises, Keyhaven Quay, Milford on Sea
Lymington, Hampshire SO41 0PB Tel: 01590 642500**

up to six sailings a day in each direction with a crossing time of approximately
30 minutes. And if you want to charter your own cruise for a special occasion,
Sean Crane can arrange that too.

BARTON-ON-SEA   Map 3 ref J8
6 miles SW of Lymington, off the A337

Within sight of Hurst Castle, Barton-on-Sea offers visitors a scenic stretch of
coastline with a beach of fine shingle and safe swimming. The town is set back
from the sea with a broad strip of green extending back to Marine Drive where
the main shops are located. Amongst them is a curious survival, a 1930s style
garage, and also an outstanding place to take tea.

As you might expect from a tea room which has been awarded the Tea Council's distinctive Guild Member Seal of Approval, **Sea Cottage Tea Shoppe** can be
relied upon for an excellent pot of tea, served in pleasant and relaxing surroundings and at a price which provides good value for money. The present
owners, Kevin and Wendy Noon, have been serving award-winning teas since
1991 and have achieved a finalist position in the 'Top Tea Place of the Year'
competition, placing them in the highest echelons in the country. Local people
enjoy coffee and tea-cakes in the morning, whatever the weather. The lunches
are freshly prepared every day with traditional and more exotic dishes to suit
every appetite. Sunday lunches are so popular that a phone call would be advis-
able. Barton on Sea enjoys commanding views across Christchurch Bay to the
Needles and the Isle of Wight, there's ample parking, and a gentle slope leads to

**The Sea Cottage Tea Shoppe, Marine Drive, Barton-on-Sea
Hampshire BH25 7DZ Tel: 01425 614086**

the shingle beach with delightful coastal walks. The Sea Cottage Tea Shoppe with its distinctive cottage frontage can be found nestled on the cliff top and is open from 10.30am to 5pm, every day except Monday, all year round.

NEW MILTON
Map 3 ref J8
4 miles W of Lymington, on the A337

If you were allowed to see only one visitor attraction in New Milton, you would have a difficult choice. One option is the town's splendid **Water Tower** of 1900. Late-Victorian providers of water services seem to have enjoyed pretending that their storage towers and sewage treatment plants were really castles of the Middle Ages. They built these mock-medieval structures all around the country, but the one at New Milton is particularly striking. Three storeys high, with a castellated parapet, the octagonal building has tall, narrow windows - ideal for Water Authority archers seeing off customers who have dared to dispute their water bill.

Devotees of vintage motor-cycles will make for a very different attraction: the **Sammy Miller Museum** to the west of the town, widely regarded as one of the best motorcycle museums in the world. Sammy Miller is a legend in his own lifetime, still winning competitions almost half a century after his first racing victory. More than 200 rare and classic motorcycles are on display here.

If you are more interested in the arts, you'll be pleased to hear about **Forest Arts** in New Milton. Hampshire is particularly fortunate in having a network of arts centres that specialises in bringing their audiences something 'just that little bit different'. Forest Arts is a typical example, a very busy multi-artform venue and a unique venue for the arts activities on offer in the New Forest District. Serving a large, scattered rural population, plus Bournemouth, Lyndhurst and Lymington, its main aim is to bring a high quality arts product to the area so that people do not always have to travel to the main cities. Music of all kinds is on offer, from jazz, salsa and blues, to traditional and classical matinée con-

**Forest Arts, Old Milton Road, New Milton, Hampshire BH25 6DS
Tel: 01425 612393**

certs. Performances are conveniently timed so that you can arrive after picking up the kids from school. Other daytime events include slide talks by experts on a wide range of topics. Forest Arts also hosts some of the best contemporary dance companies around, ensembles who have performed at The Place in London and indeed all over the world. And if you enjoy the buzz and excitement of seeing new, vibrant theatre, the type of theatre which is on offer at the Edinburgh Fringe Festival for example, Forest Arts provides that as well. Whatever your interest - drama, playwrighting, poetry writing, ballet, jazz dance, life drawing or singing, the Centre has excellent quality tutors who can help you develop your skills through evening workshops run from Monday to Thursday. In 1994, Forest Arts underwent a major building refurbishment which resulted in greatly improved facilities, amongst them a very pleasant café bar, disabled toilets, two new workshop spaces, plus a well-equipped studio theatre with 140 seats. Plans are under way to provide larger exhibition space and increased parking facilities. Residents of the area already appreciate the innovative aims of Forest Arts: visitors to the New Forest District will be doing themselves a favour if they check out the Centre's current programme which is available from local Tourist Information Centres, or by contacting the address above.

There are two other places in New Milton that deserve special mention. One is **The Hen House**, the only shop of its kind for miles around, a veritable treasure trove for anyone interested in embroidery and associated crafts. Opened in 1996, the shop is owned and run by Marlene Fielding, a retired Building Society Manager who has transformed what was once just an absorbing hobby of hers

The Hen House, Shop Unit 6, Osborne House, Osborne Road, New Milton Hampshire BH25 6AD Tel: 01425 628991

into a flourishing business. Visitors to The Henhouse will find a wide range of craft items including patchwork quilting, glass painting, parchment crafts as well as all the materials necessary for creating your own works of art. An accomplished seamstress and embroiderer, Marlene holds regular workshops and also offers either individual or class tutoring. And if you are wondering where the shop's name comes from, Marlene explains that it stems from the hundred of visits she has made to her favourite place, Scotland. Scots, it appears, use 'Hen' as an affectionate term for females!

The other special place in New Milton is an excellent eating place in the town centre, **Robert's Restaurant**, owned and run by Catherine A. Howe. Born in Yorkshire, Catherine travelled extensively around the country before settling at New Milton in 1998. A devotee of water sports, she's also a lover of music so diners in this stylish restaurant enjoy a background of classical and mood music, softly played. Catherine trained in catering and she insists on everything served at Robert's being home-made. The regular menu offers a wide choice of snacks and light meals, (cheese & leek potato cakes, for example), main meals

such as Aubergine & Artichoke Bake, Southern Fish Pie, or, in honour of Catherine's home county, a 7-inch filled Yorkshire Pudding. There's also an All Day Breakfast, daily Specials, and for dessert, a selection of home-made sweets, puddings, and Sweet Pancakes with a choice of fillings. Cream Teas are served during the season and there's always a range of freshly made pastries on offer. The restaurant is attractively decorated and furnished, with linen table-cloths, prints hung around the walls, and flowers on every table. Roberts is fully licensed and has a small bar area where you

Robert's Restaurant, 58 Lymington Road New Milton, Hampshire BH25 6PZ Tel: 01425 610081

can savour a pre-meal drink and study the wine list which offers a short but well-chosen selection of European wines, with House Wines available by the glass. Beers and soft drinks are also available. (Please note that for the comfort of all customers, Robert's Restaurant is totally non-smoking). Outside, there's a patio and garden, and, conveniently for a town centre location, parking space also. The restaurant's opening times are very convenient too, since it's open 7 days a week, from 8am until 10pm, all the year round.

BURLEY

8 miles SW of Lyndhurst, on minor road off the A31

MAP 3 REF J7

At Burley, it's very clear that you are in the heart of the New Forest, with woodland running right through the village. A pleasant way to experience the peacefulness of the surrounding forest is to take a trip with **Burley Wagonette Rides** which run from the centre of the village. Rides in the open wagons last from 20 minutes to 1½ hours and are available from Easter to October. The village is also home to **New Forest Cider** where farmhouse cider is still made the old-fashioned way from local orchard apples and cider fruit. Visitors can taste and buy draught cider from barrels stored in the former cowshed. The centre is open most times throughout the year although ideally you should time your visit to co-incide with pressing time when the grand old cider press is in operation.

Nestling on twelve acres of scenic beauty, **Burbush Farm** is a secluded country house in the heart of the New Forest offering peace and tranquillity - and a choice of either bed & breakfast or self-catering accommodation. Bed & breakfast guests stay in the spacious main house, the home of David and Carole Hayles who have lived here for some 20 years. There's a warm, welcoming atmosphere and comfortable rooms decorated to a high standard. All bedrooms have en suite bathrooms, good-sized beds (one super King size, one King size), tea and coffee facilities, and colour television. Downstairs, there's a guest lounge with an inviting log fire, and for summer days, a tennis court. Hearty English breakfasts, cooked on the trusty Aga, include award-winning New Forest sausages and all the usual options. Burbush Farm itself is set back some 500 yards from the road and framed by woodland from which deer emerge from time to time. "They come to the door" says Carole, "and are almost like pets!"

If you prefer a self-catering holiday, 'April' and 'Burbush Cottages' are two beautifully restored farm cottages situated at the bottom of a quiet private drive, approximately half a mile from the centre of Burley village. Comfortably furnished to a high standard, both cottages have received the 4-Key Highly

Burbush Farm, Pound Lane, Burley, nr Ringwood, Hampshire BH24 4EF
Tel/Fax: 01425 403238

Commended rating from the Southern Tourist Board and the English Tourist Board. Each of the well-equipped cottages (with dishwasher, microwave and freezer included) sleeps five people: one bedroom with a double bed, the other with a double and single. There are plenty of activities to keep you busy: walking, cycling, (cycles are available for hire from Burbush Farm), or golf, while the beaches within a 15 minute drive offer sailing, windsurfing and bathing. Horse riding is available in the village of Burley: alternatively if you wish to bring your own horses, they can graze on the farm paddocks.

RINGWOOD

MAP 3 REF J7

10 miles W of Lyndhurst, on the A31/A338

Wednesday morning is a good time to visit Ringwood since that is when its market square is filled with a notable variety of colourful stalls. The town has expanded greatly in recent years but its centre still boasts a large number of elegant Georgian houses, both large and small. **Ringwood Meeting House**, built in 1727 and now a Museum, is an outstanding example of an early Nonconformist chapel, complete with the original, rather austere, fittings. **Monmouth House** is of about the same period and stands on the site of an earlier house in which the luckless Duke of Monmouth was confined after his unsuccessful uprising against James II. The Duke had been discovered hiding in a ditch just outside the town and despite his abject pleas to the King to spare his life he was beheaded at Tower Hill a few days later.

Five miles west of the town stretch the great expanses of **Ringwood Forest**, which includes the **Moors Valley Country Park**. Since this area lies across the River Avon and is therefore in East Dorset, it really belongs in the next chapter but its landscape makes it clearly part of the New Forest. One of the most popular attractions in the Moors Valley Country Park is the **Moors Valley Railway**, a delightful narrow gauge steam railway with rails just 7¼ inches apart. The railway was one of the first developments undertaken at the Park and work began

Moors Valley Railway, Horton Road, Ashley Heath, nr Ringwood Hampshire BH24 2ET Tel: 01425 471415

in November 1985 laying the one and a half miles of aluminium track and converting a former cow shed into the main station. Eight thousand wooden sleepers, 500 tons of ballast and hundreds of man hours later the track was ready and the first train journey took place in 1986. Today, the railway has eleven locomotives, all in different liveries, and 33 passenger vehicles. At busy periods, there may be up to six trains on the track so signalling is taken seriously and strictly controlled in accordance with British Rail procedures. The signal box at Kingsmere, the main station, was purpose-built but all the equipment inside comes from old redundant signal boxes - the main signal lever frame for example came from the Becton Gas Works in East London.

At Kingsmere Station, in addition to the Ticket Office and the Engine and Carriage Sheds, there's also a Railway Shop, Buffet and Model Railway Shop. The route southwards runs alongside the Moors Lake, a man made feature which also serves as a flood diversion area when the River Moors, notorious for causing flooding in the area, is running high. The southern terminus of the railway is at Lakeside Station where there's a Visitor Centre, Information Point, Tearoom and Country Shop. Services operate every day from Easter to mid-September, weekends throughout the year (winter weather permitting), during Dorset schools' half term holidays and, one of the busiest periods, from Boxing Day to the end of the Christmas holiday. Throughout the year, there are special events such as open weekends, model railway exhibitions, a Steam Gala and the very special "Santa's Specials" in December when the staff dress in Victorian costume.

A mile or so south-east of Ringwood, in the hamlet of **Crow**, the **New Forest Owl Sanctuary** is home to the largest collection of owls in Europe, housed in more than 100 aviaries. There are flying displays, both inside and out, daily lectures to entertain visitors of all ages, a café and shop. In the hospital units Bruce Berry, founder of the sanctuary, and his dedicated staff have prepared hundreds of birds for release back into the world. The Sanctuary is open daily from March to November and weekends only during the winter. Tel: 01425 476487.

POULNER   Map 3 ref J7
On eastern edge of Ringwood, off the A31

Just a mile or so from the boundary of the New Forest Park, **The London Tavern** is a regular winner of the award for 'Best Pub in Ringwood for Floral Displays'. During the summer, this attractive 18th century building is made even more appealing by a fine display of many-coloured flowers in tubs and hanging baskets. The interior is just as inviting with its inglenook fireplace, old ceiling beams, wall panelling, gleaming copper and brass ornaments, vintage photographs and prints. Another pleasing feature is the Garden Room Bar which opens out onto the garden - an ideal place for children on a sunny day. (If it's not that kind of day, there are toys for them inside and even a play chalet). This child-friendly

The London Tavern, Linford Road, Poulner, Ringwood
Hampshire BH24 1TY Tel: 01425 473819

atmosphere is no doubt connected with the fact that mine hosts at The London Tavern, Graham and Karen Hodkinson, have two young children of their own. Graham, known to one and all as "Odge", and Karen have been here since 1994 and preside over a lively, sociable hostelry whose darts and dominoes teams enjoy something of a reputation. So too do the bar meals on offer here. "Odge" calls them "snacks just beyond the sandwich", a rather modest description for meals such as the home-made Chilli with Rice or the vegetarian Giant Yorkshire Pudding filled with Cajun vegetable casserole. Anyone who appreciates good, wholesome food and the atmosphere of a genuine "local" should certainly seek out The London Tavern. And after your visit, there are the unspoilt acres of the New Forest to explore, attractions such as the Owl Sanctuary at Crow or the Dorset Heavy Horse Centre about 5 miles north-west of Ringwood, historic Wimborne Minster, and the seaside resort of Bournemouth, all within easy reach.

NORTH POULNER
MAP 3 REF J7
2 miles NE of Ringwood, on minor road off the A31 or A338

Located in a Conservation Area on the very edge of the New Forest, **The Old Cottage** is indeed old, about 300 years old in fact. It was probably built as a farm labourer's cottage with walls partly of cob and a roof thatched with water reeds. This exceptionally inviting bed & breakfast establishment stands in about an acre of grounds abutting the Forest, an area of mature lawns, masses of heather,

The Old Cottage, Cowpitts Lane, North Poulner, nr Ringwood
Hampshire BH24 3JX Tel/Fax: 01425 477956 Mobile: 0860 453038

shrubs, bushes and trees, and garden seating. The Old Cottage is the home of Tony and Sue Theobald who have filled the house with sumptuous furnishings while retaining its old world cottage style. There are beamed, low ceilings, wood panelling, planked doors and cupboards, old-fashioned door latches and an abundance of nooks and crannies. The accommodation comprises 2 twin or double rooms, both en suite and with a Tourist Board rating of 4 Diamonds. The elegantly appointed rooms are well separated from each other, providing plenty of private space for guests. Sue looks after the cooking, and serves quite superb full English breakfasts in farmhouse style. The Old Cottage's location makes it an ideal holiday base for walkers, cyclists, and bird watchers, (The Owl Sanctuary at Crow is only 3 miles away), and the local beauty spot, Linford Bottom, is even closer.

LINWOOD   MAP 3 REF J7
3 miles NE of Ringwood, on minor road off the A31 or A338

Attractively sited with an extensive area of woodland to one side, open heathland to the other, this tiny hamlet is fast becoming well-known to lovers of Real Ales who take the opportunity of combining a tour of the New Forest with a visit to the **Red Shoot Inn & Brewery**. Paul and Margo Adams run this characterful hostelry with old settles and benches, open log fire and vintage milk churns serving as unusual bar stools. Paul is the brewmaster and although his first brew was produced as recently as 1998, Red Shoot ales have already acquired a dedi-

**Red Shoot Inn & Brewery, Toms Lane, Linwood, Ringwood
Hampshire BH24 3QT Tel: 01425 475792**

cated following. It was Paul's regular customers who chose the names: first there
was 'Forest Gold', followed later by 'Tom's Tipple' which has a strength of 4.8.
The brewery is housed within the main building and a viewing window allows
guests to watch the brewing process under way. To accompany your wholesome
pint, Margo offers a really inviting choice of food. The menu is extensive and
includes starters such as Deep Fried Spinach & Feta Goujons, or a tasty home-
made soup. Main dishes range from sizzling steaks, fish and poultry dishes, to
ploughman's, jacket potatoes and other 'Light Bites'. There's always a vegetarian special of the day and for your 'Just Desserts' choose from the tempting
selection of sweets and puddings marked up on the sweet board. If you prefer
wine with your meal, the inn's wine list contains nearly a score of different
varieties including House Wines available by the bottle, carafe, and large or
small glass. Children are welcome in the extensive and separate Families Area
and have their own special Activity Menu. Adults who fancy the idea of some
gentle activity of their own will find many miles of paths and bridleways criss-
crossing the nearby woodlands, part of which is named Red Shoot Wood - the
original inspiration for the inn's name.

FORDINGBRIDGE
MAP 3 REF I6
7 miles N of Ringwood, on the A338

The painter Augustus John (1878-1961) loved Fordingbridge, a pleasant riverside town with a graceful medieval 7-arched bridge spanning the River Avon.
He spent much of the last thirty years of his life at **Fryern Court**, a rather austere Georgian house just north of the town (not open to the public, but visible

from the road). Scandalous stories of the Bohemian life-style he indulged in there circulated around the town but didn't deter the townspeople from erecting a strikingly vigorous statue to his memory in a park near the bridge.

Also close to the bridge and enjoying a lovely riverside position, **The George Inn** makes good use of its location with a light and airy conservatory providing panoramic views of the Hampshire River Avon. Geoff and Jackie Lawson are the welcoming hosts at this friendly hostelry built around 1760 and named in honour of King George III who passed through Fordingbridge several times on his way to the sea bathing at Weymouth. It's said that he paid to have the bridge here rebuilt in stone and widened to allow easier passage for the royal coaches. During the smuggling epidemic of the late 18th and early 19th centuries, The George was occupied by Revenue men keeping watch over the river for contraband cargoes of tea which at that time was exorbitantly taxed. In this traditional

The George Inn, Bridge Street, Fordingbridge, Hampshire SP6 1AH
Tel: 01425 652040 Fax: 01425 650436

inn with its wooden floors and dark, ancient beams, Geoff and Jackie offer an excellent choice of real ales and fine food which ranges from light meals and snacks, (filled baguettes, jacket potatoes, and ploughmans for example), through vegetarian options, to generous main dishes such as Plaice Parisienne or a hearty 10oz Rump Steak. The regular menu is supplemented by a daily choice of homemade pies, Chef's Special Choices, and a changing selection of desserts. With so many attractive features, The George fully justifies its description of itself as "The Jewel on the Avon".

A good place to make for around tea time (and indeed any other time of day) is the **Ivy Cottage Tea Rooms** on Salisbury Road. Seymour and Lesley Harris own and run this traditional olde worlde tea room housed in a 16th century cottage, a charming building with latticed windows and exposed roof beams which are believed to have been ship's timbers. Here, home-made cakes, scones and vegetarian soups are a speciality and, in addition to a delicious Cream or Cottage Tea, the menu offers a good choice of light meals, ploughman's lunches,

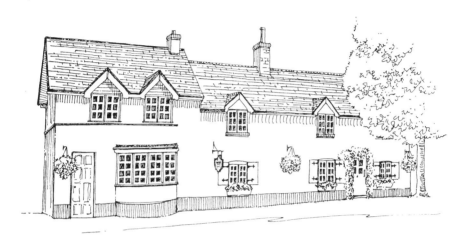

**Ivy Cottage Tea Rooms, Salisbury Road, Burgate, Fordingbridge
Hampshire SP6 1LX Tel: 01425 654515**

snacks, salads and sandwiches. The tea room is licensed, with lager, cider, red and white wine available with a full meal. Conveniently located on the A338 Fordingbridge by-pass, Ivy Cottage also has a secluded rear garden where you can enjoy your refreshment on fairweather days. The historic city of Salisbury lies about 10 miles to the north and the rural expanses of the New Forest begin just a couple of miles to the east.

On the edge of the town, there's a special treat for anyone who savours daft public notices. As a prime example of useless information, it would be hard to beat the trim little 18th century milepost which informs the traveller: "Fordingbridge: 0".

6 East Dorset

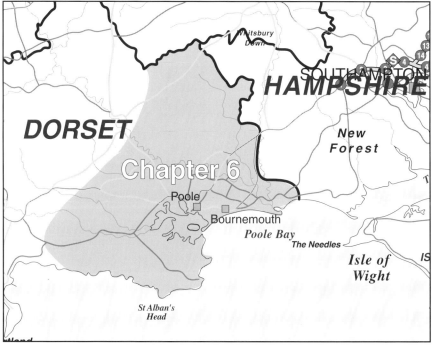

Within a comparatively small area, East Dorset provides an extraordinary variety of attractions. It contains the county's two largest towns, Bournemouth and Poole, (virtually one, nowadays), where, amongst its other attractions, you can enjoy one of the best beaches in Britain during the day and a first class symphony concert in the evening.

Across Poole Harbour, the Isle of Purbeck is famous for the marble which has been quarried here since Roman times. The Isle of Purbeck's 'capital', the engaging seaside resort of Swanage, is linked by the steam-hauled Swanage Railway to the magnificent ruins of Corfe Castle. Set on a high hill above the charming village of the same name, this is one of the grandest sights in southwest England and should not be missed. Two other historic houses in the area also deserve special mention: Kingston Lacy which boasts an incomparable collection of 17th century Old Masters, and Cloud's Hill, the comfortless cottage where the enigmatic World War I hero T.E. Lawrence spent his last years. And no visitor to East Dorset should leave without paying a visit to glorious Wimborne Minster, a triumph of medieval architecture. To the west of Swanage are two of the most spectacular natural features in the county: the enchanting Lulworth Cove and the soaring limestone arch carved by the sea known as Durdle Door. Inland, a string of villages along the River Piddle, (delicately modified in Victorian times to 'Puddle') culminates in historic Tolpuddle, honoured in trades' union history as the home of the Tolpuddle Martyrs.

BOURNEMOUTH

In 1998, no less a magazine than *Harpers & Queen* predicted that Bournemouth was on its way to becoming the "next coolest city on the planet" and another dubbed the town "Britain's Baywatch", a reference to the comely young life-guards who patrol the six miles of golden beaches. The British Tourist Authority's guide reckons that Bournemouth has "more nightclubs than Soho" as well as a huge range of hotels, shops, bars, restaurants and entertainment venues. Each year, some 5.5 million visitors are attracted to this cosmopolitan town which has been voted the greenest and cleanest resort in the UK. (Even the town centre streets are washed and scrubbed every morning).

Two hundred years ago, the tiny village of Bourne was a mere satellite of the bustling port of Poole, a few miles to the west. The empty coastline was ideal for smugglers and Revenue men were posted to patrol the area. One of them, Louis Tregonwell, was enchanted by Bourne's glorious setting at the head of three deep valleys, or chines. He and his wife bought land here, built themselves a house and planted the valleys with the pines that give the present-day town its distinctive appearance. Throughout Victorian times, Bournemouth, as it became known, grew steadily and the prosperous new residents beautified their adopted town with wide boulevards, grand parks, and public buildings, creating a Garden City by the Sea.

They also built a splendid **Pier** (1855) and, around the same time, **St Peter's Church** which is much visited for its superb carved alabaster by Thomas Earp, and tomb in which Mary Shelley, the author of *Frankenstein*, is buried along with the heart of her poet-husband, Percy Bysshe Shelley. The **Casa Magni Shelley Museum**, in Shelley House where the poet's son lived from 1849 to 1889, is the only one in the world entirely devoted to Shelley's life and works. Other museums include the **Russell-Cotes Art Gallery & Museum**, based on the collection of the globe-trotting Sir Merton Russell-Cotes; the **Rothesay Museum** which follows a mainly nautical theme but also has a display of more than 300 vintage typewriters; the **Teddy Bear Museum** in the Expocentre; and, north of the town, the **Aviation Heritage Museum** at Bournemouth International Airport, home to a collection of vintage jet aircraft which are flown on a regular basis.

As you might expect in such a popular resort, every conceivable kind of sport and recreation facility is available: anything from surfboarding to paragliding, from symphony concerts to international golf tournaments. And if you're looking for a novel experience, and a really spectacular aerial view of the town and coastline, **Vistarama**, in the Lower Gardens near the Pier, offers day or night ascents in a tethered balloon which rises up to 650ft.

Harry Ramsden's fish and chip restaurants have virtually become a national institution in the 70-odd years since a young fish frier of that name opened a shop in Bradford where he was the first to offer a sit-down fish and chip meal. When his wife contracted tuberculosis, Harry moved his business in 1928 to what was then open country at Guiseley, near Leeds. The white-painted hut,

Harry Ramsden's, East Beach, Undercliff Drive, Bournemouth
Tel: 01202 295818 Fax: 01202 296372

10ft by 6ft, in which he started is still in place today. The present building at Guiseley is on rather a different scale, holding a place in the *Guinness Book of Records* as the world's largest fish and chip restaurant, serving nearly one million customers a year. Bournemouth's Harry Ramsden's can't match that record, but you will find the same legendary quality in the dishes cooked in his traditional and unique batter. Even the standard portions are generous, the large ones even more so, and if you have a really hearty appetite try "Harry's Challenge" - a whole giant prime haddock with chips, mushy or garden peas, and beans. If you successfully meet the challenge, you will receive a signed certificate and a free dessert of your choice! (If you are travelling into Hampshire, there's also a Harry Ramsden's in Southampton).

POOLE
MAP 2 REF H8

5 miles W of Bournemouth, on the A35/A350

Once the largest settlement in Dorset, Poole is now a pleasant, bustling port. Its huge natural harbour, actually a drowned river valley, is the most extensive anchorage in Europe with a history going back well beyond Roman times. A 33ft long Logboat, hollowed from a giant oak tree and dating back to around 295 BC, has been found off **Brownsea Island**, the largest of several islands dotting the harbour. **The Quay** is a great place to relax with a drink and watch people "just messing about in boats". Nearby is the **Waterfront Museum**, which celebrates 2000 years of maritime heritage, and the internationally famed Poole Pottery which has been producing high-quality pottery for more than 125 years. Here, visitors can watch a 12-minute video summarising two millennia of ceramic production, watch the age-old processes under way, and children can 'have a go' themselves at this tricky craft. **The Pottery Shop** offers factory-direct prices and special savings on seconds, there are superb displays of the Pottery's distinctively designed creations, and a brasserie and bar overlooking the harbour. Close by, The Aquarium Complex brings you eyeball to eyeball with sharks, piranhas and crocodiles, although anyone with a horror of rattlesnakes, monster pythons, tarantulas or toads might be well-advised to have a stiff drink before paying a visit. Model train enthusiasts, on the other hand, will be delighted with the 3000ft of track of the **Great Scenic Model Railway**.

Just behind Poole Pottery, and a short walk from the Quay, stands the **Royal Oak and Gas Tavern**, or "The Gas" as it is known locally. It's a grand old Victorian building dating back to 1866 and its old-fashioned public bar is a haven for

The Royal Oak & Gas Tavern, 25 Skinner Street, Poole, Dorset BH15 1RQ
Tel: 01202 672022

characters from Old Poole. The lounge bar has been beautifully refurbished and your hosts, Bob and Maureen Kerr, offer a friendly welcome, a choice of real ales and excellent, home-made food. The emphasis, naturally, is on fish and with many local fishermen among the regulars, you can be confident of its quality!

During the season, there are "Sprat Suppers" and "The Gas" also gets involved in the annual Poole Cockle Festival in early May, and the celebrations each year when a different ship of the Royal Navy visits the port. The tavern also has a large, walled-in beer garden, (secure and ideal for children), where barbecues are held on summer evenings. In good weather, tables are also set up on the pavement outside. "The Gas" welcomes bookings for private parties and can accommodate up to 120 guests. If you want to experience the authentic flavour of this lively town and its people, then a visit to the Royal Oak is strongly recommended.

Few hotels and restaurants in Dorset have been honoured with as many accolades as **The Mansion House** in Thames Street, no more than 200 yards from Poole's bustling quayside and within easy reach of the town's many attrac-

The Mansion House, Thames Street, Poole, Dorset BH15 1JN
Tel: 01202 685666 Fax: 01202 665709

tions. Set in a quiet cobbled mews, this beautiful Georgian house was Old Poole's "Mayoral House", built in the late 1780s for the Lester family who, along with other leading merchants of the town, had made their fortune in the Newfoundland fishing trade.

During its long history, the gracious old house has suffered many vicissitudes, including a period during World War II when it became a Seaman's Mission. In 1979, however, it was tastefully converted by its present owners, Robert and Valerie Leonard, into an elegant town house hotel offering outstanding cuisine and excellent accommodation. There are 28 individually designed bedrooms, most resplendent with antiques and every amenity. In early 1999, a further 4 de luxe bedrooms were added, two of them boasting four-poster beds - ideal for wedding couples or guests celebrating special occasions.

The hotel restaurant, with its handsome cherrywood panelling, is considered one of the most beautiful dining rooms in the south of England, and the imaginative modern British cuisine served here has attracted warm recommendations from the Good Food Guide, and Egon Ronay, and been awarded 2 rosettes by the A.A. The restaurant is open for lunch and dinner daily and also hosts frequent special events, such as before and after concert suppers, (linked to the Bournemouth Orchestra's concert programme), gourmet dinners, "bring your own wine" evenings, and much more. The hotel publishes an informative newsletter detailing these and many other activities which it organises or supports. The Mansion House also offers special Christmas, New Year, midweek and winter weekend breaks at prices which represent exceptional value for money.

From the Quay there are regular ferries to **Brownsea Island** (National Trust), where there are quiet beaches with safe bathing and visitors can wander through 500 acres of heath and woodland which provide one of the few refuges for Britain's native red squirrel. Here, in 1907, General Robert Baden-Powell carried out an experiment to test his idea of teaching boys from all social classes the scouting skills he had refined during the Boer Wars. Just 20 boys attended that first camp: in its heyday during the 1930s, the world-wide Scouting Movement numbered some 16 million members in more than 120 countries.

PARKSTONE   MAP 2 REF H8
1 mile E of Poole, on the A338

For good, appetising food at tremendous value-for-money prices, do seek out **The Lantern Café** on Bournemouth Road, a mile or so east of Poole Quay. The café is owned and run by Linda a' Beckett and Peter Stevens. It specialises in hearty traditional fare such as Steak & Kidney Pie, along with lighter meals such as pasta bake, jacket potatoes and triple-decker sandwiches. At the rear, there's an enclosed, secluded patio and tea garden, ideal for a quiet cuppa.

For Linda, running this café is something of a change of pace after travelling around the world catering to the motor racing fraternity. She has kept them

well fed and watered at such famous venues as Monte Carlo, and has worked several times with the Mitsubishi Motor Rally team. But don't let that lead you to expect "fast food": Everything here is freshly cooked to order and the service is prompt and friendly.

About a mile south of the Lantern Café, you'll find one of the county's great gardens, **Compton Acres**. Amongst its varied themed areas, which include a lovely Italian Garden, the Japanese Garden enjoys an especially fine reputation. Japanese

**Lantern Café, 100 Bournemouth Road, Parkstone, Dorset, BH14 9HY
Tel: 01202 745050**

architects and workmen were brought over to England to create what is reputed to be the only completely genuine Japanese Garden in Europe, an idyllic setting in which only the most troubled spirit could not find solace. Magnificent sculptures enhance the grounds and from the Colonnade viewpoint there are grand views over Poole Harbour to the Purbeck hills beyond.

ORGANFORD   MAP 2 REF G8
5 miles W of Poole, on minor road off the A35

To the west of Poole, the tiny village of Organford stands on the edge of the tree-covered expanses of Gore Heath. Organford is so small it doesn't possess either a church or a pub, but it does have a Manor House which enjoys a wonderfully quiet and secluded position surrounded by woods. Here you'll find **Organford Manor Caravans and Touring**, an exceptionally attractive and well-equipped camping and caravan site. It's located in the grounds of the Manor which has been in the present owner's family for 4 generations. Ann Harrison's predecessors were in the fishing business, trading between the icy waters of Newfoundland and Europe.

The handsome, white-painted Manor House provides a striking centrepiece to the site which has standings for Touring Caravans by the side of the drive and, adjacent to the house, a 3-acre field for tourers and camping which is level, sheltered and well-drained. On each side of the drive, there are four acres of woodland in which are 45 privately owned static caravans, some of which are

**Organford Manor Caravans & Touring, Organford , Poole
Dorset BH16 6ES Tel: 01202 622202**

available for hire. Amongst the amenities available are toilet and shower blocks; a laundry room; some electric hook-ups; pay phone; chemical disposal points, and, during the high season, a shop. Fresh milk and farm eggs are available daily, and there's also an ice pack service. Dogs are allowed, provided they are kept on a lead. Within easy reach of the site are some of the best beaches on the South Coast, attractions such as Corfe Castle and Beaulieu Motor Museum, and a host of facilities for active pursuits: - sea and river fishing nearby, sailing and windsurfing in Poole Harbour, and many good local golf courses.

BERE REGIS   MAP 2 REF F8
11 miles W of Poole, on the A35

Most visitors to the **church at Bere Regis** are attracted by its associations with Hardy's *Tess of the D'Urbervilles*. They come to see the crumbling tombs of the once-powerful Turberville family whose name Hardy adapted for his novel. It was outside the church, beneath the Turberville window, that Hardy had the homeless Tess and her family set up their 4-poster bed. A poignant fictional scene, but the church is also well worth visiting for its unique and magnificent carved and painted wooden roof. Large figures of the Apostles (all in Tudor dress) jut out horizontally from the wall and there are a number of humorous carvings depicting men suffering the discomforts of toothache and over-indulgence. There's also a carving of Cardinal Morton who had this splendid roof installed in 1497. The church's history goes back much farther than that. In Saxon times, Queen Elfrida came here to spend the rest of her days in penitence for her part in the murder of young King Edward at Corfe Castle in 979, and there's evidence of the church's great age in the fact that around 1190 King John paid for the pillars of the nave to be "restored".

In the village itself, **The Royal Oak**, dating back to the 1600s, is a welcoming traditional pub with a relaxed atmosphere, friendly service, and a reputation for particularly fine food. Laura and Mike Jones, who took over here in late 1997, offer an excellent choice of good home-cooked meals, an interesting mix of old favourites such as home-made Steak & Guinness Pie, ("The only way to have your Guinness and eat it", says the menu), and inventive creations like the Royal Oak "Combo", a selection of barbecue ribs, hot chicken wings, potato skins with cheese and salsa, stuffed mushrooms, Kofta kebabs, and an item called "Texas toothpicks" - strips of Jalepeno peppers and onions in batter. The "Combo"

The Royal Oak, West Street, Bere Regis, Wareham, Dorset BH20 7HQ
Tel: 01929 471203 Fax: 01929 472636

comes complete with a side salad and chips. The menu also includes vegetarian choices, children's meals, and sweets such as home-made Dorset "Oak" apple cake. There's a short but well-chosen wine list, or you may prefer a glass of traditional ale.

Devotees of vintage water Jugs will consider their visit worthwhile just to see the fine collection on display in the spacious bar area. Outside, the secure beer garden is great for children, (and dogs, which are welcome here too), and The Royal Oak also boasts that essential feature of a West Country pub, a Skittle Alley, which doubles as a function room capable of seating 40 guests. The inn also has five letting rooms, all newly built and well-appointed, and all en suite. Bere Regis village itself is an essential stop for any Thomas Hardy enthusiast. Appearing in *Tess of the d'Urbervilles* as Kingsbere-sub-Greenhill, Bere Regis was the home of the Turbervilles whose family vault lies beneath the south aisle of the church. The family died out generations ago but, in Hardy's novel, their glorious past inspires Tess Durbeyfield's father to claim them as his ancestors, so setting in train the tragic sequence of events leading to Tess's death.

About three miles west of Bere Regis, the small village of **Tolpuddle** sits quietly just off the main road. In the early 19th century, Tolpuddle was a far sleepier place than it is now. Not the kind of place you would expect to foment a social revolution, but it was here that six ill-paid agricultural labourers helped lay the foundations of the British Trade Union Movement. In 1833, they formed a "confederation" in an attempt to have their subsistence wages improved. The full rigour of the landowner-friendly law of the time was immediately invoked. All six were found guilty of taking illegal oaths and sentenced to transportation to Australia for seven years. Even the judge in their case was forced to say that it was not for anything they had done, or intended to do, that he passed such a sentence, but "as an example to others". Rather surprisingly, public opinion sided with the illegal "confederation", vigorous protests eventually forcing the government to pardon the men after they had served three years of their sentence. They all returned safely to England, honoured ever afterwards in Trade Union hagiography as the "Tolpuddle Martyrs". The **Martyrs' Museum** at Tolpuddle tells an inspiring story, but it's depressing to realise that the 7 shilling (35p) weekly payment those farm-workers were protesting against actually had more buying power in the 1830s than the 1998 legally-enforced minimum wage.

About a mile west of Tolpuddle, Athelhampton House is a delightful, mostly Tudor house surrounded by a series of separate, 'secret' gardens. It's the home of Sir Edward and Lady du Cann and has the 'lived-in' feeling that adds so much interest to historic houses. One of the finest houses in the county, Athelhampton's most spectacular feature is its magnificent Great Chamber built during the reign of Elizabeth I. In the grounds there's an unusual 15th century circular dovecote. It is almost perfectly preserved, with its 'potence', or revolving ladder used to collect eggs from the topmost nests, still in place and still useable. Tel: 01305 848363.

WINTERBORNE ZELSTON   MAP 2 REF G8
7 miles NW of Poole, off the A31

Winterborne is the name of the river that wanders in serpentine fashion across East Dorset, so-named because only in winter does it run full. Along its course the river adds its name to a succession of "Winterborne" villages: Abbas, Came, Kingston, St Martin, Steepleton, Stickland, Tomson, Whitchurch, and, set alongside the A31, Winterborne Zelston. Nobody seems to know where the "Zelston" came from, but the village is well-known locally because of the **The Botany Bay Inn**, noted for its excellent cuisine. Both Deborah and David Schroetter, who have run the inn since 1996, are qualified chefs and their expertise is apparent in the wide range of interesting and tasty dishes on offer. Starters for example include a Wild Boar Pâté or you might prefer Dorset Mushrooms, poached in

The Botany Bay Inn, Winterborne Zelston, nr Wimborne
Dorset DT11 9LS Tel: 01929 459227

cider and onions and finished with strips of ham and melted cheese. Amongst the House specialities are mighty steaks, and a Gourmet Platter for two, ('Try it on your own, if you dare!!' warns the menu). You'll also find a wide range of fish, poultry and vegetarian dishes, along with salads, a children's menu and daily specials which are marked up on the blackboard. For smaller appetites, The Botany Bay also offers a good choice of Ploughman's Lunches, 'Stuffed Spuds', filled French sticks and sandwiches. But don't leave without trying one of the home-made desserts - they're particularly tempting. No wonder that anyone in the area planning a celebration meal or function thinks first of The Botany Bay!

ALMER   Map 2 ref G8
7 miles NW of Poole, on the A31

Back in 1965, the travel writer and television celebrity Ralph Wightman noted a solitary, thatched inn on the main Wimborne to Bere Regis road. *"Whether it is the name, the solitude, or a cheerful host, I cannot tell, but the cars and motor-coaches flock to **The World's End** every summer evening"*. Much has changed in the more than 35 years since he wrote those words, but this long, low building has re-mained a popular venue. It suffered badly from a fire in 1992 but the old inn has been lovingly restored, its thatched roof, panelling, beams and open fires faithfully reflecting a history that stretches back some 400 years. Lisa and Adam Walkey are 'mine hosts' at this charming hostelry which can count the World War II Army supremo General Montgomery amongst its earlier patrons. Any-one who appreciates wholesome home-cooked food, pleasantly served, will really enjoy themselves as they browse through the 9-page menu listing a compre-hensive choice of dishes. It includes just about every option: anything from a plump 12oz Rump Steak, to a tasty Somerset Pie of diced gammon with leeks in a cheese and cider sauce, topped with short crust pastry; through vegetarian

The World's End, Almer, Nr Blandford, Dorset DT11 9EW
Tel: 01929 459671

choices, bar snacks, and a children's menu. A further two pages of the bill of fare are devoted to a well-chosen and sensibly-priced selection of European and New World wines.

WIMBORNE MINSTER

Map 2 ref H8

6 miles N of Poole on the A349/A31

Happily, the A31 now by-passes this beguiling old market town set amongst meadows beside the rivers Stour and Allen. The glory of the town is **Wimborne Minster**, a distinctive building of multi-coloured stone boasting some of the finest Norman architecture in the county. The Minster is also notable for its 14th century astronomical clock, and the 'Quarterjack', a life-sized figure of a grenadier from the Napoleonic wars, which strikes the quarter hours on his bells. Inside, the unique Chained Library, founded in 1686, contains more than 240 books, amongst them a 14th century manuscript on vellum.

In the High Street, the **Priest's House** is a lovely Elizabethan house set amidst beautiful gardens. It houses the Museum of East Dorset Life which recreates 400 years of history in a series of rooms where the decoration and furnishings follow the changing fashions between Jacobean and Victorian times. There's also an archaeology gallery with hands-on activities and a recently opened Gallery of Childhood.

In King Street you can see Wimborne as it was in the early 1950s - but at one tenth the size. **Wimborne Model Town** presents a meticulous miniature version of the town, complete with an Old English fair and a working small scale model railway.

A mile or so northwest of Wimborne, **Kingston Lacy** (National Trust) is an imposing 17th century mansion and an irresistible attraction for anyone who loves the paintings of such Old Masters as Brueghel, Rubens and Van Dyck. Apart from those owned by the Queen, the pictures on display here are generally acknowledged by experts as the finest private collection in the country. Kingston Lacy's fabulous gilded-leather Spanish Room and elegant Grand Saloon, both with lavishly decorated ceilings, and a fascinating exhibit of Egyptian artefacts dating back to 3000 BC, all add to the interest of a visit. Outside, you can wander through 250 acres of wooded parkland, home to a herd of splendid Red Devon cattle, collect souvenirs from the gift shop, or enjoy refreshments in the restaurant. Tel: 01202 883402.

HOLT HEATH
MAP 3 REF I7

8 miles NE of Wimborne Minster, on minor road off the B3072 or B3078

It's well worth seeking out the tiny village of Holt Heath just to see the **Cross Keys Inn,** a lovely 16th century building smothered with flowers in hanging baskets and tubs, and with 6ft high dahlias in the garden. But there's more to the Cross Keys than just a pretty face. Inside, you'll find a lively landlady full of personality, Vivien Howard, who has been here since 1988, excellent food and drink, and a friendly atmosphere that becomes even warmer when the huge log fire is blazing away. The tempting menu includes a wide range of choices, from simple snacks and sandwiches to robust main meals amongst which you'll find "Viv's Special", a home-made Steak & Kidney Pie filled with British beef and pure Guinness. (If your children don't behave, Viv threatens, it becomes a "Steak

**The Cross Keys Inn, Mannington, Holt Heath, Wimborne
Dorset BH21 7JZ   Tel: 01202 822555**

& Kiddy Pie"!) There's also a Curry of the Day and a dessert selection amongst which you'll find a home-made Fruit Pie and Treacle Sponge Pudding. Viv also offers you the choice of an incredible 200 different kinds of spirit, "Two hundred and one", she says, "if you count the resident ghost!" Other attractions at the Cross Keys include the weekend sing-alongs and a spacious Beer Garden with plenty of room to erect a marquee for weddings or other functions. Definitely a Hidden Place to discover.

THREE LEGGED CROSS
MAP 3 REF I7

6 miles NE of Bournemouth, on the B3072

The main road really does twist and turn in the village to create a three-legged cross with a country lane. Located in the heart of this curiously-named village, **The Woodcutters** has all the welcoming atmosphere one appreciates in a traditional village pub. The present building dates back to 1927, replacing an 18th century coaching inn, the Traveller's Rest, vintage photographs of which are on display in the Woodcutters' bars. The Woodcutters' licensees Ian and Dawn Armstrong have some forty years experience between them of running pubs and although they only arrived at the Woodcutters in 1997, the popularity of the inn shows that they are clearly providing what their patrons want. "We like to think that our customers can come here to relax, muddy boots and all. We have quiz nights and sing-songs. We also have our own darts teams, ladies' and mens', who play every Monday night in the public bar. On Tuesday, it's pool; Wednesday, it's dominoes; and Friday, it's darts". And on Thursdays? That's

**The Woodcutters, Ringwood Road, Three Legged Cross, Wimborne
Dorset BH21 6RB Tel: 01202 828866**

their night off and, since Dawn and Ian do all the cooking, the usual vast menu which is chalked-up around the lounge bar, is restricted to light snacks for that one night. At other times, though, the extensive choice ranges from a tasty Game Hot Pot, through Mexican dishes, traditional favourites such as Pork Chops in Cider Sauce, burgers, sandwiches, to a humble chip butty. Servings are generous, with main meals accompanied by at least 3 vegetables, and there's a good selection of wines, lagers and beers. Children are welcome in the lounge bar until 9pm, and can either choose from their own menu, or have a smaller portion from the main menu. In good weather, they have their own secure play area in the attractive Beer Garden where barbecues are held in summer. This warm and friendly pub is open all day, 7 days a week.

CRANBORNE
12 miles NE of Wimborne Minster, on the B3078

MAP 2 REF H6

A picturesque village in a glorious setting, Cranborne sits on the banks of the River Crane with a fine church and manor house creating a charming picture of a traditional English village. The large and imposing Church of St Mary is notable for its Norman doorway, 13th century nave, and exquisite 14th century wall-paintings. **Cranborne Manor** was built in Tudor and Jacobean times for the Cecil family, now Marquesses of Salisbury, who still live there. The house is not open to the public but visitors can explore the gardens on Wednesdays during the season, and the Cranborne Manor Garden Centre, which specialises in old fashioned roses, is open all year. The present manor house stands on the site of a royal hunting lodge built by King John for his hunting forays in Cranborne Chase. Much of the huge forest has disappeared but detached areas of woodland have survived and provide some splendid walks.

This small village is well-known locally for its excellent "Restaurant with Rooms". After the *Daily Telegraph*'s hotel reviewer, Paddy Burt, had stayed incognito at **La Fosse at Cranborne** she declared herself "completely won over by Mrs La Fosse's charm and desire to please", by the bowls of freshly-cut-up fruit awaiting her at breakfast - "and also by the bill"! Misled by the hotel's name, Paddy Burt had arrived "confidently expecting a dash of *ooh-la-la*" and a temperamental Gallic chef but happily discovered that her hosts, Sue and Mac La Fosse, are neither French nor temperamental.

Their appealing "Restaurant with Rooms" provides outstanding value for money and also arranges frequent special themed nights such as "Californian Dream" (a 4th of July dinner party complemented with Californian wines) and "Posh School Dinner" for Fathers' Day. In fact, most nights at La Fosse seem rather special with a typical menu offering starters such as Baked Crab Claws Szechuan and a choice of main dishes which makes a final decision very difficult: how *do* you choose between, say, a Supreme of Salmon roasted with an almond crust on a champagne sauce or a Tournedos of Pork Fillet with smoked oysters and a Chinese oyster sauce? The restaurant is open for dinner from

**La Fosse at Cranborne, London House, The Square, Cranborne
Dorset BH21 5PR Tel: 01725 517604 Fax: 01725 517778**

Tuesday to Saturday, and lunch from Tuesday to Sunday (except on Saturdays). La Fosse at Cranborne also has 5 very well-appointed rooms, all en suite and with reduced rates for diners. It's an ideal place for a weekend away from the cooking and there are some excellent walks in the neighbourhood to help you work up an appetite. Sue and Mac will be pleased to send you details of forthcoming special nights as well as their rates for accommodation. Tucked away in the Dorset countryside, La Fosse at Cranborne is a Hidden Place which abundantly repays a little effort in seeking it out.

SWANAGE
10 miles S of Poole, on the A351

Map 2 ref H10

Picturesquely set beside a broad, gently curving bay with fine, clear sands and beautiful surrounding countryside, Swanage is understandably popular as a family holiday resort. A winner of 'Southern England in Bloom', the town takes great pride in the spectacular floral displays in its parks and gardens, and its other awards include the prestigious European 'Blue Flag' for its unpolluted waters, and the Tidy Britain Group's 'Seaside Award'. Swanage offers its visitors all the facilities necessary for a traditional seaside holiday, including boat-trips, (with sightings of bottle-nosed dolphins if you're lucky), water-sports, sea angling and an attractive, old-fashioned pier. The **Mowlem Theatre** provides a seasonal programme of films, shows and plays, and on Sunday afternoons the Recreation Ground resounds to the strains of a brass band. On the clifftops, **Durlston Country Park** covers some 260 acres of delightful countryside; on the front, the Beach Gardens offer tennis, bowls and putting, or you can just rent a beach hut or bungalow and relax. One attraction not to be missed is a ride on the **Swanage Railway** along which magnificent steam locomotives of the old Southern Railway transport passengers some 6 miles through lovely Dorset countryside to Norden, just north of Corfe Castle.

Swanage Railway

In the town itself, the **Town Hall** is worth seeing for its ornate façade, the work of Christopher Wren. Wren didn't build it for Swanage, however. It was originally part of Mercers Hall in Cheapside, London. When the Mercers Hall was being demolished, a Swanage man scavenged the fine frontage and rebuilt it here. He also brought the graceful little Clock Tower which stands near the pier. The tower used to adorn the Surrey end of London Bridge. No wonder older residents of the town refer to Swanage as "Little London".

Ideally situated in the centre of the town, **The Anchor Inn** is reputed to be the oldest pub in Swanage. This charming old building, with its typical Purbeck stone roof tiles, dates back to the mid-1500s, and when alterations were carried out recently, the walls were found to be made of stone, rubble, and pebbles from the beach. Originally, the building comprised three small cottages, with

one room up, one down: later they were combined to become an inn, known by the sign of the Anchor. The inn also served as the local Market House, with business conducted here on a Friday - mostly by barter. During the stage-coach era, the Royal Mail coach left from The Anchor at 9am for Wareham, returning at 6pm the same day. It was during this period, too, that the Press Gangs were active and on one occasion when a gang arrived seeking crews for the ships in Poole Harbour, local men barricaded themselves inside The Anchor until the Press Gang finally gave up. This historic and appealing old hostelry is now run by Bob and Linda Brett who have created a

The Anchor, 30 High Street, Swanage, Dorset, BH19 2NU. Tel: 01929 423020

warm and friendly atmosphere befitting an inn with such a long history of hospitality. They have Real Ales on tap, and serve delicious home-made meals, bar snacks (hot and cold), sandwiches and daily specials, all at value-for-money prices; another good reason for visiting this attractive old inn.

The Herston Conservation Area is one of the oldest parts of Swanage and here you'll find **Plum Tree Cottage**, a charming example of a late 18th-century Purbeck cottage, built in the traditional style with walls 2ft thick and a stone-clad roof. It's the home of Janet and Berny Howells who, after working and travelling abroad, settled here in 1997. Having spent a year on the restoration they now offer excellent bed and breakfast accommodation with present day facilities amidst their interesting collections from times past. They have three attractively furnished double bedrooms with colour television and tea making facilities, each with its own bathroom or shower room.

A generous English or Continental breakfast is included in the tariff, packed lunches are available to order, and 4 course candlelit dinners can be arranged on request. The cosy breakfast room is available in the evening to watch television or relax by the fire. If you prefer a self-catering holiday, Janet and Berny can provide that too in one of their other cottages nearby. Next door to them is Topsail Cottage, another lovely old building, which is said to have been built for smugglers in exchange for barrels of rum.

Plum Tree Cottage, 60 Bell Street, Swanage, Dorset BH19 2SB
Tel: 01929 421601

Back down the hill on the High Street, facing across the valley to Ballard Down and the cliffs at Swanage Bay, is Royal Oak Cottage which is even older and also listed. Both cottages have two bedrooms and are equally suitable for families or couples. On the ground floor of each is a bathroom, fully equipped kitchen and a well-furnished lounge with beams, exposed stone walls, an open fire, and a sofa bed for those who would have difficulty with steep stairs. And if you really want to get away from it all, they also have a caravan for two over at Knitson Farm. Staying at one of these beautifully restored cottages on the outskirts of this Victorian seaside town, close to open countryside, nature reserves, the Priest's Way and South West Coastal Path, provides an ideal base for exploring other hidden places in the Isle of Purbeck.

Located in a quiet cul de sac, and just minutes from the sea, shops and the steam railway station, **"Perfick Piece"** is a welcoming bed & breakfast establishment which provides exactly what its name suggests. Elaine and Peter Hine have been running their small friendly guesthouse since December 1994 and endeavour to create a genuine "home from home" atmosphere. They have 3 letting rooms, (1 double, 1 twin, and a family room with en suite facilities), all very attractively furnished and equipped, and with lots of thoughtful little extras such as playing cards, books and even a corkscrew! There's a residents' lounge, with Sky TV, and everywhere you'll see evidence of Elaine's passion for collecting cuddly soft toys, and Peter's interest in trains and commemorative cars. Evening meals are available by arrangement and the Hines also offer special weekend, Christmas, and New Year Breaks. There's forecourt parking space for 3 cars, and dog owners will be pleased to know that smaller dogs are also welcome at "Perfick Piece".

Collectors of curiosities will want to make their way to **Tilly Whim Hill**, just south of Swanage, which is also well-known for its murky Caves. High above the Caves stands the Great Globe, a huge round stone, some 10 feet in diameter and weighing 40 tons, its surface sculpted with all the countries of

**"Perfick Piece", Springfield Road
Swanage, Dorset BH19 1HD
Tel: 01929 423178 Fax: 01929 423558**

the world. At its base, stone slabs are inscribed with quotations from the Old Testament Psalms, Shakespeare and other poets. They include moral injunctions such as "Let prudence direct you, temperance chasten you, fortitude support you", and the information that, "if a globe representing the sun were constructed on the same scale, it would measure some 1,090 feet across".

A couple of miles north of Swanage, **Studland Bay** offers a lovely 3-mile stretch of sandy beach, part of it clearly designated as an exclusive resort for nudists only.

LANGTON MATRAVERS
2 miles W of Swanage, on the B3069

Map 2 ref H10

Before tourism, the main industry around Swanage was quarrying the famous Purbeck stone that has been used in countless churches, cathedrals and fine houses around the country. The **Purbeck Stone Industry Museum** at Langton Matravers tells the story of Purbeck Marble, a handsome and durable material which was already being cut and polished back in Roman times. This sizeable village is also home to **Putlake Adventure Farm** where visitors are encouraged to make contact with a variety of friendly animals, bottle feed the lambs, or have a go at milking cows. There are pony and trailer rides, picnic and play areas, a farm trail, gift shop and tea room.

Established for 40 years as a camping site, **Tom's Field** has long been highly regarded for its unique character and attractive setting amidst the Purbeck Hills. John and Sarah Wootton first camped here back in 1970: twenty-two years later they bought the site. Lying within an Area of Outstanding Natural Beauty, Tom's Field is bounded by old stone walling and the camping pitches offer a variety of aspects - some sheltered and some more open, affording delightful views across to Swanage Bay. The toilet block also has a room for clothes washing and baby care, and a chemical disposal point. There are also facilities for disabled visitors. A shop on the site provides basic foodstuffs and generally useful items, and also

Tom's Field Camping, Langton Matravers, Swanage BH19 3HN
Tel: 01929 427110

holds good stocks of camping accessories, Camping Gaz, and some Calor. There is a freezer facility for freezer packs. Tom's Field has 4 acres of land and takes tents and motor-vans, but please note that towed caravans cannot be accepted. An attractive feature of the site's location is the proximity of many excellent walks. Access to the Coastal Path is via a footpath within the site and can be reached in approximately 20 minutes, at a point close to the remarkable rock formation known as Dancing Ledge. It's also possible to walk to Swanage along the Coastal Path and then catch a bus back to the village. With its excellent facilities and lovely location, Tom's Field is ideal for family holidays and as a base for hikers, climbers, water sports, and field study groups.

CORFE CASTLE
MAP 2 REF H9

6 miles NW of Swanage, on the A351

One of the grandest sights in the country is the impressive ruin of **Corfe Castle** (National Trust), standing high on a hill and dominating the attractive grey stone village below. Once the most impregnable fortress in the land, Corfe dates back to the days of William the Conqueror, with later additions by King John and Edward I. The dastardly John threw 22 French knights into the castle dungeons and left them to starve to death. Later, Edward II was imprisoned here before being sent to Berkeley Castle and his horrible murder.

Corfe remained important right up until the days of the Civil War when it successfully withstood two sieges before it fell into Parliamentary hands through treachery. A month later, Parliament ordered the castle to be 'slighted' - rendered militarily useless.

Although Corfe now stands in splendid ruin, you can see a smaller, intact version at the **Model Village** in West Street. This superbly accurate replica is built from the same Purbeck stone as the real thing and the details of the miniature medieval folk going about their daily business are wonderful. Surrounded by lovely gardens, this intriguing display is well worth a visit.

NORDEN
MAP 2 REF G9

7 miles NW of Swanage, on the A351

About half a mile north of Corfe Castle, Norden Station is the northern terminus of the **Swanage Railway** and there's a regular bus service from the station to the castle. The hamlet of Norden itself is actually another mile further to the northeast, a delightful place surrounded by pine trees and heathland. If you are interested in natural curiosities, follow the brown and white signs for the Blue Pool. Originally a clay pit, tiny particles of clay in the pool diffract light and create an astonishing illusion of colour, varying from sky blue to deepest azure. There's a tea house, shops and museum here and the tree-lined shore is a popular picnic place.

Back in Norden itself, **The Halfway Inn** with its thatched roof and cob walls looks particularly welcoming and inviting, and in this case appearances are definitely not deceptive. Rod and Claire Darroll-Brough, aided by their daughter Amanda, run this charming inn, parts of which date back to the 16th century. Panelled ceilings and old beams, an abundance of nooks and crannies, and a fireplace in each room all add to the appealing atmosphere. Naturally, an inn of this antiquity has its resident ghost, an amiable lady who has often been seen by guests in the lounge. There's nothing insubstantial however about the fare on offer here, an extensive range of fresh, home-made dishes that includes traditional pub favourites such as Steak & Kidney Pudding along with contemporary offerings like Cajun Chicken or Seared Tuna Supreme. Speciality salads (Toasted Goat's Cheese, for example), light meals and sandwiches, daily specials and

The Halfway Inn, Norden, Nr Corfe Castle, Wareham
Dorset BH20 5DU Tel: 01929 480402

children's meals all add to the choice. And if you enjoy wine with your meal, the Halfway Inn's wine list contains some 30 different options, from both Europe and the New World, a few of them also available in half-bottles.

WAREHAM
Map 2 ref G9

10 miles NW of Swanage, on the A351/A352/A35

Situated between the rivers Frome and Piddle, Wareham is an enchanting little town lying within the earthworks of a 10th century encircling wall. Standing close to an inlet of Poole Harbour, Wareham was an important port until the River Frome clogged its approaches with silt. Then, in 1726, a devastating fire consumed the town's timber buildings, a disaster which produced the happy result of a rebuilt town centre rich in handsome Georgian stone-built houses.

Wareham's history goes back much further than those days. It was Roman conquerors who laid out its street plan: a stern grid of roads which faithfully follows the points of the compass. Saxons and Normans helped build the **Church of St Mary**, medieval artists covered its walls with devotional paintings of remarkable quality. It was in the grounds surrounding the church that King Edward was buried in 879 AD after his stepmother, Queen Elfrida, contrived his murder at Corfe Castle. Elfrida added insult to injury by having the late King buried outside the churchyard, in unhallowed ground.

EAST STOKE
Map 2 ref G9

4 miles W of Wareham, off the A352

Set in quiet and peaceful surroundings, **Luckford Wood House** offers excellent bed and breakfast accommodation in a warm and informal environment, as

Luckford Wood House, East Stoke, Wareham
Dorset BH20 6AW Tel: 01929 463098 Fax: 10929 405715

well as camping facilities in a picturesque setting. The house stands on a working farm run by John and Lesley Barnes and many visitors have remarked on the "excellent farmland views". John and Lesley have also received many compliments for the "superb" full farmhouse breakfasts cooked by John, which begin with a copious choice of juices, cereals, yoghurts, and fresh fruit, and offer a choice of main courses which includes cold smoked ham or succulent kippers, both served with poached eggs and tomatoes. "Ruinous" declared one visitor with satisfaction. A Continental style breakfast of croissants with a selection of cheeses and cooked meats, etc. is also available. To meet the guests' individual needs, breakfast is served from 6am until 12 noon, and can even be served in your bedroom by special request.

There are 3 large and spacious letting rooms at Luckford Wood House, all en suite, and all comfortably appointed with all modern amenities, including television and a refreshment tray. East Stoke village lies close to the River Frome and near many beauty spots and places of historical interest. Corfe Castle, Lulworth Cove and Lawrence of Arabia's Cottage are all within easy reach, as are the seaside resorts of Swanage and Weymouth, and the historic county town of Dorchester. Other leisure facilities nearby include gliding, shooting/stalking, fishing, walking and golfing.

WINFRITH NEWBURGH

MAP 2 REF F9

8 miles W of Wareham, on minor road off the A352

This charming little village stands on a minor road that leads to one of the county's best-known beauty spots, **Lulworth Cove**. An almost perfectly circular bay, the Cove is surrounded by towering 440ft cliffs. Over the centuries, the sea has gnawed away at a weak point in the limestone here, inadvertently creating a breathtakingly beautiful scene. Best to visit out of season, however, as parking places nearby are limited.

About a mile to the west of Lulworth Cove stands another remarkable natural feature which has been sculpted by the sea. **Durdle Door** is a magnificent archway carved from the coastal limestone. There's no road to the coast at this

point, but you can reach it easily by following the **South West Coast Path** from Lulworth Cove. Along the way, you will also see another strange outcrop, a forest of tree-stumps which have become fossilised over the centuries.

A couple of miles inland, **Lulworth Castle** (English Heritage) looks enormously impressive from a distance: close-up, you can see how a disastrous fire in 1929 destroyed most of it. Amongst the remains, though, is a curious circular building dating from 1786: the first Roman Catholic church to be established in

Durdle Door, Lulworth Bay

Britain since Henry VIII's defiance of the Pope in 1534. Sir Thomas Weld was given permission to build this unique church by George III. The King cautiously added the proviso that Sir Thomas' new place of worship should not offend Anglican sensibilities by looking like a church. It doesn't, and that's a great part of its appeal.

Many visitors to this area prefer to rent a cottage rather than stay at a hotel. Choosing a holiday cottage can be a chancy business, but if you select one of those approved by **Dorset Coastal Cottages** you can be confident that you will be staying in an attractive, well-equipped and well-maintained holiday home. Charles and Jennie Smith holidayed in Dorset for 20 years before coming to live here. They now run Dorset Coastal Cottages, a specialist holiday agency offering a selection of much loved, privately owned holiday homes in the Dorset coastal region. They know all the owners and have personally approved all the homes described in their brochure.

Their selection of cottages fits in well with the nature of rural Dorset. They are spread between Studland and Lyme Regis, with rather more in the eastern half of the county than the west. The vast majority are within 5 miles of the coast, none are further than 10 miles, and all are in or near traditional villages. The cottages are old, half are thatched, and three-quarters have open fires. Some are conversions of farm buildings or Victorian schools, others are traditional

Dorset Coastal Cottages, The Manor House, Winfrith Newburgh Dorchester, Dorset DT2 8JR Tel: 01305 852988 Fax: 01305 854988

cottages which have been carefully restored and brought up to date whilst retaining their cosiness, character and charm. Two of the properties are actually the former dairy and granary of the Smiths' Manor House in the picturesque village of Winfrith Newburgh. All the cottages are equipped to a set standard with a fully equipped kitchen, a comfortable sitting room with television, (and in most cases, with an open fire), good quality beds, and a well-maintained garden with outdoor furniture. Electricity, gas, logs/coal or oil, are all included in the rent. During the season, bookings are for a minimum of a week, but 3-day short breaks are available during the autumn, winter and spring. Comprehensive details of each property and its location are provided in Dorset Coastal Cottages' brochure which also includes vouchers offering discounts on entry to various Dorset attractions.

MORETON
MAP 2 REF F9

10 miles W of Wareham, on minor road off the B3390

Thomas Hardy may be Dorset's most famous author, but in this small village it is another distinguished writer, (also a scholar, archaeologist and military hero), who is remembered. In 1935 T.E. Lawrence, "Lawrence of Arabia", left the RAF where he was known simply as Aircraftsman T.E. Shaw and retired to a spartan cottage he had bought ten years earlier. It stands alone on the heath outside Moreton village and here Lawrence lived as a virtual recluse, without cooking facilities and with a sleeping bag as his bed. He was to enjoy this peaceful, if comfortless, retreat for only a few weeks. Lawrence loved speeding along the Dorset lanes on his motor-cycle and one lovely spring day his adventurous driving led to a fatal collision with a young cyclist. The King of Iraq attended the hero's burial in the graveyard at Moreton and the home Lawrence occupied for such a short time, **Cloud's Hill** (National Trust), is now open to the public.

Tucked away in the Dorset countryside, this little village nevertheless has a direct railway link to London. The railway arrived here in the 1840s and that was when an enterprising local man, William Brown, spotted his opportunity and built **The Frampton Arms** directly opposite the new station. Like many landlords of his day, William was involved in other businesses as well. Hunt's Directory of 1851 listed him as offering "Flys and Post Horses" for hire, and also

The Frampton Arms, Moreton, Nr Dorchester, Dorset DT2 8BB
Tel: 01305 852253 Fax: 01305 854586

as a coal merchant. Over the years, the ownership of The Frampton Arms has changed many times but since 1982 has been in the very capable hands of John and Janette Paulson who during that time have continually improved and extended the premises whilst still retaining the character of this attractive listed building. The pub sports the Frampton family crest over the doorway and once inside you will find a friendly atmosphere and an excellent choice of food and drink. One of the two bars is dedicated to the World War II planes which flew from nearby Warmwell airfield, with original photographs of Spitfires and Hurricanes adorning the walls. Two other notable features of this interesting building are its light and airy conservatory restaurant, which offers an extensive menu of freshly-prepared, beautifully-presented dishes, and a wonderful skittle alley which has its own bar, and also serves as a function room and even, on occasion, as a cinema. Outside there is a beer garden with a play area for children: when the weather is not so kind, there's an indoor games room to keep them amused. The Frampton Arms also has 3 guest bedrooms, (2 doubles and a family room, all en suite), ideal if you are looking for reasonably priced accommodation in the area.

7 North Dorset

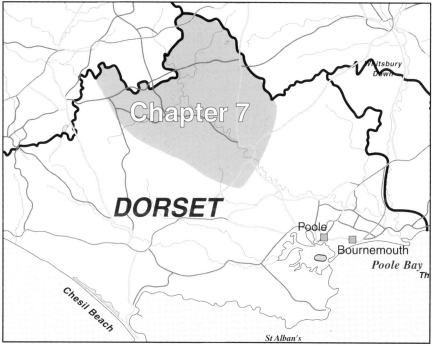

© MAPS IN MINUTES ™ (1998)

Largely agricultural, north Dorset represents rural England at its most appealing. It's a peaceful, unspoilt area embracing half a dozen small market towns and many attractive villages. The area's most glorious building is Sherborne Abbey and the same small town also contains Sir Walter Raleigh's Sherborne Old Castle as well as several other striking medieval houses. Blandford Forum, the administrative centre of the district, has a pleasing town centre, mostly Georgian, and in Shaftesbury, Gold Hill became one of the most familiar streets in the county as a result of being featured in the classic TV commercial for Hovis bread.

Running along the northwestern border of the district, Blackmoor Vale is still much as Thomas Hardy described it in *Tess of the d'Urbervilles*, "The Vale of Little Dairies". The landscape here is on an intimate scale, tiny fields bordered by ancient hedgerows which have escaped the wholescale uprooting inflicted by agribusiness elsewhere.

North Dorset is a place to explore for its enchanting countryside and beguiling little towns. There are very few tailor-made tourist attractions. One of the rare exceptions to that rule, the Dorset Rare Breeds Centre near Gillingham, reflects the agricultural pre-occupations of the area.

BLANDFORD FORUM

Blandford Forum, the administrative centre of North Dorset, is beautifully situated along the wooded valley of the River Stour. It's a handsome town, thanks mainly to suffering the trauma of a great fire in 1731. The gracious Georgian buildings erected after that conflagration, most of them designed by local architects John and William Bastard, provide the town with a quite unique and soothing sense of architectural harmony.

Three important ancient buildings escaped the fire of 1731: the **Ryves Almshouses** of 1682, the **Corn Exchange**, and the splendid 15th century **Old House in The Close**. The old parish church did not survive the fire, but its 18th century replacement, crowned by an unusual cupola, now dominates the market-place. It's well worth stepping inside the church to see the massive columns of Portland stone, and the elegant pulpit, designed by Sir Christopher Wren, removed here from St Antholin's Church in the City of London.

CHARLTON MARSHALL   MAP 2 REF G7
3 miles SE of Blandford Forum, on the A350

Built in 1860, **Poppy Cottage** - offering bed and breakfast accommodation - is a charming little flint-and-brick house with a slate roof and a fenced garden that's a safe haven for children and dogs. Trees and bushes provide shade, and patio furniture invites you to while away the odd hour in the mature garden.

There's an inviting home-from-home feel the moment you go through the porch into a cosy lounge with traditional furnishings and an open fireplace. From the well-equipped kitchen, steep stairs lead up to the two bedrooms, (1 double, 1 single), which share a combined bathroom and toilet. A Z-bed or bed settee is available for extra accommodation, and a cot will be provided free of charge - children of all ages are welcome. Poppy Cottage is situated on the edge of Charlton Marshall, which stands in the beautiful Stour Valley by the A350, on the road from Blandford Forum to Poole. It's part of a small community (Charlton on the Hill) of about a dozen properties and is very rural and peaceful, with no passing traffic.

The cottage, which stands up a narrow unmade road, is run by June and John Dunn who made the break from the London area five years ago, having

Poppy Cottage, "Fountains", 19 River Lane, Charlton Marshall
Dorset DT11 9NZ Tel: 01258 452013

enjoyed it as a weekend retreat. Walking and fishing are favourite pastimes at this most delightful and relaxing spot.

SHILLINGSTONE

MAP 2 REF F7

6 miles NW of Blandford Forum, on the A357

Lost in lovely countryside on a private road going nowhere, **Pennhills Farm** stands half a mile from the village of Shillingstone, which lies on the A357 between Blandford Forum and Sturminster Newton. Sitting in the garden is delightful enough for some, but this is great walking and cycling country, with the River Stour close by. The Hod and Hambledon Hills are a short walk away and all around there is an abundance of wildlife and picturesque scenery. A favourite trail is the Wessex Ridgeway, which runs from Ashmore to Cerne Abbas and right through to Lyme Regis. Peaceful it certainly is, but if you want to spice things up a bit there are some exciting drives for off-road and 4x4 vehicles.

The house itself is of high-quality modern design, with plenty of timber in its construction and a look that has something of a Swiss chalet about it. The views are superb from the comfortably appointed bedrooms (one on the ground floor) and there's a great feeling of peace and contentment out on the patio or in the garden on a summer's evening. When the temperature drops, a log fire

**Pennhills Farm, Sandy Lane, off Larchards Lane, Shillingstone
Nr Blandford Forum, Dorset DT11 0TF Tel: 01258 860491**

beckons in the lounge. Rosie Watts and her family guarantee the friendliest of receptions, and children are very welcome - pets, too, by arrangement. A splendid country breakfast, with farm eggs and home-produced sausages, sets up walkers in fine style, and good evening meals are available locally.

SHAFTESBURY   MAP 3 REF G5
12 miles N of Blandford Forum, on the A350/A30

Set on the side of a hill 700ft high, Shaftesbury was officially founded in 880 AD by King Alfred who fortified the town and also built an Abbey of which his daughter was first Prioress. A hundred years later, the King Edward who had

Gold Hill, Shaftesbury

been murdered by his step-mother at Corfe Castle was buried here and the Abbey became a major centre of pilgrimage. Very little of Shaftesbury Abbey remains but the associated Museum contains many interesting artefacts excavated from the site.

Shaftesbury is a pleasant town to explore on foot. In fact, you *have* to walk if you want to see its most famous sight, **Gold Hill**, a steep, cobbled street, stepped in places and lined with 18th century cottages. Already well-known for its picturesque setting and grand views across the Vale of Blackmoor, Gold Hill became even more famous when it was featured in the classic television commercial for Hovis bread. Also located on Gold Hill is the Shaftesbury Local History Museum which vividly evokes the story of this ancient market town.

One of the liveliest arts centres in the country, the **Shaftesbury Arts Centre** is, remarkably, completely owned by its membership and administered entirely by volunteers. The results of their efforts are anything but amateur, however. From its beginnings as a Drama Club almost half a century ago, the organisation has evolved into an all-embracing Arts Centre, fully licensed for public performances. One of the most popular features of the Centre is its Gallery which is open daily with a regularly changing variety of exhibitions - ranging from paintings, etchings and sculpture, to batiks, stained glass, embroideries and quilting.

The Centre's Drama Group is responsible for 3 major productions each year - plays in Spring and Autumn, and a pantomime or Christmas Show each January. These are performed in the well-equipped theatre which also serves as a cinema for the Centre's Film Society, screening

Shaftesbury Arts Centre, 13 Bell Street, Shaftesbury Dorset SP7 8AR Tel: 01747 854321

a dozen or more films during the season from September to April on Friday evenings. The Art Group caters for people with an interest in the visual arts, both professionals and amateurs. It provides workshops, lectures and demonstrations relating to drawing and painting, and organises visits to galleries.

The group arranges 3 exhibitions a year for the sale of members' works, including an open-air exhibition on Park Walk in August. During the winter months, the Art Group meets on Monday afternoons for portrait, figure and still life drawing and painting. Other activities include a Camera Group which has demonstration evenings by professional photographers, various competitions, and slide show talks by members; a Junior Drama Group for anyone from first school age to adults who want to learn about acting; a Music & Light Opera Group which stages a show each year in early summer, and presents a programme of Christmas music in December; a Calligraphy Group, and even a Yoga Group. Membership is open to all, and subscription rates are extremely reasonable.

Conveniently located on the main A30 Yeovil to Salisbury road, **The Roadside Lodge/L.A. Pizzas** offers a staggering choice of pizzas, burgers, fish and chicken dishes, ethnic food, as well as sandwiches, a children's menu and vegetarian meals. The Lodge is owned and run by a young and enthusiastic couple, Gary and Jeanne Cooper, who have brought a freshness and vitality to this bright, modern restaurant. Pizzas are made and cooked to order, with almost a dozen varieties available, or you can create your own from a wide choice of toppings. The ethnic foods on offer include popular favourites such as Chicken Tikka Masala, Lamb Rogan Josh, and Vegetable Balti, and amongst the modestly priced desserts are Kansas Kiss Cake and Apple & Blackcurrant Roll. Meals can be enjoyed either in the restaurant itself, in the patio garden, or as takeaways. Gary and Jeanne also provide a delivery service in the Shaftesbury area, and to other places by appointment. The Lodge completes its excellent service by opening 7 days a week, from 7am to 11pm.

**The Roadside Lodge/L.A. Pizzas, Salisbury Road, Shaftesbury
Dorset SP7 8BU Tel: 01747 855455**

About 3 miles northwest of Shaftesbury, the **Dorset Rare Breeds Centre** harbours the county's largest collection of rare and endangered farm animals. They range from knee-high Soay sheep to mighty Suffolk Punch horses weighing a ton or more. All of these native breeds are at great risk and the Centre hopes to alert animal lovers to the imminent threat.

KINGTON MAGNA Map 2 ref F5
6 miles W of Shaftesbury off the A30

If you've ever fancied the idea of adding character to your bedroom with a stylish Victorian iron and brass bedstead, the people to get in touch with are John and Dorrie Peat at **Farmhouse Antiques**. John and Dorrie have a large

choice of original iron and brass bedsteads, as well as Victorian and Edwardian decorative iron and brass bedheads. They are meticulously restored to their original splendour and are available in a whole range of traditional colours. The bedsteads come in all sizes so you can virtually order one "tailor made" to your requirements, along with made-to-measure bases. And should you happen to have a brass bed which is in need of

**Farmhouse Antiques, Kington Magna, Gillingham
Dorset SP8 5EE Tel/Fax: 01747 838217**

refurbishment, Farmhouse Antiques can look after that as well. Visitors are welcome, by appointment, to their workshop in an old stone barn in a farmyard in the heart of the Dorset countryside. A delivery service is also available.

MARNHULL Map 2 ref F6
7 miles SW of Shaftesbury, on minor road off the B3092

The scattered village of Marnhull claims to be the largest parish in England, spread over a substantial area, with a circumference of 23 miles. The village itself is well worth exploring for its part-Norman St Gregory's church with a fine

15th century tower, and who knows what you might find along Sodom Lane? This now-prosperous village appears in *Tess of the d'Urbervilles* as 'Marlott', the birthplace of his heroine. The thatched Tess's Cottage (private, but visible from the lane) is supposedly the house Hardy had in mind.

The Crown at Marnhull also features in the novel, re-christened "The Pure Drop Inn". Once you've seen its creamy stone walls and low-hanging thatched roof, only the most hardened teetotaller, surely, could resist stepping inside for a pure drop. As in those far-off days, The Crown is still an important focus of village life, a lively social centre for Marnhull's flourishing cricket and football clubs, with its Skittles Alley and Function Room providing a natural first choice for many local organisations and private groups. The thatched wing of the inn is the oldest part, dating back to the 17th century. Since then, The Crown has spread itself in a leisurely way along Crown Road, the most recent extension

**The Crown Hotel, Crown Road, Marnhull, Dorset DT10 1LN.
Tel: 01258 820224**

being the Crown Room at its eastern end, built in the early 1800s. Inside, the old stone-flagged floors and open fires evoke an atmosphere of olde-worlde hospitality, a mood enhanced by the inn's friendly hosts, Jill and Nigel Dawe. Jill is in charge of the kitchen and offers a tasty selection of freshly-prepared home-made meals and snacks, ranging from a gargantuan 16 oz steak to well-filled jacket potatoes, baguettes and sandwiches. Vegetarian meals and a children's menu are also available, and this family-friendly inn also offers a children's garden and play area. You may well want to linger in this attractive village: if so, The Crown has four guest rooms for bed & breakfast visitors.

STALBRIDGE
MAP 2 REF E6

10 miles W of Sherborne, on the A357

The 15th century church here has a striking 19th century tower which provides a landmark throughout the Vale of Blackmoor. Perhaps even more impressive is the town's **Market Cross** standing 30ft high and richly carved with scenes of the Crucifixion and Resurrection. Just outside the town, Stalbridge Park (private) sheltered Charles I after his defeat at Marston Moor. The house (now demolished) was built by Richard Boyle, 1st Earl of Cork, and it was here that his 7th son, the celebrated physicist and chemist Robert Boyle carried out the experiments that eventually led to his formulation of Boyle's Law.

Like many arts ventures, the **Guggleton Farm Arts Project** owes its existence to the vision of one person: in this case, Isabel de Pelet, who was a full time housewife until a few years ago when she changed the direction of her life. After completing a course at art college, Isabel was enthused by the idea of creating a centre which would provide studio space for recently graduated artists, and so give them the time to establish themselves professionally, helped by the support and contacts opened up through the Arts Project. A mere four years ago, Isabel found the appropriate premises in some near-derelict farm buildings, and today Guggleton Farm is a vibrant artistic community of sculptors, painters and ceramicists. At the centre of the project is a small Gallery where exhibitions are

Guggleton Farm Arts Project, Station Road, Stalbridge
Dorset DT10 2RQ Tel: 01963 362289

staged at least 8 times a year, and this space is also available for other shows and activities, as well as doubling up as a Community Arts workshop and small lecture room. A regular programme of events and practical courses continues throughout the year, open to local people and visitors alike. The project is a triumphant vindication of Isabel's credo that "artists working alongside, and within an active Community Arts Programme, create a positive way to further mutual understanding and form experiences that will both enrich and stimulate all those who involve themselves". For anyone with an interest in contemporary art, Guggleton Farm is definitely a place to seek out.

STURMINSTER NEWTON
8 miles NW of Blandford Forum, on the A357

MAP 2 REF F6

This unspoilt market town is an essential stop for anyone following in Thomas Hardy's footsteps for it was at Sturminster Newton that he and his first wife Emma had their first real home together. From 1876 until 1878, they lived in "a pretty cottage overlooking the Dorset Stour, called Riverside Villa". Here, Hardy wrote *The Return of the Native* and often referred to their time at **Sturminster Newton** in his poems. It was, he said, "our happiest time". The house is not open to the public but is visible from a riverside footpath.

At the heart of this charming little town stands **The White Hart**, a wonderfully picturesque old inn with a thatched roof and, to one side, a broad entrance through which stage coaches used to clatter. Built around 1708, this appealing hostelry still has its ancient beamed ceilings and open log fire, and a curious collection of vintage bottle openers on display adds to the olde-worlde atmos-

The White Hart, Market Cross, Sturminster Newton
Dorset DT10 1AN Tel: 01258 472593

phere. Mine hosts, Pete and Jan Bennett, have made The White Hart a lively social centre, with pool, darts, and a skittle alley all available, and with regular quiz nights adding to the entertainment. Jan is in charge of the kitchen and her menu of "Hearty Pub Grub!" offers a good choice of simple, wholesome food, well-prepared, and at attractive prices. There's also a "Snack Attack" menu which includes an all day breakfast, jacket potatoes, ploughman's, filled baguettes, and other light meals.

For fairweather days, there's a pleasant Beer Garden to the rear where visitors can also admire the colourful birds at home in Pete's aviary. And if you are planning to stay in this lovely part of the county, The White Hart has 3 letting rooms, (2 doubles, 1 twin), ideal as a base for exploring Dorset and east Somerset.

Until Elizabethan times, Sturminster and Newton were separate villages standing on opposite sides of the River Stour. Shortly after the graceful Town Bridge linked the two communities, a Mill was built some 250 yards upstream. Once again restored to working order, **Newton Mill** offers guided tours explaining the milling process, and the delightful setting attracts many amateur and professional artists and photographers. Incidentally, the fine old 6-arched bridge still bears a rusty metal plaque carrying the dire warning: "Any person wilfully injuring any part of this county bridge will be guilty of felony and upon conviction liable to be transported for life by the court. P. Fooks".

SHERBORNE   MAP 1 REF D6
16 miles W of Shaftesbury, on the A352

One of the most beautiful towns in England, Sherborne beguiles the visitor with its serene atmosphere of a "Cathedral City", although it is not a city and its lovely **Abbey** no longer enjoys the status of a cathedral. Back in AD 705 though, when it was founded by St Aldhelm, the Abbey was the Mother Cathe-

Sherborne Abbey

dral for the whole of southwest England. Of that original Saxon church only minimal traces remain: most of the present building dates back to the mid-1400s which, by happy chance, was the most glorious period in the history of English ecclesiastical architecture. The intricate tracery of the fan vaulting above the nave of the Abbey looks like the supreme culmination of a long-practised art: in fact, it is one of the earliest examples in England. There is much else to admire in this majestic church: 15th century misericords in the choir stalls which range from the sublime, (Christ sitting in majesty on a rainbow), to the scandalous, (wives beating their husbands); a wealth of elaborate tombs amongst which is a lofty 6-poster from Tudor times, a floridly baroque late-17th century memorial to the 3rd Earl of Bristol, and another embellished with horses' heads in a punning tribute to Sir John Horsey who lies below alongside his son.

As well as founding the Abbey, St Aldhelm is also credited with establishing **Sherborne School** which numbered amongst its earliest pupils the two elder brothers of King Alfred, (and possibly Alfred himself), and in later times the Poet Laureate Cecil Day-Lewis and the writer David Cornwell, better known as John le Carré, author of *The Spy Who Came in from the Cold* and many other thrillers.

Perhaps the best-known resident of Sherborne however is Sir Walter Raleigh. At a time when he enjoyed the indulgent favour of Elizabeth I he asked for, and was granted, the house and estate of **Sherborne Old Castle** (English Heritage). Sir Walter soon realised that the medieval pile with its starkly basic amenities was quite unsuitable for a courtier of his sophistication and ambition. He built a new castle alongside it, **Sherborne New Castle**, a strange three-storeyed, hexagonal structure which must rate, from the outside, as one of the most badly-designed, most unlikeable mansions to be erected in an age when other Elizabethan architects were creating some of the loveliest buildings in England. Inside Sir Walter's new castle, it is quite a different story: gracious rooms with elaborately-patterned ceilings, portraits of the man who single-handedly began

Sherborne Castle

the creation of the British Empire, and huge windows which at the time Sir Walter ordered them proclaimed a clear message that its owner had the wealth to pay the enormous cost of glazing such vast expanses. After Sir Walter's execution, the castle was purchased in 1617 by Sir James Digby and it has remained with his descendants ever since. They added exquisite gardens designed by "Capability" Brown and in the late 1800s re-decorated the interior in Jacobean style. Amongst the castle's greatest treasures is the famous painting by Robert Peake depicting Elizabeth I on procession, being carried on a litter and surrounded by a sumptuously dressed retinue. The old cellar of the castle is now a museum housing an eclectic display of items, most gruesome of which is the skull of a Royalist soldier killed in the seige of 1645 with a bullet still lodged in his eye socket. Sherborne New Castle, incidentally, is one of several locations claiming to be the genuine setting for the old story of Sir Walter enjoying a pipe of tobacco and being doused with a bucket of water by a servant who believed his master was on fire. Sherborne Castle is open from April to October, and also offers visitors an attractive lakeside tearoom, a well-stocked gift shop, and various special events throughout the year. For more details, telephone 01935 813182.

Located in the old walled kitchen gardens of Sherborne Castle, **Castle Gardens** offers a huge selection of healthy and colourful plants and garden products. This quality product range is backed by dedication to customer service through a large, qualified and friendly staff who are able to answer and assist in all areas of gardening. Castle Gardens provides a great deal more to gardeners through its Gold Club. Members receive regular newsletters detailing special offers and forthcoming events and there is also an extensive programme of day trips and holidays. (A recent trip, for example, explored the gardens of the Loire Valley in France).

For members from farther afield there is the Connoisseur Plant Club, which evrey year offers members 8 collections, listed in colourful newsletters, of more unusual and interesting plants available by mail order. All of these activities have been master-minded by Mike and Louise Burks and Tony Rash who built and have been running the centre with their team since 1987 (and a twin venture at Brimsmore Gardens, near Yeovil) and whose enthusiasm and energy have made them a magnet for gardeners for miles around. Both centres are open 7 days a week, from 9am

Castle Garden Centre, New Road, Sherborne, Dorset DT9 3SA
Tel: 01935 814633

to 6pm and, in addition to the services already mentioned, also offer a 2 year guarantee on all hardy plants, pest and disease identification, plant search, gift wrapping, and delivery within a 25 mile radius - all free of charge.

This appealing small town with a population of around 8500 has much else to interest the visitor. The **Almshouse of Saints John the Baptist** and **John the Evangelist**, near the Abbey, was founded in 1437 and the original buildings completed in 1448 are still in use as an almshouse, accepting both men and women. The almshouse chapel boasts one of the town's greatest treasures, a late-15th century Flemish altar tryptich which can be viewed on afternoons during the summer. Close by, the **Conduit House** is an attractive small hexagonal building from the early 1500s, originally used as a lavatorium, or washroom, for the Abbey monks' ablutions. It was moved here after the Reformation and has served variously as a public fountain and a police phone box. The Conduit House is specifically mentioned in Hardy's *The Woodlanders* as the place where Giles Winterborne, seeking work, stood here in the market place "as he always did at this season of the year, with his specimen apple tree". Another striking building is the former **Abbey Gatehouse** which frames the entrance to Church Lane where the **Sherborne Museum** has a collection of more than 15,000 items of local history. Particularly notable are two major photographic collections recording events and people in the town since 1880.

Tucked away in a little side street, **The Digby Tap** is a genuine Hidden Place,

The Digby Tap, Cooks Lane, Sherborne, Dorset DT9 3NS
Tel: 01935 813148

and well worth seeking out. The attractive old stone building dates back to the 1700s, reputedly the second oldest pub in Sherborne. The Digby Tap's authentic old world atmosphere, with its stone-flagged floors and ancient oak beams, provided an appropriate location for a BBC Television play, *Murder of Quality*, starring Denholm Elliot, Glenda Jackson and Joss Ackland. The pub gets its name from the days when it was the alehouse for workers on the Digby Estate, (the Digby family, incidentally, is commemorated by its own sumptuous chapel in the Abbey).

Peter Lefevre, who runs this lively and friendly hostelry, offers his patrons an excellent choice of Real Ales, (including Exmoor, Smiles, and Teignworthy), and a tasty choice of home-made snacks and meals. There's always a daily home-made soup, jacket potatoes, snacks such as cheesy stuffed mushrooms, or home-made pâté, and a daily special - a carbonara pasta in herby sauce, perhaps. The Digby Tap is a popular watering-hole with the local Rugby Club: devotees of the game will be interested in the many club ties which adorn the beams.

STOURTON CAUNDLE Map 2 ref E6
6 miles E of Sherborne, on minor road off the A3030, or A357

For a fascinating insight into Dorset rural life, you really must make your way to the charming little village of Stourton Caundle and its equally delightful pub, **The Trooper**, some 300 years old. It's owned and run by Larry and Sue Skeats and well-known for its busy Skittle Alley, excellent Real Ales, and tasty snack lunches served in the low-ceilinged bar with ancient settles all around, and nooks and crannies everywhere. That's only part of the attraction, though, because at the rear of the pub is Larry's personal museum of country bygones, an astonishing collection of agricultural and domestic artefacts which range from a

milk churn bearing a beautifully-painted rustic scene, through strange and mysterious farming tools, to brightly-coloured root pulpers, along with much, much more. An admitted magpie, Larry acquired hundreds of "unconsidered trifles" in the course of his 40-year career as a shepherd, during which time he also became a familiar figure

The Trooper, High Street, Stourton Caundle
Dorset DT10 2JW Tel: 01963 362405

on country life television programmes such as *Out of Town* and *Country Ways*, hence his fine collection of shepherding memorabilia, sheep bells and shepherd's crooks. Few museums can boast such a wealth of material; fewer still are in the care of such a knowledgeable curator. Not all the exhibits are connected with the healthy outdoor life: Larry also collects ashtrays. To date, he has some 500 of them - and also a fine collection of vermin traps!

MILBORNE PORT

MAP 2 REF E6

3 miles NE of Sherborne, on the A30

Surrounded by mature gardens and 3½ acres of grounds, **The Old Vicarage** at Milborne Port is a gracious, listed Victorian house, originally built in 1870. It's now owned by Jörgen Kunath and Anthony Ma, formerly of the highly acclaimed "Noughts & Crosses Restaurant" in West London. At The Old Vicarage they offer bed and breakfast throughout the week, and also special weekend

The Old Vicarage, Sherborne Road, Milborne Port, Dorset DT9 5AT
Tel: 01963 251117 Fax: 01963 251515

breaks which include an outstanding 4-course dinner on the Friday and Saturday evenings. Served in the (non-smoking) conservatory overlooking the garden, Anthony's menus (changed daily) provide a unique blend of traditional and innovative cuisine, making good use of fresh local produce and Dorset specialities such as vinney cheese or air dried Dorset ham. The Old Vicarage is able to offer visitors a choice of accommodation. In the main house, there are 3 large en suite bedrooms, all decorated with style and panache, and all enjoying delightful views of open country or the gardens. The Coach House, with its rustic charm, has 4 smaller en suite bedrooms with a sun terrace overlooking the garden. All guests are welcome to make themselves at home in the spacious lounge which is tastefully decorated with a wealth of interesting antiques.

8 In and Around Dorchester

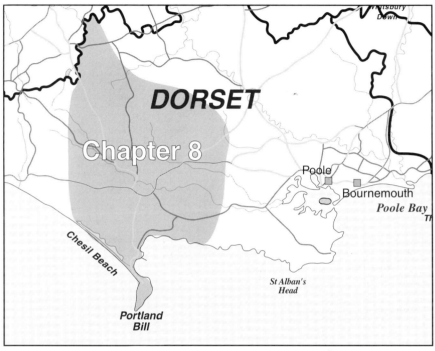

DORCHESTER

One of England's most appealing county towns, Dorchester's known history goes back to AD74 when the Romans established a settlement called Durnovaria at a respectful distance from the River Frome. At that time the river was much broader than it is now and prone to flooding. The town's Roman origins are clearly displayed in its street plan, in the beautiful tree-lined avenues known as **The Walks** which follow the course of the old Roman walls, at **Maumbury Rings**, an ancient stone circle which the Romans converted into an amphitheatre, and in the well-preserved **Roman Town House** behind County Hall in Colliton Park. As the town's most famous citizen put it, Dorchester "announced old Rome in every street, alley and precinct. It looked Roman, bespoke the art of Rome, concealed dead men of Rome". Thomas Hardy was in fact describing "Casterbridge" in his novel *The Mayor of Casterbridge* but his fictional town is immediately recognisable as Dorchester. One place he describes in great detail is **Mayor Trenchard's House**, easily identified as what is now Barclays Bank in South Street which bears a plaque to that effect. Hardy made his home in Dorchester in 1883 and two years later moved in to Max Gate (National Trust) on the outskirts of the town, a strikingly unlovely "two up and two down" Victorian villa designed by Hardy himself and built by his brother at a total cost of £450. Here he would entertain a roll-call of great names - Robert Louis Stevenson, G.B. Shaw, Rudyard Kipling and H.G. Wells amongst many others, to tea at 4 o'clock.

For many visitors, the most accessible introduction to the town and the county will be found at the excellent **Dorset County Museum** in High Street West. Designated Best Social History Museum in the 1998 Museum of the Year Awards, the museum houses a comprehensive range of exhibits spanning the centuries, from a Roman sword to a 19th century cheese press, from dinosaur footprints to a stuffed Great Bustard which used to roam the chalk uplands of north Dorset but has been extinct in this country since 1810. Founded in 1846, the museum moved to its present site in 1883, into purpose-built galleries with lofty arches of fine cast ironwork inspired by the Great Exhibition of 1851 at the Crystal Palace. The building was designed by G. R. Crickmay, the architect for whom Thomas Hardy worked in 1870, and the great poet and novelist is celebrated in a major exhibit which includes a fascinating reconstruction of his study at Max Gate, his Dorchester home. The room includes the original furnishings, books, pictures and fireplace. In the right hand corner are his musical instruments, and the very pens with which he wrote *Tess of the d'Urbervilles, Jude the Obscure,* and his epic poem, the *Dynasts* are also here. More of his possessions are displayed in the Gallery outside - furniture, his watch, music books,

The Dorset County Museum, High Street West, Dorchester, Dorset DT1 1AX Tel: 01305 262735 Fax: 01305 257180

and some of his notebooks. Also honoured in the Writers Gallery is William Barnes, the Dorset dialect poet, scholar and priest, who was also the first secretary of the Dorset Natural History and Archaeological Society which owns and runs the museum.

Other galleries display the rich and varied environment of Dorset in the past and present. There's a fossil tree, around 135 million years old, from Portland, skeletons of Iron Age warriors from Maiden Castle cemetery, part of a Roman mosaic from Dorchester, a 12th century ivory carving of a King found near Milborne St Andrew, a 19th century Dorset bow waggon, and much, much more. The museum also stages regularly changing temporary exhibitions on topics as varied as whales to sculpture, Dorset in wartime to abstract art.

Just outside the museum stands the Statue of William Barnes and, at the junction of High Street West and The Grove, is the Statue of Thomas Hardy. Opposite the Museum, the Antelope Hotel and the 17th century half-timbered building beside it (now a tea-room) were where Judge Jeffreys (1648-89) tried 340 Dorset men for their part in Monmouth's Rebellion of 1685. As a result of this "Bloody Assize", 74 men suffered death by being hanged, drawn and quartered, and a further 175 were transported for life. Jeffreys' ferociousness has been attributed to the agony he suffered from gallstones for which doctors of the time could provide no relief. Ironically, when his patron James II was deposed, Jeffreys himself ended up in the Tower of London where he died. A century and a half after the "Bloody Assizes", another infamous trial took place in the Old Crown Court and Cells nearby. Here, 6 farm labourers who later became known as the **Tolpuddle Martyrs** were condemned to transportation for their part in organising a "Friendly Society" - the first agricultural trade union. The **Court and Cells** are now open to the public where they are invited to "stand in the dock and sit in the dimly-lit cells...and experience four centuries of gruesome crime and punishment".

Also in High Street West is the **Tutankhamun Exhibition**, an impressive reconstruction of the young Pharaoh's tomb and treasures, including his famous golden mask, with "sight, sound and smell combining to re-create the world's greatest discovery of ancient treasure". Close by, at the **Teddy Bear House**, visitors join Mr Edward Bear and his family of human-size bears as they relax around the house or busy themselves making teddies in the **Old Dorset Teddy Bear Factory**. Hundreds of the cuddly creatures are on sale in the exhibition's period shop.

One of Dorchester's most historic pubs is **The Borough Arms** in High East Street, and it's run by a couple who must be amongst the youngest licensees in the county, Martin and Beverley West, both in their mid-thirties. From the front, the inn doesn't look particularly large, but once you step inside you find that the rooms, with floors of ancient flagstones, follow one after another, ending in a high-walled outside area which, by the time you read this, should have been transformed into a garden and children's play area. This secluded area is prob-

The Borough Arms, 36 High East Street, Dorchester, Dorset DT1 1HN
Tel: 01305 260512

ably a legacy of the days when the Borough Arms, which dates back to the 1600s, was a coaching inn. The deceptively spacious interior even finds room to accommodate a popular Skittle Alley. Martin and Beverley, who only took over the tenancy recently, plan to begin serving bar snacks and modest tasty meals: again, these may well be on offer by the time this book is published. During the Borough Arms' long history many of the great and the good have supped here, including Dorchester's most famous resident, Thomas Hardy. A much-repeated story recounts that one day he was passing by as an auction was under way in the inn. Pausing to look through the window, he noticed an old friend and raised his hand to greet him. Continuing along the street, the great novelist and poet was unaware that he had just bought the lot up for sale.

Just around the corner from The Borough Arms is the **Dinosaur Museum** which was declared Dorset's Best Family Attraction in 1997. Actual fossils, skeletons and life-size reconstructions combine with audio-visual and hands-on displays to inform and entertain. Somewhat surprisingly, this is the only museum in Britain dedicated exclusively to these fascinating creatures. The museum is open daily throughout the year. Also well worth a visit is **The Keep Military Museum** housed in an interesting, renovated Grade II listed building. Audio technology and interactive computerised displays tell the remarkable story of those who have served in the regiments of Dorset and Devon. An additional bonus is the spectacular view from the battlements across the town and surrounding countryside.

In the short time since they arrived at **The White Hart Hotel**, located in the centre of the town, Trish Jones and David Tysoe have firmly established a reputation for serving their guests good food and fine ales at sensible prices. Set beside a millstream of the River Frome, the hotel dates back to the late 18th century and it maintains the traditions of those more hospitable days. Trish is in charge of the kitchen and her menu includes an excellent choice of meals that ranges from a simple platter of breaded mushrooms, served with a blue cheese or garlic & herb dip, to a hearty fillet steak complete with all the trimmings. In between, you'll find tasty fish dishes; succulent preparations of chicken, (the Chicken Tricia, which comes in a creamy sauce topped with cheese, is particularly recommended); 3-egg omelettes stuffed with the filling of your choice; and vegetarian options such as Vegetable Kiev and Pancake Rolls, (a vegetarian version of Spring Rolls), served with salad. Picky kids will almost certainly be won over by the White Hart's inventive Children's Menu of "Snappy Meals" which includes such irresistible offerings as Golden Whale (served with potato Smiles and peas) and Chick'n Teddies. Outside, there's a patio and beer garden, and if you are thinking of staying in this lovely corner of the county, the White Hart has 8 letting rooms: a family room, a twin bedroom, 2 doubles, and 4 singles.

The White Hart Hotel, 53 High Street East, Dorchester, Dorset DT1 1HU
Tel: 01305 263545

There can be few churches in the country with such a bizarre history as that of **Our Lady, Queen of Martyrs & St Michael**. It was first erected in Wareham, in 1888, by a Roman Catholic sect who called themselves the Passionists, a name derived from their obsession with Christ's passion and death. When they found that few people in Wareham shared their fixation, they had the church moved in 1907, stone by stone to Dorchester where it was re-assembled and then served the Catholic community for almost 70 years. By the mid-1970s the transplanted church had become too small for its burgeoning congregation. The Passionists moved out, ironically taking over an Anglican church whose communicants had become too few to sustain it. A decade later, their abandoned church was acquired by an organisation called World Heritage which has transformed its interior into a reconstruction of the tomb of Tutankhamun. With the help of a running commentary, visitors can follow the footsteps of the archaeologist Howard Carter who discovered the real tomb in 1922, a tour which ends beside a life-size facsimile of the youthful Pharoah's mummy constructed from a genuine skeleton covered with organic-substitute flesh and animal skin.

Another oddity in the town is an 18th century sign set high up in a wall bearing the information that Bridport is 15 miles distant and Hyde Park Corner, 120. It was placed in this position for the convenience of stage-coach drivers, although one would have thought that they, of all people, would have already known the mileage involved.

Just a mile or so northeast of the town, **Kingston Maurward Gardens** are of such historical importance that they are listed on the English Heritage register of Gardens. The 35 acres of classical 18th century parkland and lawns sweep majestically down to the lake from the stately Georgian house. The Edwardian Gardens include a croquet lawn, rose garden, herbaceous borders and a large display of tender perennials, including the National Collection of Penstemons and Salvias. There's also an Animal Park with an interesting collection of unusual breeds, nature trails, plant sales and the Old Coach House Restaurant serving morning coffee, lunches and teas.

Of even greater historical significance is **Maiden Castle**, a couple of miles southwest of Dorchester and one of the most impressive prehistoric sites in the country. This vast Iron Age fortification covering nearly 50 acres dates back some 4000 years. Its steep earth ramparts, between 60 and 90 feet high, are nearly 2 miles round and together with the inner walls make a total of 5 miles of defences. The settlement flourished for 2000 years until AD44 when its people were defeated by a Roman army under Vespasian. Excavations here in 1937 unearthed a war cemetery containing some 40 bodies, one of which still had a Roman arrowhead embedded in its spine. The Romans occupied the site for some 30 years before moving closer to the River Frome and founding Durnovaria, modern Dorchester. Maiden Castle was never settled again and it is a rather forbidding, treeless place but the extensive views along the Winterborne valley by contrast are delightful.

MARTINSTOWN
Map 1 ref D9

3 miles SW of Dorchester, on the B3159

For centuries Martinstown was known as Winterborne St Martin, taking its name from the river that runs through the village and its 15th century church.

On the Black Downs southwest of Martinstown stands **Hardy's Monument** (National Trust) which commemorates, not Thomas Hardy the great novelist of Wessex, but Sir Thomas Hardy the flag-captain of *HMS Victory* at Trafalgar to whom the dying Lord Nelson spoke the immortal words, "Kiss me, Hardy", (or possibly, "Kismet, Hardy"). This stunningly graceless memorial has been variously described as a "huge candlestick", a "peppermill", and most accurately as a "factory chimney wearing a crinoline". But if you stand with your back to it, there are grand views over Weymouth Bay.

ABBOTSBURY
Map 1 ref D9

8 miles SW of Dorchester, on the B3157

Surrounded by hills, picturesque Abbotsbury is one of the county's most popular tourist spots and by any standards one of the loveliest villages in England. Its most striking feature as you approach is the 14th century **St Catherine's Chapel**, perched on the hill-top. Only 45ft by 15ft, it is solidly built to withstand the Channel gales with walls more than 4ft thick. St Catherine was believed to be particularly helpful in finding husbands for the unmarried and in medieval times spinsters would climb the hill to her chapel chanting a dialect jingle which concludes with the words *"Arn-a-one's better than Narn-a-one"* - anyone is better than never a one.

Abbotsbury takes its name from the important **Benedictine Abbey** that once stood here but was comprehensively cannibalised after the Reformation, its stones used to build the attractive cottages that line the village streets. What has survived however is the magnificent **Great Abbey Barn**, 247ft long and 31ft wide, which was built in the 1300s to store the Abbey's tithes of wool, grain and other produce. With its thatched roof, stone walls and a mightily impressive entrance it is one of the largest and best-preserved barns in the country. It now houses a Terracotta Warriors exhibition and is surrounded by a Childrens Farm where youngsters can feed the animals. The Barn is open all year round.

Set in a delightful thatched converted stable block near the centre of Abbotsbury village, the **Dansel Craftwork Gallery** is Britain's leading showcase for contemporary craft work in wood and one of the Craft Council's Selected Shops. Featuring a superb collection of high quality handmade items from the best of British designer craftsmen, the Gallery has recently been described as a "Mecca for woodworkers". All the pieces on display are carefully selected, with the emphasis on good design and quality of finish. The story of the Gallery goes back to 1979 when Danielle and Selwyn Holmes set up a workshop and showroom here, initially dedicated to their own creations but soon welcoming the

**Dansel Craftwork Gallery, Rodden Row, Abbotsbury, Dorchester
Dorset DT3 4JL Tel: 01305 871515**

work of other artists working in wood. Today, more than 200 British woodworkers are represented in the Gallery, almost certainly the largest such concentration of its kind in the country. The range, too, is extensive: from individually designed furniture, through elegant jewellery boxes, to colourful toys, (including such mind-bending puzzles as 3-dimensional jigsaws), to one-off decorative pieces in which the woodworker has given full rein to his/her inventiveness and versatility. As Paul Atterbury of BBC Television's *Antique Roadshow* remarked: "If the Antiques Roadshow is still running in 50 years time, maybe the next generation of experts will be enthusing over wooden objects made or sold at Abbotsbury in the 1990s".

About a mile south of the village is the famous **Abbotsbury Swannery**, established in Saxon times to provide food for the Abbey during the winter months. More than 600 free-flying swans have made their home here and visitor figures rocket from the end of May to the end of June - the baby swans' hatching season. There's also a children's Ugly Duckling Trail and the oldest known duck decoy still working. Just to the west of the village, Abbotsbury Sub-Tropical Gardens enjoy a particularly well-sheltered position and the 20 acres of grounds contain a huge variety of rare and exotic plants and trees. Other attractions include an 18th century walled garden, beautiful lily ponds and a children's play area.

STINSFORD   Map 2 ref E9
2 miles E of Dorchester, off the A35

It was in St Michael's Church at Stinsford that Thomas Hardy was christened and where he attended services for much of his life. He sang hymns to the accompaniment of the village band, (amongst whom were several of his relatives), which played from a gallery at the back of the church. The gallery was demolished in Hardy's lifetime, but many years later he drew a sketch from memory which showed the position of each player and the name of his instrument. A copy of this drawing is on display in the church, alongside a tablet commemorating the Hardys who took part.

HIGHER BOCKHAMPTON   Map 2 ref E8
3 miles NE of Dorchester, on minor road off the A35

In the woods above Higher Bockhampton, reached by a series of narrow lanes and a 10-minute walk, is a major shrine for devotees of Thomas Hardy. **Hardy's Cottage** is surrounded by the trees of Puddletown Forest, a setting he evoked so magically in *Under the Greenwood Tree*. The delightful thatched cottage and gardens are now owned by the National Trust and the rooms are furnished much as they would have been when the great novelist was born here in 1840. Visitors can see the very room in which his mother gave birth only to hear her child proclaimed still-born. Fortunately, an observant nurse noticed that the infant was in fact breathing and so ensured that such classics of English literature as *Tess of the D'Urbervilles* and *The Return of the Native* saw the light of day. This charming cottage was Hardy's home for the first twenty-two years of his life until he set off for London to try his luck as an architect. In that profession his record was undistinguished, but in 1871 his first novel, *Desperate Remedies,* was published. An almost farcical melodrama, it gave few signs of the great works that would follow but was sufficiently successful for Hardy to devote himself thereafter to writing full time.

ANSTY   Map 2 ref F7
9 miles NE of Dorchester, off the A354

Philip and Shirley Scott have been in the business for 25 years, and the **Fox Inn**, which they have recently taken over, is one of the best known public houses in the county. The building dates back more than 200 years and was once the home of the Woodhouse family of brewers. It became an inn in 1915. The setting, in rolling countryside, can justly be called idyllic and its location makes it the ideal base for a driving, cycling or walking holiday.

The area is rich in history and interest as well as beauty and among the major local attractions are the lovely church in the hamlet of Hilton, the rare breeds farm at Milton Abbas and Milton Abbey, and the superb viewpoint of Bulbarrow Hill (899'). It is equally possible to arrive at the Fox Inn and simply stay put! The accommodation is of a very high standard: all 14 rooms have en suite facilities, and the star of the show is the honeymoon suite with a four-poster bed. Guests can relax in the tranquil and mature gardens or while away an hour or two in the heated swimming pool. After that a drink could be in

The Fox Inn, Ansty, Near Dorchester, Dorset DT2 7PL
Tel: 01258 880328

order, and the flagstoned bars are just the place; one bar features the private collection of prints and photographs of the Woodhouse family. A full bar menu is available, with anything from deep-fried mushrooms or prawn salad to hot baguettes, filled jacket potatoes, breaded plaice and home-made steak and Guinness pie. In the Woodhouse Restaurant more formal evening meals are served, with imaginative offerings such as medallions of monkfish served on lentils with a herb sauce, or roast rack of lamb on a creamy leek and potato fondue with a rich port jus. The Sunday carvery is a popular feature.

LOWER BURTON   MAP 2 REF E8
1 mile N of Dorchester, off the A352

The Sun Inn is a 17th century hostelry built on land owned at one time by Henry VIII and later by the Earl of Ilchester. From 1885 until 1923 it did double duty as the blacksmith's base. Later owned by Devenish brewery, it is now a free house, run by Robin Maddox and his wife Karem. It stands in the Dorset countryside less than a mile from Dorchester on the old Sherborne road at Lower Burton (Burton is one of ten Saxon land units in the area and means 'near fortification' - in this case probably Poundsbury Camp). Leaded lights, oak beams, wooden tables and log fires paint a traditional picture in the bar, where decorative touches include lots of pottery and china ornaments.

Food is taken very seriously here, and the menu is supplemented by a chef s daily specials board. Garlic mushrooms, whitebait or mozzarella chili sticks

The Sun Inn, Lower Burton, Dorchester, Dorset DT2 7RZ
Tel: 01305 250445

with salsa could start your meal, followed perhaps by smoked haddock and prawns in white sauce or a chargrilled steak of swordfish. To satisfy a real country appetite the mammoth mixed grill includes steak, gammon, lamb, pork, liver, sausage and black pudding! There are always several vegetarian options and children's meals, plus snackier items such as ploughman's salads, filled baguettes and jacket potatoes. The Sunday roast is a popular attraction, and there are regular special menu evenings. A decent wine list includes bottles from France, Spain, Italy and the New World. Dorchester has a long connection with ale, and here there's a good selection of cask ales. Food is served lunch and dinner seven days a week. Families are welcome and there's a large car park and a play area in the garden, where there's plenty of space for enjoying the fresh air of a balmy Dorset evening.

CERNE ABBAS

MAP 1 REF E8

7 miles N of Dorchester, on the A352

This pretty village beside the River Cerne takes its name from **Cerne Abbey**, formerly a major Benedictine monastery of which an imposing 15th century gatehouse, a tithe barn of the same period, and a holy well still survive, all well worth seeing. So too are the lofty, airy church with grotesque gargoyles and medieval statues adorning its west tower, and the old Market House on Long Street. In fact, there is much to see in this ancient village, from the remains of the Abbey, the Tithe Barn and 14th century houses to the **Cerne Abbas Giant** himself, and a stroll around the streets will set you up nicely for a spot of refreshment at **The Singing Kettle Tearoom**. If you should decide on a longer stay, bed and breakfast accommodation is also available. Owned and run by

Terry and Pat Dean, it's located in the main street at the centre of the village at the corner of Duck Street, overlooking what used to be a coaching stop. The white-painted building, which is Grade II listed is thought to date from about 1750, and little has been lost with the recent renovations and the addition of modern facilities. The ground floor is occupied by the tea room, delightfully traditional in style, which leads out to the secluded garden. (The garden can also be reached from Mill Lane, to the rear). The first floor is private accommodation, and above it are two twin-bedded garrets as guests's bedrooms which have en suite facilities.

The Singing Kettle, 7 Long Street
Cerne Abbas, Dorset DT2 7JF
Tel: 01300 341349

One room is blue, the other pink, and both are beautifully furnished in cottage style. Terry does the cooking for the tea room where seats for 36 are supplemented by seats in the split-level garden which has a lawn, shrubs, flowers and a water feature. Inside or out, there's an atmosphere of timeless charm which appeals to visitors of all ages. The menu, available all day, presents a choice of simple, wholesome snacks, from savouries on toast and jacket potatoes with various fillings to omelettes, broccoli and cheese bake, battered cod, and sandwiches plain or toasted. For the sweet tooth, locally baked cakes are listed on the blackboard: the Kettle's speciality is Dorset apple cake, served warm with clotted cream or ice cream. Cakes and home-made preserves are on sale to take away, along with mugs, tea towels and other little gifts.

Just to the north of the village is the famous **Cerne Abbas Giant** (National Trust), a colossal 180ft-high figure cut into the chalk hillside. He stands brandishing a club, naked and full-frontal, and there can be absolutely no doubt about his maleness. An ancient tradition asserts that any woman wishing to become pregnant should sit, or preferably sleep the night, on the Giant's huge erect penis. The age of this extraordinary carving

Cerne Abbas Giant

is hotly disputed but a consensus is emerging that it was originally created by ancient Britons as a fertility symbol and that the Giant's club was added by the Romans. (There are clear similarities between the Giant and the representation of Hercules on a Roman pavement of AD 191, preserved at Sherborne Castle). As with all hill-carvings, the best view is from a distance, in this case from a layby on the A352. A curious puzzle remains. The Giant's outlines in the chalk need a regular scouring to remove grass and weeds. Should this be neglected, he would soon fade into the hillside. In medieval centuries, such a non-essential task of conservation could only have been authorised by the locally all-powerful Abbots of Cerne. What possible reason did those Christian advocates of chastity have for carefully preserving such a powerful pagan image of virility?

A couple of miles south of the Giant, the village of **Godmanstone** is of interest to collectors of unusual pubs. Dorset can boast many cosy, intimate pubs, but the **Smith's Arms** at Godmanstone is in a class of its own, claiming to be the smallest inn in the country with a frontage just 11 feet wide. This appealing 14th century thatched building was originally the village smithy and, according to tradition, Charles II happened to stop here to have his horse shod. Feeling thirsty, the King asked for a glass of ale and was not best pleased to be told that as the blacksmith had no licence, no alcoholic drink was available. Invoking the royal prerogative, Charles granted a licence immediately and this tiny hostelry has been licensed ever since. Given the cramped interior, elbow-bending at the Smith's Arms can be a problem at busy times, but fortunately there is a spacious terrace outside.

MINTERNE MAGNA
Map 1 ref E7

8 miles N of Dorchester, on the A352

A couple of miles north of the Cerne Giant, Minterne Magna is notable for its parish church, crowded with memorials to Napiers, Churchills and Digbys, the families who once owned the great house here and most of the Minterne valley. The House itself, rebuilt in the Arts & Crafts style around 1900 is not open but its splendid **Minterne Gardens** are. The gardens are laid out in a horseshoe below the house and landscaped in the 18th century style of Capability Brown They contain an important collection of Himalayan rhododendrons and azaleas, along with Cherries, Maples and many other fine and rare trees. The gardens are open daily from late March to early November.

STOCKWOOD
Map 1 ref D7

12 miles N of Dorchester, off the A37

Ruth and Andrew House, both Dorset born and bred, put out the welcome mat at **Church Farm**, their lovely Georgian house. It stands just off the A37 (see signs for Stockwood, Chetnole and Leigh just north of Holywell) surrounded by woodland and streams on a working farm of 180 acres with a herd of dairy cows

Church Farm, Stockwood, Near Dorchester, Dorset DT2 ONG
Tel. 01935 83221

and a few beef animals. The house is thought to be Hardy's 'Little Hintock' in *The Woodlanders*. Modern overnight accommodation comprises two double rooms and a twin, all with en suite facilities, centrally heated and furnished to an impressively high standard. A full English breakfast can be enjoyed in the dining room overlooking the gardens and fields. Children are welcome, but no pets and no smoking. Why Church Farm? Because standing in the garden is a delightful surprise in the shape of one of England's smallest churches, measuring just 30 feet by 12. It is dedicated, uniquely, to Edwold, the younger brother of the Anglian king and martyr Edmund. The tiny church dates from the early 15th century, with some 17th century additions, and one of its most charming features is a pretty little bell turret with four columns supporting a stone dome. Services are no longer held, but the church remains consecrated and is looked after by the Churches Conservation Trust.

WINTERBORNE CAME
Map 2 ref E9

1 mile SE of Dorchester, on minor road off the A352

This tiny hamlet is a place of pilgrimage for admirers of Dorset's second most famous man of letters who is buried in the graveyard here. William Barnes was Rector of Winterborne Came from 1862 until his death in 1886 and in the old Rectory (not open to the public) he entertained such luminaries of English literature as Alfred Lord Tennyson and Hardy himself. Although Barnes was highly respected by fellow poets, his pastoral poems written in the distinctive dialect of the county never attracted a wide audience. At their best, though, they are marvellously evocative of the west Dorset countryside:

The zwellen downs, wi' chalky tracks
A-climmen up their zunny backs,
Do hide green meads an zedgy brooks...
An' white roads up athirt the hills.

Winterborne Came's unusual name, incidentally, derives from the fact that in medieval times the village was owned by the Abbey of Caen in France.

WEST KNIGHTON
MAP 2 REF E9
3 miles SE of Dorchester, on minor road off the A352

The New Inn at West Knighton is as pretty as a picture, a long low building with grey walls covered with ivy and colourful creepers. Some 300 years old, it served for many years as a coaching inn, and is now a lively village pub run by Clive and Sandie Woodrow. An enthusiastic, self-taught chef, Sandie is in charge of the kitchen and her versatile menu includes an intriguing range of chicken and beef dishes, as well as "bubble and squeak", (how often can one find this

The New Inn, West Knighton, Dorchester, Dorset DT2 8PE
Tel: 01305 852349

tasty dish nowadays?), baguettes, jacket potatoes, omelettes, and a special selection for children. Food is served either in the 30-seater restaurant, The Gallery, where a brick built fireplace dividing the dining area is a notable feature, or in the Long Bar. As well as pool and darts, The New Inn also has its own skittle alley, which also doubles as a function room. Outside, there's a pleasant beer garden, children's play area, and ample parking space. Clive and Sandie are both keen walkers and, very conveniently, the Jubilee Trail passes through the village. There are many other footpaths and bridleways nearby, including an attractive 5 mile circular route through Black Hill woods which starts almost at the Inn door.

WEYMOUTH   Map 1 ref E10
8 miles S of Dorchester, on the A354

No wonder the good citizens of Weymouth erected a statue of George III to mark the 50th year of his reign in 1810. The troubled king had brought great kudos and prosperity to their little seaside resort by coming here to bathe in the sea water. George had been advised that sea-bathing would help cure his "nervous disorder" so, between 1789 and 1805, he and his royal retinue spent a total of 14 holidays in Weymouth. Fashionable society naturally followed in his wake. The imposing statue is unusual in being painted. Not far away, at the head of King Street, his grand-daughter Victoria's own 50th year as Queen is commemorated by a colourful Jubilee Clock erected in 1887. Nearby, the picturesque **Harbour** is always busy - fishing boats, paddle steamers, pleasure boats, catamarans servicing the Channel Islands and St Malo in France, and if you're lucky you may even see a Tall Ship or two.

One of the town's premier tourist venues is **Brewers Quay**, an imaginatively redeveloped Victorian brewery offering an enormous diversity of visitor attractions amidst a labyrinth of paved courtyards and cobbled streets. There are no fewer than 22 different establishments within the complex, ranging from craft shops and restaurants through a fully automated Ten Pin bowling alley to the "Timewalk Journey" which promises visitors that they will "See, Hear and Smell over 600 years of Weymouth's spectacular history".

Tall Ship, Weymouth

From Brewers Quay, a path leads through Nothe Gardens to **Nothe Fort**, built between 1860 and 1872 as part of the defences of the new naval base being established on Portland. Ten huge guns face out to sea; two smaller ones are directed inland. The fort's 70 rooms on three levels now house the **Museum of Coastal Defence** which has many interesting displays illustrating past service life in the fort, history as seen from the Nothe headland, and the part played by the people of Weymouth in World War II. Nothe Fort is owned and operated by the Weymouth Civic Society which also takes care of **Tudor House**, just north of Brewers Quay. One of the town's few remaining Tudor buildings, the house originally stood on the edge of an inlet from the harbour and is thought to have been a merchant's house. It's now furnished in the style of an early-17th century middle class home and the guided tour gives some fascinating insights into life in those days.

With its distinctive circular "tower", the **Queen's Hotel** will be a familiar sight to anyone who has arrived at Weymouth railway station, just opposite. Originally built in Victorian times, the hotel was completely re-modelled in 1939 in the hope of benefitting from the expected surge of tourists using the grand new railway station which was completed in the same year. The local newspaper, the *Southern Times*, breathlessly revealed that the hotel's owners had spent "not far short of £7,000" on the rebuilding. The bar accommodation, the reporter noted, was "an immense improvement on the old", with a long saloon bar facing King Street, a public bar overlooking Park Street, and with "lavatory accommodation provided for *each* bar"! Sadly, all this investment was grievously blighted by the beginning of World War II just one month after The

Queen's Hotel, 7 King Street, Weymouth, Dorset DT4 7BJ
Tel: 01305 786326

Queen's re-opened. Some sixty years later, however, the hotel is thriving once again, under the capable management of Mark Downton who took over here in 1991. It's a lively pub with enthusiastic pool, darts, cribbage and quiz teams, satellite TV, and a separate secure area for children which is equipped with various video games and a miniature skittles alley.

The Queen's is a good place to eat, too, with food served weekdays from 11am until 10pm; Sundays from 12 noon until 10pm. The menu offers a wide choice of wholesome, traditional pub food, along with vegetarian meals, a children's menu, and a selection of bar meals which includes an all day breakfast, jacket potatoes, sandwiches and other light snacks. There's a patio for sunny days, a regular "Happy Hour" from 9.30-10.30pm each evening, and if you are looking for accommodation in the town, The Queen's has 3 guest bedrooms, all well-equipped with colour television and tea/coffee making facilities. A fairly recent addition to the hotel's amenities is its Bistro, which is open every evening from 5pm until 10pm, and offers a wide range of food, plus daily specials.

Only yards from the waters of Weymouth Bay, **Lodmoor Country Park** is another popular attraction. Access to most of the park is free and visitors can take advantage of the many sport and recreation areas, wander around the footpaths and nature reserve, or enjoy a picnic or barbecue. Set within the Park and surrounded by beautiful gardens complete with a bird aviary, **Model World** is a quite unique attraction which has been more than 25 years in the making. Back in 1972, Colin Sims conceived the idea of creating a model village and during the course of the next nine years constructed hundreds of finely detailed hand-made models from a variety of materials: stone, concrete, specially treated wood and plastics to withstand all kinds of weather. All built to a scale of 1:32 of life size, together the models create a complete world in miniature. Some of the models replicate actual buildings of special interest to the area, (such as Stonehenge, the cottage

Model World, Lodmoor Country Park
Preston Road, Weymouth, Dorset
Tel: 01305 781797

where Thomas Hardy was born and Weymouth Seafront as it looked in 1920), but most are imaginative constructions based on traditional buildings. Amongst them are the medieval "Castle Lod" and "Lodmoor Manor House", a Cathedral, water-mill, Oast House, and windmill. More contemporary exhibits include "Weymouth International Airport", and an "Inter-Galactic Explorer Class" space ship. Children are particularly fascinated by the models which can be activated at the touch of a button and the special sound effects: the Castletown Fire Brigade extinguishing a fire, a fairground in full swing, an 'O' gauge railway, and many more. This outstanding and affordable family attraction is open daily from 10am, from May to October.

Opened in 1988 by Princess Anne, and with two separate attractions under one roof, **Deep Sea Adventure** is a fascinating family attraction telling the story of underwater exploration and marine exploits from the 17th century through to the modern day. This entertaining and educational exhibition fills 3 floors of an imposing Victorian Grain Warehouse with a wealth of animated and interactive displays recounting compelling tales of shipwreck survival and search & rescue operations, a "Black Hole" in which you can experience what it is like to be a deep sea diver, and a unique display which tells the epic story of the Titanic in the words of the officers, crew and survivors, along with the original Titanic signals and one of the largest models of the doomed ship in the world. A major recent addition to Deep Sea Adventure is **Sharky's**, a huge, all-weather adventure play area for children of all ages, (with a height limit of 5ft), and with a separate area for toddlers. (During school term-time, Sharky's Shrimps toddler mornings also provide a perfect way to challenge, stimulate, and wear out your pre-schoolers). The complex also includes a Gift Shop, **Sharky's Galley** offering a delicious selection of meals for both parents and children, and a licensed bar. An outstanding venue for a family outing, Deep Sea Adventure is open daily from 9.30am, (closing at 8pm in the summer, 7pm in the winter). There are baby-changing facilities and good disabled access and toilets.

Deep Sea Adventure & Sharky's
9 Custom House Quay, Weymouth
Dorset DT4 8BG Tel: 01305 760690

**Tamarisk Hotel, 12 Stavordale Road, Weymouth, Dorset DT4 0AB
Tel: 01305 786514**

Centrally situated in a peaceful cul-de-sac with only a short walk to the sands, harbour and shops, the **Tamarisk Hotel** is a friendly, family run hotel which delights in the catering, comfort and well-being of its guests. Families are most welcome, with children at reduced rates if sharing their parents' room, and arriving guests are offered complimentary Afternoon Tea. This stylishly furnished and decorated hotel is owned and run by Hilary and Martin Brain whom many Dorset lovers of good food will remember from their years at the Lobster Pot Restaurant in Portland. They have brought the same concern for good food to the Tamarisk, offering regularly-changing menus with a varied choice of quality traditional English dishes. Special diets can also be catered for and the hotel has a licensed bar for residents, a comfortable lounge with colour television, and its own large private car park. All 14 bedrooms have colour television, tea/coffee making facilities, and most enjoy an en suite bath/shower and toilet. Hilary is an avid player of bridge and is happy to organise special weekend breaks for other enthusiastic amateurs. Weymouth's historic harbour, with its ferry services to Guernsey and St Malo, the splendid beach, and the town's many other attractions are all within walking distance, and a host of historic sites, charming villages and superb coastal scenery are just a short drive away.

With its colourful hanging-baskets, tubs and window-boxes, the exterior of **The New Inn** on Littlemoor Road seems like the Chelsea Flower Show in miniature. This stunning floral display earned Mark and Malindi Bailey first prize in the Inn Partnership Exterior Awards of 1998, a competition designed to encourage licensees to take as much pride in the exterior of their pubs as they do in the bar and lounge areas. The judges also consider the creativity, tidiness and overall appearance of the pub exterior. For Mark and Malindi, the award was all the more welcome since they had only taken over the inn less than a year earlier. The interior of The New Inn, if not so floral, is equally inviting with lots of old

The New Inn, Littlemoor Road, Weymouth, Dorset DT3 5NY
Tel: 01305 812418 Fax: 01305 813936

photographs, line drawings, and quasi-caricatures of locals and visitors displayed around the bar. Young and enthusiastic, Mark and Malindi have made this a lively pub with active darts and pool teams, regular quiz nights, and live entertainment on Fridays. It's also a family-friendly pub, with children allowed in the snug bar area and with their own play area in the large garden outside. Well-behaved dogs are also welcome. Essential elements of The New Inn's popularity are its well-tended cask ales and its range of good wholesome food. A speciality of the house is its "Sizzling Platters" - dishes such as Chicken Balti or Country Gammon served on special cast iron sizzle platters. There's a good choice of other dishes, too, with additional daily specials listed on the chalkboard. A pleasantly sociable feature of the fare on offer is the selection of "Starters to Share" and "Combi Platters". Four of you, for example, can share a tureen of home-made soup of the day; while for two people there are generously-stacked Combi Platters, one of which is a Medieval Platter bearing a whole roast chicken, BBQ ribs, sage & onion stuffing, and a jug of rich gravy!

When George Afedakis first saw the **Dughill Hotel** in 1990, he fell in love with this grand old Victorian building and promised his wife Paulette that one day they would own it. It took a little longer than he expected but his cherished dream was finally realised in 1998. George hails from Crete, (where he met and

Dughill Hotel, 53-55 Dorchester Road, Weymouth
Dorset DT4 7JT Tel: 01305 784282

married Paulette, who is English), and has introduced some traditional Greek dishes to the Dughill's menu, along with choices to suit all tastes. A separate taverna, which is also open to non-residents, is only the second of its kind in Dorset, and provides the setting for special Greek Weekends when the menus, wines, spirits and music all have a Greek flavour. George and Paulette also plan to organise holidays for visitors from Greece, as well as trips to Greece for British holiday-makers. The spacious hotel, with its 9ft high ceilings adorned with moulded architraves, manages to be both rather grand and very relaxing at the same time. There are 15 guest rooms, (9 double/family rooms, 6 twins), all with satellite television and refreshment trays, eight of them en suite. Families are welcome and outside there's a swimming pool, and a children's games garden where they can play in complete safety. Also within the main building are 3 self-catering apartments, each with its separate entrance. Sleeping 3, 6, or 7 people respectively, these apartments are all fully equipped with modern fixtures and fittings. This outstanding hotel is located just a 10-minute walk, or 2-minute drive, from the centre of Weymouth with its many attractions, and within easy reach of the lovely Dorset countryside, historic towns such as Dorchester and Lyme Regis, and the West Dorset Heritage Coast.

ISLE OF PORTLAND
MAP 1 REF E10

3 miles S of Weymouth, on the A354

Portland is not really an island at all, but a 4½ mile long peninsula, well known to devotees of shipping forecasts and even more famous for the stone from its quarries. Numerous buildings in London are constructed of Portland stone, amongst them St. Paul's Cathedral and Buckingham Palace, and the stone was also favoured by sculptors such as Henry Moore. There are good cliff-top walks with grand views of **Chesil Beach**, a vast bank of pebbles worn smooth by the sea which stretches for some 10 miles to Abbotsbury. Inexplicably, the pebbles are graded in size from west to east. Fishermen reckon they can judge whereabouts on the beach they are landing by the size of the pebbles. In the west they are as small as peas; at Portland they have grown to the size of cooking apples! The area of water trapped behind the beach is known as **The Fleet**.

CHICKERELL
MAP 1 REF D10

3 miles W of Weymouth, on the B3157

A warm stone building dating back over 250 years, the **Turks Head Hotel** has long held a prominent position in the village of Chickerell - first as a private dwelling, then as the village bakery and, during World War II, housing a fire engine in its outbuildings. This charming old building has now been sympathetically converted into a hotel and restaurant, whilst still retaining a wealth of original features and old world character, complementing its warm and friendly atmosphere. The village stands less than a mile from the Fleet and Chesil Beach, and its long association with the sea inspired the hotel's name: the "Turks Head" knot was used by local fishermen, as depicted on the sign-board in the forecourt. This outstanding hotel has a renowned restaurant offering extensive menus

Turks Head Hotel, 8 East Street, Chickerell, Weymouth, Dorset DT3 4DS
Tel: 01305 783093 Fax: 01305 786668
e-mail: bookings@turksheadhotel.demon.co.uk

which include a wonderful choice of locally caught fish dishes, along with meat, poultry and vegetarian options. An excellent wine list, with some 50 varieties to choose from, offers a wide range of European and New World wines, some of them available by the glass, half-bottle, or litre. The Turks Head also offers first class accommodation in spacious rooms with large en suite bathrooms. Each room has its own character, but all provide everything expected by the discerning guest, including colour television & video, tea/coffee-making facilities, trouser press and hairdrier. Whether you are looking for superb food and drink, or quality accommodation, the Turks Head is a Hidden Place you should certainly seek out.

OSMINGTON MILLS
Map 2 ref E9

5 miles NE of Weymouth, on minor road off the A353

The memory of Osmington Mills' notorious history in trading contraband liquor lingers in the name of **The Smugglers Inn**. Unlike many similarly-named hostelries, this one really was a regular haunt for smugglers. Dating back to the 13th century, this former fisherman's cottage enjoyed a secluded position and the nearby beach provided safe landing. The inn's landlord in the early 1800s was Emmanuel Carless who, together with his French partner, Pierre Latour or 'French Peter', ran a thriving business importing thousands of gallons of brandy each year. Unfortunately, the liquor was so inferior locals refused to drink it and the spirit had to be carried inland on stage coaches, disguised as luggage, to be distilled again. No such problems with the alcoholic beverages served at The Smugglers nowadays, or with the excellent choice of freshly-prepared food. Specialities of the house include fresh Weymouth Bay lobster but David and Jacqui Southward's enticing à la carte menu also offers a wide selection of meat, poul-

The Smugglers Inn, Osmington Mills, Weymouth, Dorset DT3 6HF
Tel: 01305 833125

try and vegetarian dishes along with a choice of the day's sweets listed on a blackboard. Or you can choose from an extensive bar menu - anything from a large filled bap to a substantial 8oz steak. Children under 10 have their own special choices. Outside, there's a large beer garden with splendid views across Weymouth Bay to the town and Portland Bill, a magnificent vista immortalised by John Constable in his painting, *Weymouth Bay*, now on display in the National Gallery.

There are several "White Horses" carved into hillsides around the country, but the **White Horse** at Osmington, apart from being one of the largest, (354ft high and 279ft wide), is the only one which also has a rider. Wearing a tall cocked hat and carrying a whip, the horseman represents George III. The king was a frequent visitor to nearby Weymouth and his royal patronage naturally attracted many free-spending courtiers to the town. The town fathers of Weymouth decided to express their appreciation by paying the local militia to scrape a hillside and form an unrecognisable, if undoubtedly loyal, tribute to His Majesty. Like all the other White Horses in England, it looks much better when seen from a few miles away; close up, it is meaningless.

9 In and Around Lyme Regis

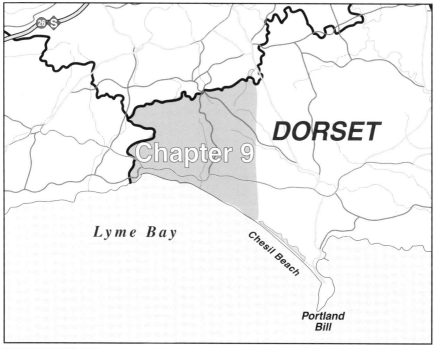

DORSET

Chapter 9

Lyme Bay

Chesil Beach

Portland
Bill

© MAPS IN MINUTES ™ (1998)

LYME REGIS

Known as "The Pearl of Dorset", this captivating little town enjoys a setting unrivalled in the county, an area of outstanding natural beauty where the rolling countryside of Dorset plunges to the sea. The town itself is a maze of narrow streets with many charming Georgian and Regency houses, and the picturesque harbour will be familiar to anyone who has seen the film *The French Lieutenant's Woman*, based on the novel by Lyme resident, John Fowles. The scene of a lone woman standing on the wave-lashed Cobb has become one of the cinema's most enduring images.

The Cobb, which protects the harbour and the sandy beach with its clear bathing water from south-westerly storms, was first recorded in 1294 but the town itself goes back at least another 500 years to Saxon times when there was a salt works here. A charter granted by Edward I allowed Lyme to add "Regis" to its name but during the Civil War the town was staunchly anti-royalist, routing the forces of Prince Maurice and killing more than 2000 of them. Some 40 years later, James, Duke of Monmouth, chose Lyme as his landing place to start the ill-fated rebellion that would end with ferocious reprisals being meted out to the insurgents by Judge Jeffreys. Happier days arrived in the 18th century when Lyme became a fashionable resort, famed for its fresh, clean air. Jane Austen and her family visited in 1803 and part of her novel *Persuasion* is set in the town.

A few years later, a 12-year-old girl called Mary Anning was wandering along the shore when she noticed bones protruding from the cliffs. She had discovered the first ichthyosaur to be found in England. Later, as one of the first professional fossil collectors, she also unearthed locally a plesiosaur and a pterodactyl. The 6-mile stretch of coastline on either side of Lyme is world famous for its fossils and some fine specimens of local discoveries can be seen at the **Philpot Museum** in Bridge Street and at **Dinosaurland** in Coombe Street which also runs guided 'fossil walks' along the beach.

Just around the corner from Dinosaurland, in Mill Lane, you'll find one of the town's most interesting buildings. It was in January 1991 that a group of Lyme Regis residents got together in an effort to save the old **Town Mill** from destruction. There has been a mill on the River Lym in the centre of the town for many centuries, but most of the present buildings date back to the mid-17th century when the mill was rebuilt after being burned down during the Civil War siege of Lyme in 1644. Today, the restored Town Mill is one of Lyme's major attractions, housing two Art Galleries which stage a wide range of exhibitions, concerts, poetry readings and other live performances. There is also a stable building which houses craft workshops.

Under the eaves of the old Bakehouse, **Attic Gallery** is home to Hilary Highet's ever-changing collection of wonderful hand-framed knitwear and much more. Here you'll find a lovely shop full of light, colour and texture offering something really different from the High Street. Hand-painted silk scarves, ties, clothing and jewellery are for sale or can just be admired. You can also commission a piece of knitwear in the colour and size of your choice. Periodic exhibitions featuring selected textile and jewellery designers are also held here. In the corner of the Gallery you can see work in progress on the knitting machine.

On the way down, you will smell the delicious Italian rasted coffee and dishes being prepared in Monique Pasche's outstanding café-brasserie, **Le Moulin**. Swiss-born, Monique opened her delightful restaurant in 1997 and the excellent cuisine on offer, mostly with a distinctive Mediterranean flavour, has earned Le Moulin an enviable reputation – and an award. The dishes change frequently, according to seasonal availability of local produce (fish, game and organic fare) but among the favourites are home-made houmous, Tagen Samak (Egyptian style baked cod and spicy tomato); and wonderful desserts such as Melon & Strawberry crumble or rich chocolate roulade. You can also enjoy coffee, lunch or tea in the

Le Moulin: Tel: 01297 445757 The Attic Gallery: Tel: 01297 442122.
Both located at The Town Mill, Mill Lane, off Coombe Street
Lyme Regis, Dorset DT7 3PU.

secluded Miller's Garden, which is being landscaped to a design shown on a plan dated 1820, with plants of a type grown around that time. No-one who comes to Lyme Regis should leave without paying at least one visit to these exceptionally well-restored buildings set in such unique surroundings. The Town Mill site is open to the public most days between Easter and Christmas, from 10am to 5pm and admission is free. The Attic Gallery and Le Moulin are both open from April to December but closed on Mondays, except for Bank Holidays. Please phone for enquiries or bookings.

Visitors to the Town Mill who enjoy walking will find a delightful riverside walk leading either to the inland village of Uplyme or back through the town to the harbour. The **South West Coast Path** also passes through Lyme: if you follow it eastwards for about 5 miles it will bring you to **Golden Cap**, the highest point on the south coast with spectacular views from every vantage point. Or you can take a pleasant stroll along **Marine Parade**, a traffic free promenade stretching for about a mile from The Cobb.

Also on Marine Parade and set virtually at the water's edge, **The Cobb Arms** is a favourite with local boatmen, fishermen and lifeboat personnel - a genuine community pub and meeting centre with an atmosphere that appeals to locals and visitors alike. It's also very much a family-run pub with a whole extended family involved. Firstly, there are the licensees, Linda and John McClements. Then there's Linda's sister and brother-in-law, Colin, who serve behind the bar.

**The Cobb Arms, Marine Parade, Lyme Regis, Dorset DT7 3JF
Tel: 01297 443242**

Linda's son, Simon, works in the kitchen, and her daughter, Ashleigh, who is only 10 years old, is presumably waiting in the wings. All this family involvement adds to the warm and welcoming atmosphere in this 100 year-old pub, along with its good selection of pub games, (including table skittles), excellent ales, and outstanding food. The speciality of the house is fresh crab served in every conceivable variety, but the menu also offers a wide choice of meat, fish, and poultry dishes, along with vegan and vegetarian options, and an unusually extensive children's menu. The Cobb Arms also has 3 letting rooms, all en suite, and all fully equipped with amenities such as television and a refreshment tray. It would be difficult to find a more convenient base from which to explore this appealing little town, and the many nearby attractions of west Dorset and east Devon.

For its size, Lyme Regis has an extraordinary range of activities on offer, too many to list here although one must mention the famous week-long Regatta and Carnival held in August. Bands play on the Marine Parade, there are displays by Morris Men and folk dancers, and an annual Town Criers Open Championship. Lyme has maintained a Town Crier for over a thousand years without a break and the current incumbent in his colourful 18th century costume can be seen and heard throughout the town during the summer months.

Enjoying a prime location in this ancient and unspoilt town, **The New Haven Hotel** offers visitors excellent bed and breakfast accommodation. Langmoor and Lister Gardens are just around the corner, Marine Parade and the beach

**The New Haven Hotel, 1 Pound Street,
Lyme Regis, Dorset DT7 3HZ
Tel/Fax: 01297 442499
E-mail: pettitnewhaven@tesco.net**

about 300 yards away, the Harbour and famous Cobb just a little further. Pamela Petitt and Michael have been welcoming guests to their spacious home, parts of which date back to the 17th century, for some 11 years now. Pamela's enthusiasms are handicrafts and the cinema and, like Michael, a former police Inspector, is also an avid motor-cyclist. Both love meeting people and make sure their visitors are extremely well looked after. Especially at breakfast time. The menu offers more than half a dozen choices of main dish, including a hearty traditional English breakfast, and whole kippers or smoked mackerel, (when available). They will also happily cater for vegans, vegetarians and coeliacs. In addition, you'll find a choice of 5 different teas, many herbal teas, fresh ground coffee, or hot chocolate, and, a particularly tasty item, home-made marmalade and jams to go with your white or wholemeal toast. This outstanding establishment also welcomes children and dogs and, since the Petitts know the town and the surrounding area well, they can guide you to the many attractions in west Dorset and east Devon that lie within easy reach.

Without getting your feet wet, you can't get much closer to the sea at Lyme Regis than at **Jane's Café** which is right beside the beach with fantastic panoramic views looking along the coast. Jane Austen, in whose honour the café is named, must have known this spot well: the garden in which she penned many of her memorable lines is just opposite. Jane's Café specialises in wholesome traditional snacks and main meals: fish & chips, chicken, scampi, burgers, pasties, pies, filled rolls and sandwiches, accompanied if you wish by a glass of white wine or chilled lager. Around tea-time, make your way here for a generous Cream Tea, or Apple Pie with clotted cream or ice cream, or just a simple toasted

Jane's Café, 29 Marine Parade, Lyme Regis, Dorset DT7 3JF
Tel: 01297 442331

tea cake. For those who prefer to take their refreshment alfresco on the beach, Jane's Café also has a takeaway outlet, set apart from the main dining area, where you can choose from the same menu.

Just 200 yards from the town's main street, **Ocean View** is a substantial Edwardian building where Fran and Mike Wantling offer excellent bed and breakfast accommodation. Ocean View, and its next door twin, were erected in 1904 by a local builder for his two daughters. Shortly after they moved in, the two girls quarrelled and despite being next-door neighbours never spoke to each other again. Happily, there's a much more warm and friendly atmosphere at Ocean View these days. The house has been recently refurbished to a homely and comfortable standard, and the 3 letting rooms, (2 double, 1 twin, each one colour-co-ordinated and enjoying a sea view), are all en suite, with central heating, colour TV, and refreshment tray. A full English breakfast is served between 8.30am and 9.30am in a relaxed atmosphere, with options avail-

Ocean View, Silver Street, Lyme Regis,
Dorset DT7 3HR Tel: 01297 442567

able for vegans and vegetarians. Children over 10 years "with well-behaved parents!" are welcome, and so are dogs (by arrangement), and Ocean View has its own off-road parking. Please note that the house is non-smoking.

Overlooking Lyme Bay and the picturesque coastal town of Lyme Regis, **The Victoria Hotel** was built in 1906 to provide accommodation for travellers and seaside visitors using the new rail link. The grand old building fell on hard times in the early 1990s, but in the summer of 1996 it was purchased by the Moss family who set in motion a major refurbishment programme, providing the Victoria with en suite bathrooms, a stylish new restaurant, and an open plan bar/dining area. The hotel re-opened in December 1996 and rapidly became

**The Victoria Hotel, Uplyme Road, Lyme Regis, Dorset DT7 3LP
Tel: 01297 444801 email: vichotel@globalnet.co.uk**

one of the most popular eateries in Lyme Regis. There's an exciting choice of bar snacks, catering for both traditional and more adventurous tastes and, in the non-smoking restaurant, an à la carte menu which offers a wide range of fish and seafood, game and prime char-grilled steaks, with an unrivalled selection of home-made desserts to complete your meal. The menu changes daily but to give you an idea of the kind of fare on offer, sample dishes include Fillets of John Dory with king prawns, spring onions and ginger, and Chargrilled ribeye steak with a soft green peppercorn and brandy sauce. Vegetarian dishes are individually prepared from fresh seasonal produce, but please do book these in advance. (Given the restaurant's popularity, it's a good idea in any case to make a reservation). The hotel's quality wine list contains some forty wines from around the world, selected to suit all tastes and pockets. If you are planning to stay in the area, The Victoria has 6 guest rooms, (4 doubles and 2 twins, all en suite with either a bath or a shower). Those at the front of the building enjoy wonderful views over Lyme Bay and the surrounding countryside. Downstairs, there's a residents' lounge with comfortable couches and a superb view over an unspoiled, wooded valley and meadows. The Victoria Hotel may have lost its way in the 1980s, but now in the safe hands of the Moss family it is certainly back on track.

CHARMOUTH   MAP 1 REF B8
2 miles NE of Lyme Regis, on minor road off the A35

What better recommendation could you give the seaside village of Charmouth than the fact that it was Jane Austen's favourite resort? "Sweet and retired" she called it. To quote Arthur Mee, "She loved the splendid sweep of country all round it, the downs, the valleys, the hills like Golden Cap, and the pageantry of the walk to Lyme Regis". Charmouth remains an attractive little place with a wide main street and a quiet stretch of sandy beach that gradually merges into shingle.

A rather romantic story is attached to the unusual naming of **Rainbow Connection**, Ann and Alan Smith's ceramic crafts and gift shop in The Street. "Rainbow Connection" is the name of the waltz that was being played when they first met: they had it played again at their wedding. So the title of that tune became a natural choice when they were looking for a meaningful name for their shop selling an intriguing collection of ceramic creations. The inspiration for this collection started with the medieval world of dragons and wizards, and then grew to include frogs and elephants and other animals. The final products range from dramatically-fashioned pieces, such as an

Rainbow Connection, "Devonedge", The Street, Charmouth, Dorset DT6 6PZ Tel: 01297 560165

18-inch tall flying dragon, to dainty little fridge magnets - all of them hand-painted with the same meticulous care. The creation of such imaginative work looks like a difficult art to master, but if you attend one of Ann and Alan's regular workshops, you might well find that you too have a talent for it. Even if you haven't, you will almost certainly want to take home one of the unique and distinctive pieces on display at Rainbow Connection.

WHITCHURCH CANONICORUM   Map 1 ref B8
6 miles NW of Bridport, on minor road off the A35

Clinging to the steep hillside above the valley of the River Char, Whitchurch Canonicorum is notable for its enchanting setting and for its **Church of St Candida and Holy Cross**. This noble building with its Norman arches and an imposing tower built around 1400 is remarkable for being one of only two churches in England still possessing a shrine to a Saint. (The other is that of Edward the Confessor in Westminster Abbey). St Candida was a Saxon woman named Wite - the Anglo-Saxon word for White, which in Latin is Candida. She lived as a hermit but was murdered by a Viking raiding party in AD 831. During the Middle Ages a major cult grew up around her memory. A large shrine was built of golden Purbeck stone, its lower level pierced by 3 large ovals into which the sick and maimed thrust their limbs, their head or even their whole body, in the hope of being cured. The cult of St Wite thrived until the Reformation when all such "monuments of feigned miracles" were swept away. That might have been the end of the story of St Wite but during the winter of 1899-1900 the foundations of the church settled and cracked open a 13th century tomb chest. Inside was a lead casket with a Latin inscription stating that "Here rest the relics of St Wite" and inside the casket the bones of a small woman about 40 years old. The shrine still attracts pilgrims today, the donations they leave in the openings beneath the tomb now being devoted to causes which aid health and healing.

Another major visitor attraction in Whitchurch Canonicorum is the **Five Bells Inn**. A plaque above its front door bears the date 1905, but there has been a hostelry on this site for some 400 years. Lawrence and Pat Hawkins arrived here in 1997 and have made this typical country pub, tucked away in the south Dorset hills, a popular venue for both locals and visitors. Many are attracted by the friendly and welcoming atmosphere; many others come because they know about Pat's cooking: aware that all the daily specials, set meals and sweets are home-made. Pat's menu includes a good choice of daily specials, wholesome salads, ploughmans lunches, basket meals, a 5-item breakfast, generously-filled sandwiches, jacket potatoes likewise, and vegetarian options. There's also a special menu for children, or they can choose half-price children's portions from the grown-ups' menu. In the evening, the Five Bells offers substantial meals such as 8oz steaks or a 2-course Chef's special, and if you are anywhere near Whitchurch Canonicorum around Sunday lunchtime, you should certainly seek

Five Bells Inn, Whitchurch Canonicorum, nr Bridport, Dorset DT6 6PH
Tel: 01297 489262

out this Hidden Place for its extraordinary value-for-money Sunday roast. Should you happen to be travelling through Dorset with a caravan in tow, you will find the Five Bells Inn particularly attractive: it offers a 7-acre site where you can park your caravan and then stroll across to the inn for a pint or two and a meal.

BRIDPORT   Map 1 ref C8

9 miles E of Lyme Regis, on the A35

With its broad streets, (inherited from the days when they were used for making ropes), Bridport is an appealing little town surrounded by green hills and with a goodly number of 17th and 18th century buildings. Most notable amongst these are the medieval **Prior's House**, the stately Georgian **Town Hall**, and the pleasing collection of 17th century houses in the street running south from the Town Hall. If you visit the town on a Wednesday or Saturday you'll find its three main streets chock-a-block with dozens of stalls participating in the regular **Street Market**. The Town Council actively encourages local people who produce goods at home and not as part of their regular livelihood to join in. So there's an extraordinary range of artefacts on offer, anything from silk flowers to socks, fossils to fishing tackle. Another popular attraction is **Palmers Brewery** in West Bay Road. Established in 1794, part of the brewery is still thatched.During the season, visitors are welcomed on Tuesdays and Wednesdays for a tour of the historic brewery, the charge for which includes a commemorative Certificate and also a glass or two of beer. (More details on 01308 427500). **Bridport Mu-**

seum is good on local history and family records and also has an interesting collection of dolls. You can also learn about two distinguished visitors to the town. One was Joan of Navarre who landed at Bridport in 1403 on her way to marry Henry IV; the other, Charles II who arrived in the town after his defeat at the Battle of Worcester. He was fleeing to France, pretending to be the groom in a runaway marriage. As he attended to his horses in the yard of an inn, an ostler approached him saying "Surely I know you, friend?" The quick-thinking king-to-be asked where the ostler had been working before. When he replied "In Exeter", Charles responded "Aye, that is where we must have met", excused himself and made a speedy departure from the town. If the ostler's memory for faces had been better, he could have claimed the £1000 bounty for Charles' capture and subsequent English history would have followed a very different course.

Conveniently located near the town's main car and coach park, the **Cafe Royale** provides an excellent service, staying open 7 days a week, all year round. It's been run since 1995 by Shirley Bartlett, a Dorchester-born young lady with indefatigable energy and a wealth of local knowledge. Her menu specialises in good, traditional English food, offering such old favourites as liver & bacon, Shepherd's Pie, and fish & chips. There's also an All Day Breakfast, snacks and sandwiches, vegetarian options, and children's portions are available, too. A short walk from the cafe brings you to the centre of this attractive town with its broad main streets - a legacy of the days when Bridport was a major centre for rope-making, providing the Royal Navy with its huge cables and hawsers. Rope-walks were set up in the road so that the hemp could be twisted to make the finished product. The local museum has a large display on this traditional industry and also explains the origin of the "Bridport daggers", a dark reference to the hangman's ropes which were also made here.

Cafe Royale, Bridport Bus Station, Tannery Road, Bridport
Dorset DT6 1QX Tel: 01308 422012

WEST BAY   MAP 1 REF C9
1 mile S of Bridport, on minor road off the A35

When Bridport's own harbour silted up in the early 1700s, the townspeople
built a new one at the mouth of the River Brit and called it West Bay. During the
19th century, hundreds of ships docked here every year, and West Bay had its
own shipbuilding industry until 1879. The little town never became a fashionable resort but the beach, backed by 100ft high sandstone cliffs, is much enjoyed
by holiday-makers, and there's still a stall at the little harbour where you can
treat yourself to a tub of cockles.

Occupying a lovely position right next to the beach, with no road to cross,
the **Bridport Arms Hotel** is ideal for families with young children. Known as
the "Inn on the Beach", this is an historic old thatched building which in parts
dates back as far as the 1500s. Its picturesque qualities have earned it two rôles
in the BBC-TV series "Harbour Lights" starring Nick Berry and Tina Hobky. The

Bridport Arms Hotel, West Bay, Bridport, Dorset DT6 4EN
Tel: 01308 422994

inn appears as both "The Piers Hotel" and the "Bridehaven" public house. Do
watch out for it! The hotel's resident proprietors, Carla and John Jacobs, have
been here since 1984 and offer all their guests a warm welcome to their attractive old hostelry. There are two characterful bars offering real ale and a wide
range of meals which are also available in the comfortable restaurant, lunchtimes and evenings. The menu offers some particularly tasty dishes using locally
caught fish, (including a delicious home-made Fish Pie), but also a good choice

of meat and vegetarian meals, jacket potatoes, ploughman's, and sandwiches, along with a special menu for children. If you are planning to stay in the area, the Bridport Arms has 13 bedrooms, all comfortably furnished and centrally heated, with most offering en suite facilities. Rooms in the cottage annexe are also available at reduced prices. The hotel is open all year, with special out of season breaks available.

Just before you reach the main harbour at West Bay, turn left, and there on your left is the **Seagulls Licensed Restaurant**, an excellent eating-place which has been owned and run by Douglas and Christina Fairlie since 1994. Seagulls stands on its own as a restaurant: its sole purpose is to provide good, wholesome food based on fresh local produce, and offered at attractive prices. The restaurant is located virtually on the sea front - it's just a short step to the wa-

Seagulls Licensed Restaurant, 1/3 Station Road, West Bay Bridport, Dorset DT6 4EW Tel: 01308 425099

ter's edge, so it's appropriate that fish is one of the specialities of the house. Plaice, Cod, Scampi, Haddock and Tiger Prawn dishes are always on the menu, and the fresh fish of the day is marked up on the blackboards. But there's also a good choice of meat, poultry, and vegetarian options: an authentic mild Chicken Curry, for example, made with breast meat only and enhanced with traditional spices; a Steak & Ale Pie with a puff pastry lid; or tomato pasta parcels, filled with cheese and served in a creamy tomato sauce topped with mozzarella; and many other enticing home-made specials are always available. At lunchtimes, there's a tasty "Light Bite" menu which includes such tempting bonne-bouches as garlic mushrooms cooked in double cream and served on toast; strips of haddock coated in a herby crumb, deep fried, and served with a dish of mixed salad and French bread; or jacket potatoes, with a choice of fillings and a salad which comes with a very special home-made dressing. And on Sundays there's a traditional roast. This outstanding restaurant is open throughout the year.

ASKERSWELL   MAP 1 REF C8
4 miles E of Bridport, off the A35

Selecting a holiday cottage can be fraught with difficulties, but if you book a holiday through **Court Farm Cottages** you can do so with confidence. The unspoilt and picturesque village of Askerswell stands at the head of the Asker valley, beneath the Iron Age hill fort of Eggardon Hill, and for more than 300 years Court House has stood alongside the village's parish church. It's a peaceful place where visitors can enjoy attractive accommodation created by the conversion of a Grade II listed stone-built barn into luxury cottages. Whilst retaining the atmosphere and many original features of the old building, the accommodation offers a high standard of comfort, including a fully-fitted kitchen, comfortable lounge and dining areas, a modern bathroom and spacious bedrooms. Additional attractions include the amenity of a large, lawned garden with picnic tables and barbecue, a games room, launderette with free use of a washing machine, tumble drier and ironing facilities, and a payphone. Cots and high-chairs are available, if required, and babysitting can also be arranged. The village is ideally situated just 3 miles from the coast, and is within easy

**Court Farm Cottages, Askerswell, Dorchester,
Dorset DT2 9EJ Tel: 01308 485668**

reach of Weymouth and Lyme Regis (both about 15 miles away), and many historic houses and places of interest. The rolling Dorset hills and coastal path are ideal for walking and touring, and open up outstanding views of the surrounding countryside.

BEAMINSTER

MAP 1 REF C8

6 miles N of Bridport, on the A3066

In Hardy's novel, when Tess Durbeyville arrives in Beaminster, ("Emminster" in the novel), she finds a delightful little market town. Outwardly, nothing much

has changed: the 17th century almshouse, the majestic church tower in gold-tinted Hamstone, and the charming **Market Square** with its stone roofed market cross are all much the same as they were then. What have disappeared are the many small industries that thrived in those days - rope and sailcloth, embroidered buttons, shoes, wrought ironwork and clockmaking were just some of the artefacts produced here.

Beaminster Market Cross

As you drive into Beaminster, you will find the 16th century **Pickwick's Inn** dominating the town square. Pickwick's has a very long and interesting history. It was originally built in the 1400s, and first became a public house in the 1500s, known as The Kings Arms. Although Beaminster suffered three major fires in the 17th and 18th centuries, the building remained mercifully untouched. In later years, it served successively as an antique shop and a restaurant, then returned full circle to its original function as a pub in 1984. This free house is a charming place, and under Simon and Ann Thorne, it continues to offer excellent hospitality to anyone who cares to drop in. As well as stocking a wide range of beers, real ales, wines and spirits, Pickwick's Inn is renowned for the delicious home-cooked dishes that are available at both lunchtimes and evenings throughout the week. The menu changes regularly and makes use of high quality fresh ingredients in an interesting and imaginative manner. The inn offers a wonderful selection of puddings, but Simon and Ann are always ready to take suggestions for inclusion in the next menu. Reasonably priced, it is easy to see why Pickwick's Inn is so popular with locals and visitors alike. The Inn offers cosy and friendly

Pickwick's Inn, The Square, Beaminster, Dorset DT8 3AS
Tel: 01308 862094

bed and breakfast accommodation in the heart of this historic town, and Simon and Ann are also happy to make special arrangements for a party, reception, or other event held in their intimate restaurant.

Visitors to Beaminster's imposing 15th century church tend to be overwhelmed by the grandiose, over-lifesize sculptures of the Strode family who lived at Parnham House, a gem of Tudor architecture about a mile south of the town. The splendidly restored manor house has extensive gardens where visitors can play croquet and picnic. There's also a tea room and craft shop. Tel: 01308 862204

About as far west as you can get in Dorset, **Forde Abbey** enjoys a lovely setting beside the River Axe. Founded as a Cistercian monastery more than 800 years ago, it is now the home of the Roper family. The Abbey church has gone but the monks of those days would still recognise the chapter house, dormitories, kitchen and refectories. The Upper Refectory is particularly striking with its fine timbered roof and carved panelling. The gardens, extending to 30 acres with origins in the early 1700s, are landscaped around this enchanting house - a fitting place to bring our tour of the county to an end.

TOURIST INFORMATION CENTRES

Centres in **bold** are open all the year around.

Aldershot
Military Museum, Queen's Avenue, Aldershot, Hampshire GU11 2LG
Tel: 01252 20968

Alton
7 Cross & Pillory Lane, Alton, Hampshire GU34 1HL
Tel: 01420 88448 Fax: 01420 543916

Andover
Town Mill House, Bridge Street, Andover, Hampshire SP10 1BL
Tel: 01264 324320

Basingstoke
Willis Museum, Old Town Hall, Market Place, Basingstoke
Hampshire RG21 7QD Tel: 01256 817618 Fax: 01256 356231

Blandford Forum
West Street, Blandford Forum, Dorset DT11 7AW
Tel: 01258 454770

Bournemouth
Westover Road, Bournemouth, Dorset BH1 2BU
Tel: 01202 451700

Bridport
32 South Street, Bridport, Dorset DT6 3NQ
Tel: 01308 424901 Fax: 01308 421060

Christchurch
23 High Street, Christchurch, Dorset BH23 1AB
Tel: 01202 471780

Cowes
Fountain Quay, Cowes, Isle of Wight PO31 3AR
Tel: 01983 291914

Dorchester
11 Antelope Walk, Dorchester, Dorset DT1 1BE
Tel: 01305 267992 Fax: 01305 266079

Eastleigh
The Point, Town Hall Centre, Leigh Road, Eastleigh
Hampshire SO50 9DE Tel: 01703 641261

Southampton International Airport, Wide Lane, Eastleigh
Hampshire SO18 2NL Tel: 01703 627235

Fareham
Westbury Manor Museum, West Street, Fareham PO16 0JJ
Tel: 01329 221342 Fax: 01329 282959

Fleet
Harlington Centre, Harlington Way, Fleet, Hampshire GU13 8BY
Tel: 01252 811151 Fax: 01252 812191

Fordingbridge
Visitor Information Centre, Salisbury Street, Fordingbridge
Hampshire SP6 1AB Tel: 01425 652222

Gosport
1 High Street, Gosport, Hampshire PO12 1BX
Tel: 01705 522944 Fax: 01705 511687

Havant
1 Park Road South, Havant, Hampshire, PO9 1HA
Tel/Fax: 01705 480024

Hayling Island
Central Beachlands, Seafront, Hayling Island, Hampshire PO11 0AG
Tel: 01705 467111 Fax: 01705 463297

Lyme Regis
Guildhall Cottage, Church Street, Lyme Regis, Dorset DT7 3BS
Tel: 01297 442138 Fax: 01297 443773

Lymington
St Barb Museum & Visitor Centre, New Street, Lymington
Hampshire SO41 9BH Tel: 01590 672422

Lyndhurst and New Forest
New Forest Museum & Visitor Centre, Main Car Park, Lyndhurst
Hampshire SO43 7NY Tel: 01703 284404

Newport
South Street, Newport, Isle of Wight PO30 1JU
Tel: 01983 525450

Petersfield
County Library, The Square, Petersfield, Hampshire GU32 3HH
Tel: 01730 268829 Fax: 01730 266679

Poole
Tourism Centre, The Quay, Poole, Dorset BH15 1HE
Tel: 01202 253253 Fax: 01202 684531

Portsmouth
The Hard, Portsmouth, Hampshire PO1 3QJ
Tel: 01705 826722

102 Commercial Road, Portsmouth, Hampshire PO1 1EJ
Tel: 01705 838382

Clarence Esplanade, Southsea, Portsmouth, Hampshire PO5 3ST
Tel: 01705 832464

Ringwood
The Furlong, Ringwood, Hampshire BH24 1AZ
Tel: 01425 470896

Romsey
1 Latimer Street, Romsey, Hampshire, SO51 8DF
Tel: 01794 512987

Rownhams
Rownhams Service Area, (M27 Westbound), Rownhams
Hampshire SO1 8AW Tel: 01703 730345

Ryde
Western Esplanade, Ryde, Isle of Wight PO33 2LW
Tel: 01983 562905

Sandown
8 High Street, Sandown, Isle of Wight PO36 0DG
Tel: 01983 403886

Shaftesbury
8 Bell Street, Shaftesbury, Dorset SP7 8AE
Tel: 01747 853514

Shanklin
67 High Street, Shanklin, Isle of Wight PO37 6JJ
tEL: 01983 862942

Sherborne
3 Tilton Court, Digby Road, Sherborne, Dorset DT9 3NL
Tel: 01935 815341 Fax: 01935 817210

Southampton
Leisure & Visitor Centre, Civic Centre Road, Southampton
Hampshire SO14 7LP Tel: 01703 221106 Fax: 01703 832082

Swanage
The White House, Shore Road, Swanage, Dorset BH19 1LB
Tel: 01929 422885 Fax: 01929 423423

Ventnor
34 High Street, Ventnor, Isle of Wight PO38 1RZ
Tel: 01983 853625

Wareham
Trinity Church, South Street, Wareham, Dorset BH20 4LU
Tel: 01929 552740 Fax: 01929 554491

Weymouth
King's Statue, The Esplanade, Weymouth, Dorset DT4 7AN
Tel: 01305 785747 Fax: 01305 788092

Wimborne Minster
29 High Street, Wimborne Minster, Dorset BH21 1HR
Tel: 01305 765221 Fax: 01305 765223

Winchester
Guildhall, The Broadway, Winchester, Hampshire SO23 9LJ
Tel: 01962 840500 Fax: 01962 850348

Yarmouth
The Quay, Yarmouth, Isle of Wight PO41 4PQ
Tel: 01983 760015

INDEX OF TOWNS AND VILLAGES

INDEX OF PLACES OF INTEREST

N

O

T

INDEX OF PLACES TO STAY, EAT, DRINK & SHOP

THE HIDDEN PLACES
Order Form

To order any of our publications just fill in the payment details below and complete the order form *overleaf*. For orders of less than 4 copies please add £1 per book for postage and packing. Orders over 4 copies are P & P free.

Please Complete Either:

I enclose a cheque for £ .... made payable to Travel Publishing Ltd

Or:

Card No: ☐☐☐☐ ☐☐☐☐ ☐☐☐☐ ☐☐☐☐

Expiry Date: ☐☐ ☐☐

Signature: ....

NAME: ....

ADDRESS: ....

....

....

POSTCODE: ....

TEL NO: ....

Please send to:
Travel Publishing Ltd
7a Apollo House
Calleva Park
Aldermaston
Berks, RG7 8TN

THE HIDDEN PLACES
—— Order Form ——

	Price	Quantity	Value
Regional Titles			
Cambridgeshire & Lincolnshire	£7.99	....	....
Channel Islands	£6.99	....	....
Cheshire	£7.99	....	....
Chilterns	£7.99	....	....
Cornwall	£7.99	....	....
Devon	£7.99	....	....
Dorset, Hants & Isle of Wight	£7.99	....	....
Essex	£7.99	....	....
Gloucestershire	£6.99	....	....
Heart of England	£4.95	....	....
Highlands & Islands	£7.99	....	....
Kent	£7.99	....	....
Lake District & Cumbria	£7.99	....	....
Lancashire	£7.99	....	....
Norfolk	£7.99	....	....
Northeast Yorkshire	£6.99	....	....
Northumberland & Durham	£6.99	....	....
North Wales	£7.99	....	....
Nottinghamshire	£6.99	....	....
Peak District	£6.99	....	....
Potteries	£6.99	....	....
Somerset	£6.99	....	....
South Wales	£7.99	....	....
Suffolk	£7.99	....	....
Surrey	£6.99	....	....
Sussex	£6.99	....	....
Thames Valley	£7.99	....	....
Warwickshire & West Midlands	£6.99	....	....
Welsh Borders	£5.99	....	....
Wiltshire	£6.99	....	....
Yorkshire Dales	£6.99	....	....
Set of any 5 Regional titles	**£25.00**	....	....
National Titles			
England	£9.99	....	....
Ireland	£8.99	....	....
Scotland	£8.99	....	....
Wales	£8.99	....	....
Set of all 4 National titles	**£28.00**	....	....

For orders of less than 4 copies please add £1 per book for postage & packing. Orders over 4 copies P & P free.

THE HIDDEN PLACES
—— Reader Comment Form ——

The *Hidden Places* research team would like to receive reader's comments on any visitor attractions or places reviewed in the book and also recommendations for suitable entries to be included in the next edition. This will help ensure that the *Hidden Places* series continues to provide its readers with useful information on the more interesting, unusual or unique features of each attraction or place ensuring that their stay in the local area is an enjoyable and stimulating experience.

To provide your comments or recommendations would you please complete the forms below and overleaf as indicated and send to: The Research Department, Travel Publishing Ltd., 7a Apollo House, Calleva Park, Aldermaston, Reading, RG7 8TN.

Your Name:

Your Address:

Your Telephone Number:

Please tick as appropriate: Comments ☐   Recommendation ☐

Name of *"Hidden Place"*:

Address:

Telephone Number:

Name of Contact:

THE HIDDEN PLACES
Reader Comment Form

Comment or Reason for Recommendation:

....

....

....

....

....

....

....

....

....

....

....

....

....

THE HIDDEN PLACES
—— Reader Comment Form ——

The *Hidden Places* research team would like to receive reader's comments on any visitor attractions or places reviewed in the book and also recommendations for suitable entries to be included in the next edition. This will help ensure that the *Hidden Places* series continues to provide its readers with useful information on the more interesting, unusual or unique features of each attraction or place ensuring that their stay in the local area is an enjoyable and stimulating experience.

To provide your comments or recommendations would you please complete the forms below and overleaf as indicated and send to: The Research Department, Travel Publishing Ltd., 7a Apollo House, Calleva Park, Aldermaston, Reading, RG7 8TN.

Your Name:

Your Address:

Your Telephone Number:

Please tick as appropriate: Comments ☐ Recommendation ☐

Name of *"Hidden Place"*:

Address:

Telephone Number:

Name of Contact:

THE HIDDEN PLACES
—— Reader Comment Form ——

Comment or Reason for Recommendation:

....

....

....

....

....

....

....

....

....

....

....

....

MAP SECTION

The following pages of maps encompass the main cities, towns and geo-graphical features of Dorset, Hampshire and the Isle of Wight, as well as many of the interesting places featured in the guide. Distances are indicated by the use of scale bars located below each of the maps

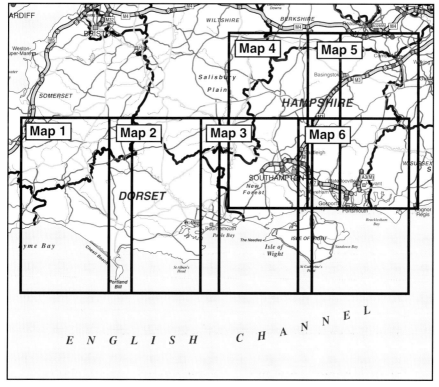

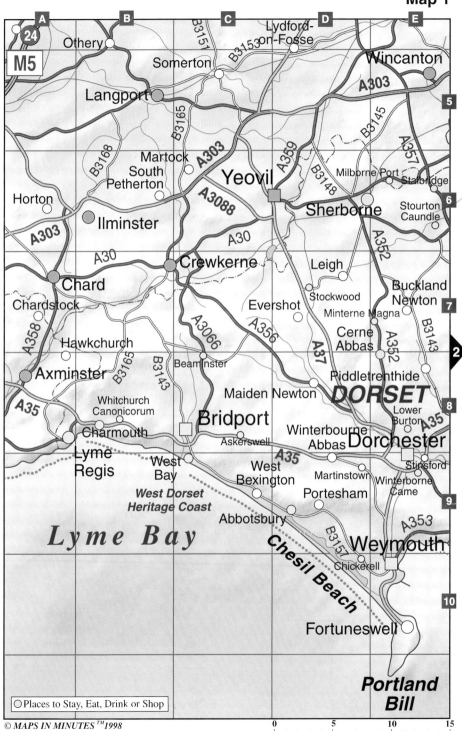

Map 1

Map 2

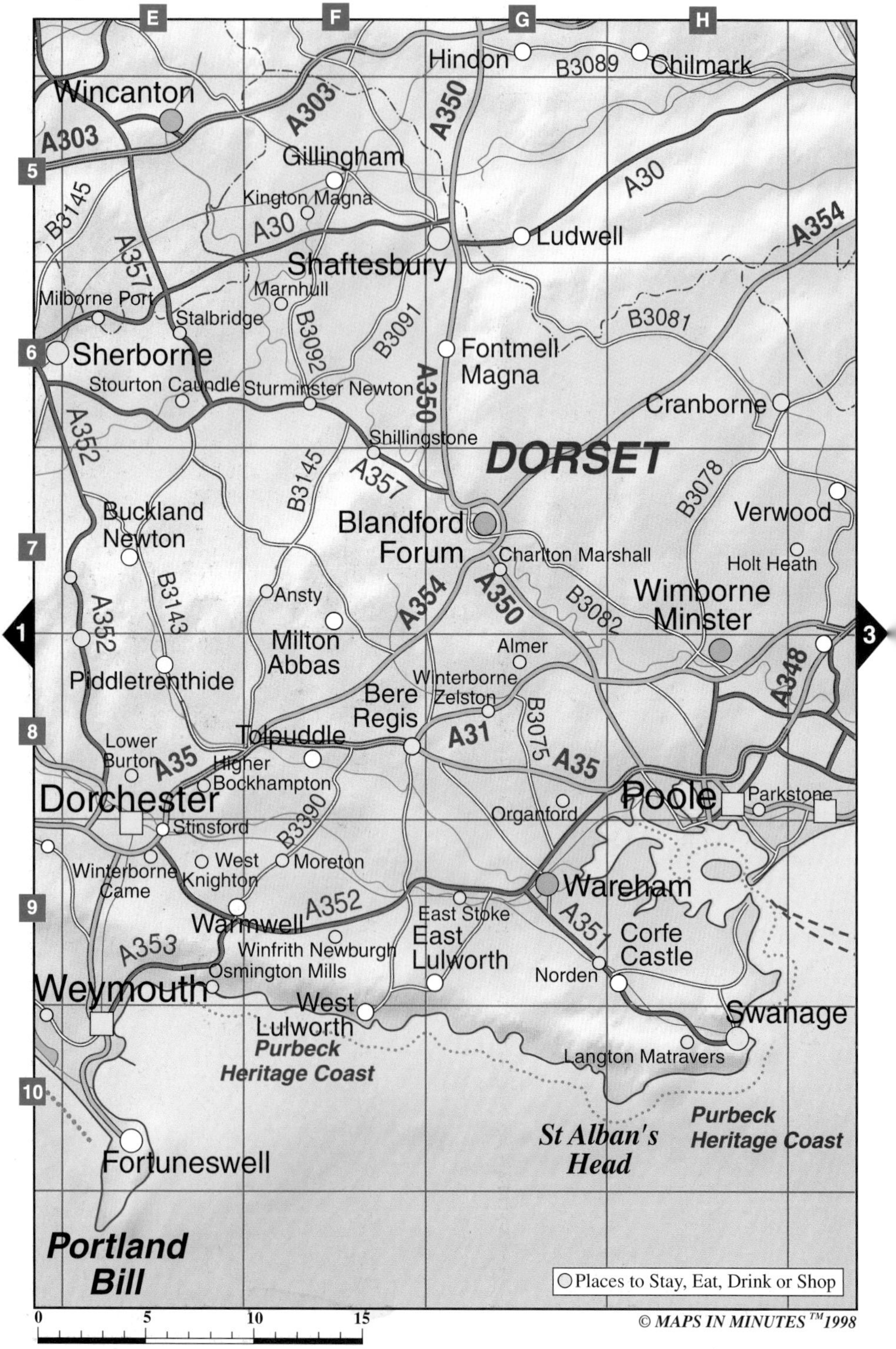

E · F · G · H

Hindon
B3089
Chilmark

Wincanton

A303

A350

A303

A350

A30

5

B8145

Gillingham

Kington Magna

A30

Ludwell

A354

A357

Shaftesbury

Milborne Port

Marnhull

Stalbridge

B3092

B3091

Fontmell
Magna

B3081

6

Sherborne

Stourton Caundle

Sturminster Newton

A350

Cranborne

A352

Shillingstone

DORSET

B3078

Verwood

Buckland
Newton

B3145

A357

Blandford
Forum

Charlton Marshall

Holt Heath

7

B3143

Ansty

A354

A350

B3082

Wimborne
Minster

A352

1

Milton
Abbas

Almer

3

A348

Piddletrenthide

Winterborne
Zelston

Bere
Regis

A31

B3075

A35

8

Lower
Burton

A35

Higher
Bockhampton

Tolpuddle

Dorchester

Stinsford

B3390

Organford

Poole

Parkstone

West
Knighton

Moreton

9

Winterborne
Came

Warmwell

A352

East Stoke

Wareham

A353

Winfrith Newburgh

East
Lulworth

A351

Corfe
Castle

Weymouth

Osmington Mills

West
Lulworth

Norden

Swanage

*Purbeck
Heritage Coast*

Langton Matravers

10

*Purbeck
Heritage Coast*

*St Alban's
Head*

Fortuneswell

**Portland
Bill**

○ Places to Stay, Eat, Drink or Shop

0 · 5 · 10 · 15

© *MAPS IN MINUTES* ™ *1998*

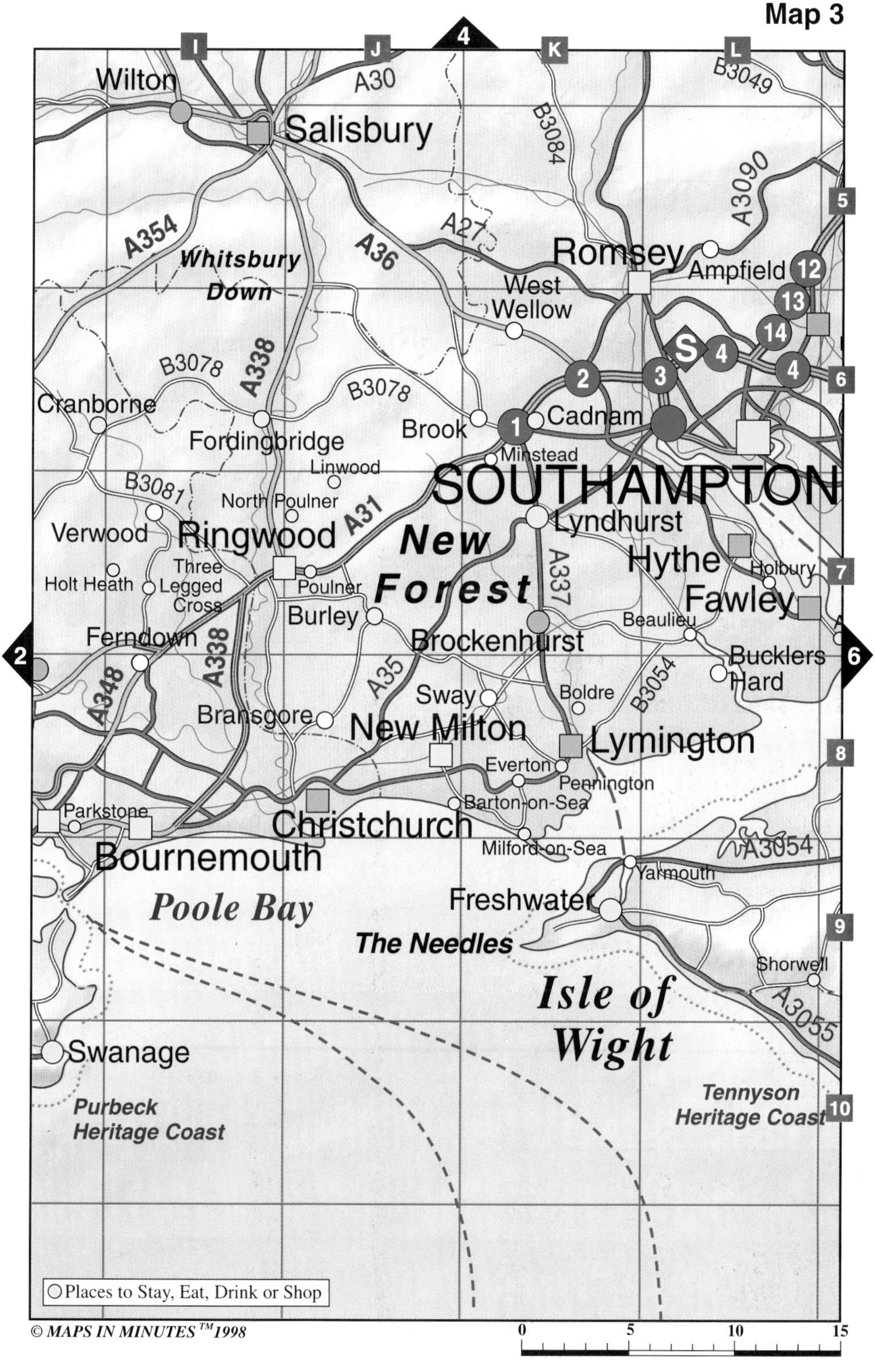

Map 3

I J **4** K L

Wilton
A30
Salisbury
B3049
B3084
A3090
5

A354
Whitsbury
Down
A36
A27
Romsey
Ampfield **12**
West
Wellow
13
S
14
Cranborne
B3078
A338
B3078
2
3
4
4
6
Fordingbridge
Brook
Cadnam
1
Minstead
SOUTHAMPTON
Linwood
B3081
North Poulner
Lyndhurst
Verwood
Ringwood
A31
New
Hythe
Holbury
7
Three
Holt Heath
Legged
Poulner
Forest
Fawley
Cross
Burley
Beaulieu
A
Ferndown
A338
A337
Bucklers
Hard
6
A348
A35
Brockenhurst
B3054
2
Bransgore
Sway
Boldre
Lymington
8
New Milton
Everton
Pennington
Christchurch
Barton-on-Sea
Bournemouth
Milford-on-Sea
Yarmouth
A3054
Parkstone
Poole Bay
Freshwater
9
The Needles
Shorwell
Isle of
Swanage
Wight
A3055
Purbeck
Heritage Coast
Tennyson
Heritage Coast
10

○ Places to Stay, Eat, Drink or Shop

0　　　　5　　　　10　　　　15

Map 4

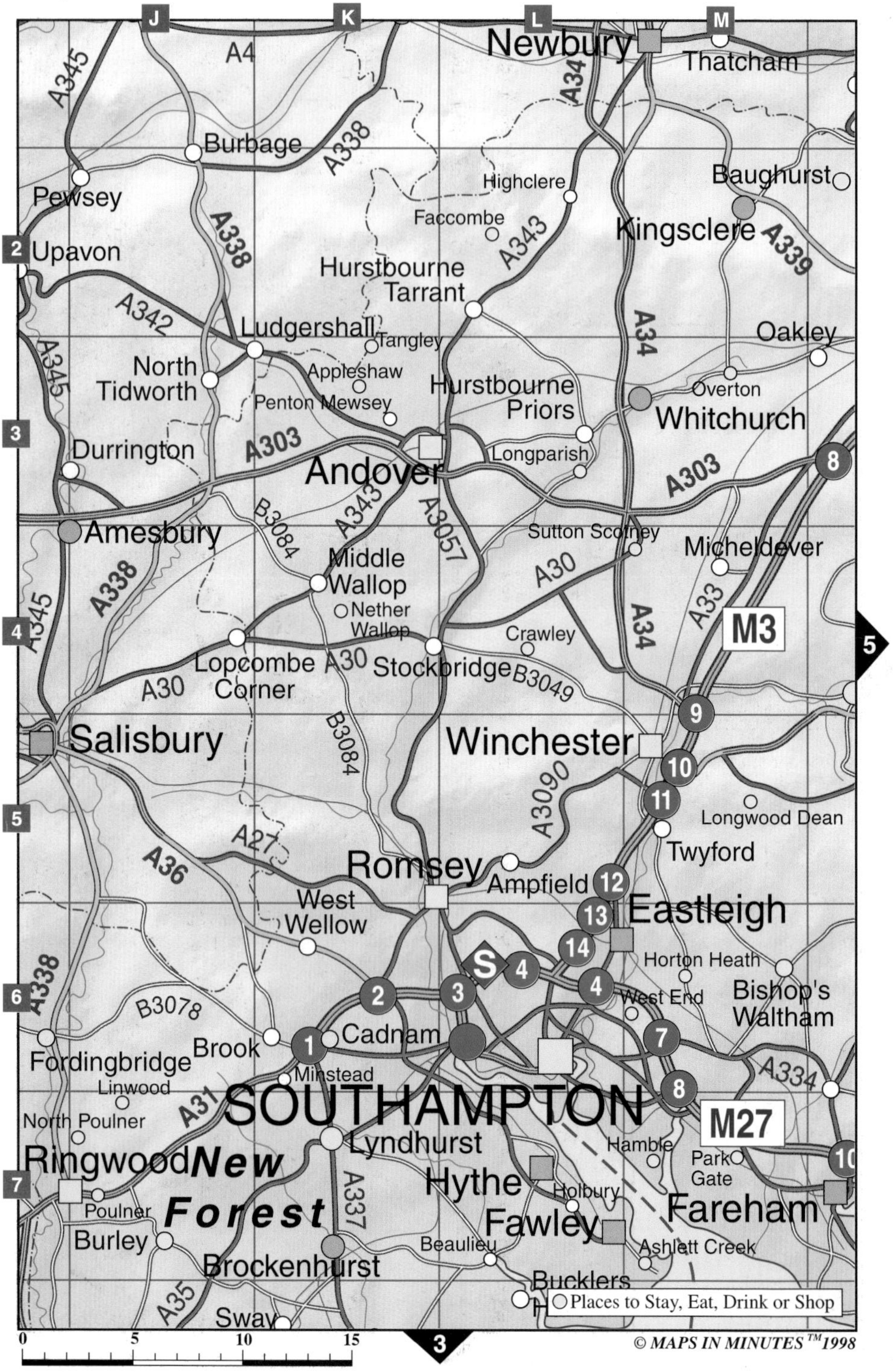

J K L M

A4
A345
A345
A338
A338
A342
A345
A338
A345

Newbury
Thatcham

Burbage

Baughurst

Pewsey
Highclere

Faccombe
A343

Kingsclere
A339

Upavon

Hurstbourne
Tarrant

Oakley

Ludgershall
Tangley
Appleshaw
North
Tidworth
Penton Mewsey
Hurstbourne
Priors
Overton
Whitchurch

A34

Durrington
A303
Andover
Longparish
A303

8

Amesbury

B3084
A343
A3057
Sutton Scotney
Micheldever

Middle
Wallop
Nether
Wallop
A30
Crawley
A34
A33
M3

A338
A345

Lopcombe
Corner
A30
A30
Stockbridge
B3049

9

Salisbury
B3084
Winchester

10

A3090

11

Longwood Dean

A36
A27
Romsey
Twyford

West
Wellow
Ampfield
12

13
Eastleigh

S
4
14
Horton Heath

A338
B3078
2
3
4
West End
Bishop's
Waltham

Fordingbridge
Brook
1
Cadnam
7
A334

Linwood
Minstead
8

North Poulner
A31
SOUTHAMPTON
M27

Ringwood New
Lyndhurst
Hamble
Park
Gate
10

Poulner
A337
Hythe
Holbury
Fareham

Burley
Forest
Fawley
Beaulieu
Ashlett Creek

Brockenhurst
Bucklers

A35
Sway
○ Places to Stay, Eat, Drink or Shop

0 5 10 15
3
© *MAPS IN MINUTES* ™ 1998

Map 5

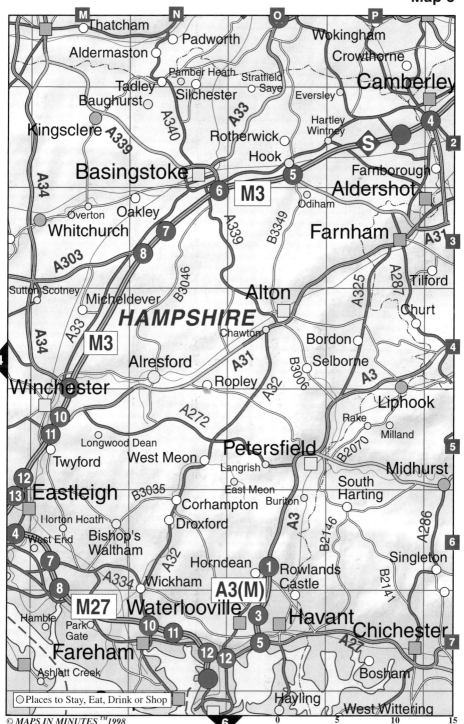

Places to Stay, Eat, Drink or Shop

Map 6

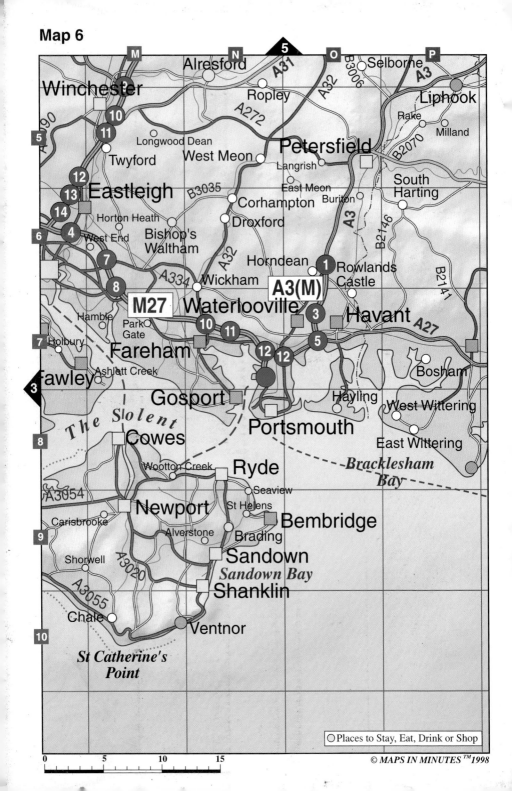

© *MAPS IN MINUTES* ™1998

0   5   10   15